SECRETS OF THE INNER LIGHT

Stepping Into Your Divine Destiny

C. David Lundberg

Heavenlight Press

SECRETS OF THE INNER LIGHT

Stepping Into Your Divine Destiny

Copyright © 2025
By C. David Lundberg and Heavenlight Press

All rights reserved, except as permitted under the U.S. Copyright Act of 1976, no part of this publication may be reproduced, distributed, or transmitted in any form or by any means, or stored in a database or retrieval system, without the prior written permission of the publisher.

Quotations and other materials used by kind permission
of the Summit Lighthouse.

AI was *not* used in the creation of this book.

Print ISBN: 978-0-9796308-4-2
eBook ISBN: 978-0-9796308-5-9

Updated May 2025

Cover Design: Indigo Artz
Cover Art: Based on a painting by Nicholas Roerich

This book is dedicated to God's One Divine Family living on Earth, in the hope that it will make a contribution to a greater understanding of ultimate reality and our innate divinity. Let God's Light, Love, Wisdom, and Power flow through every reader of these teachings, creating a higher level of consciousness of God's many wonderful blessings.

This book is based on the magnificent truth teachings within the *Corona Class Lessons*. Our Beloved Master Jesus Christ had this to say about the *Corona Class Lessons*:

> *I desire students of my life and teachings to know that this book of the Law will enable you to be experts in my divine doctrine. My soul hungers and thirsts for those who truly know me and speak of me and of my words and my teachings that I gave two thousand years ago and have not left off giving to my saints who know my voice....*
> *This work of truth shall swallow up error. And when seen as the keystone to all teachings of the ascended masters, it provides you with a foundation and an open door for speaking to people and groups as out of the Holy Spirit.*[1]

Contents

Introduction   vii

Part One
KEYS TO JOY AND FREEDOM

1. GOD'S GRAND DESIGN	3
2. MISUNDERSTANDINGS CONCERNING JESUS	13
3. LOSING ALL FEARS	29
4. FAITH RULES	35
5. WE ARE GOD'S CHILDREN WITH UNLIMITED POTENTIAL	43
6. THE CHRIST CONSCIOUSNESS	51
7. EMPOWERING HUMILITY	59
8. FREEDOM FROM SIN	65
9. THE PERFECT YOU	77
10. YOU ARE UNIQUE	89
11. THE POWER OF HABITS	103
12. DISCIPLESHIP AND MASTERY	115
13. OUR EMPOWERING BEAUTIFUL VISION	133
14. JESUS DYING FOR OUR SINS	143
15. TRANSCENDING MORTALITY—BEING "BORN AGAIN"	149
16. LOSING LIFE TO FIND IT	157
17. THE RIVER OF LIFE	169
18. SHARING THE LIGHT	173
19. THE HOLY GRAIL—DRINKING FROM THE CUP OF LIGHT	187
20. TRANSFIGURATION	193

Part Two
WORKING WITH THE LIGHT

WORKING WITH THE LIGHT	207
Daily Protection	212
God's Will and Soul Purification	214
Meditation on Light	216
God's Consuming Fire	219
Heart, Head and Hand Decrees	221
Strengthening the Heart	223
Healing and Wholeness	224
The "I AM" Way of Jesus	225
Call to Overcome the Lower Self	229
Call for Forgiveness	229
Divine Assistance—Asking for Help	231
Sharing the Light	234
Humility	235
Calls for Perfection	237
Our Unique Being in God	238
Identification with God	238
I AM Lord's Prayer	240
Christ Vision—Increasing our Perception	240
The Power of Faith	241
The Blessing of Transfiguration	242
Prayer of Praise for Service	247
Join with Others	248
Our Path of Overcoming Darkness	249
APPENDIX	251
Glossary	285
Acknowledgements	301
Notes	303
About the Author	315

Introduction

The Joy of Being a Spiritual Seeker
Hidden Keys
Challenges Along the Way
Divine Solutions Offered in This Book

THE JOY OF BEING A SPIRITUAL SEEKER

Although I am now in my eighth decade, I still remember looking up at the sky as a toddler, wondering who and what God is. I have been looking for answers ever since, and have discovered that many spiritual truths lie beyond the boundaries of what is offered by traditional and orthodox religions. This book contains what I believe to be the most important, powerful, and beautiful spiritual teachings that can guide us along the path of our spiritual destiny. I've done my best to present them in a clear, concise, and logical order. This path leads us to discovering who we really are and what our unique mission is in life. This helps us to find true freedom and guides us to personally experience the many joys of inner spiritual bliss.

Introduction

There are countless books about the nature of God, finding God, and the characteristics and purposes of the various world religions. I have earnestly studied many of them. I have accompanied my research with prayer, meditation, and personal reflection. And I have discussed and debated many spiritual issues with members of these various traditions.

Most religions and spiritual teachings share the idea that we are unique individuals, yet at the same time, we are One in spirit. The progressive unfolding of the chapters in this book will lead readers to an understanding of this Oneness—not just in theory, but also in how to *experience it*. It is a joy to discover the great blessings of God, who is the Universal divine consciousness as well as our Creator who lives within every human heart.

Few spiritual teachings surpass the revelations and the beauty that are found in the book *Corona Class Lessons*. It is a comprehensive book, loaded with the key teachings of the Ascended Masters. It contains a massive amount of information. *Secrets of the Inner Light* is a smaller, simpler book that includes a "detailed overview" of the information in *Corona Class Lessons,* presented in a logical sequence.

The teachings within *Corona Class Lessons* are attributed to our beloved Jesus Christ, as well as to the Ascended Master Kuthumi, who is best-known for his life as Saint Francis of Assisi. (Kuthumi is known also as Kuthumi Lal Singh. One of his previous embodiments was as a Tibetan Mahatma.) Their statements were delivered directly during the 1970s and '80s through Elizabeth Clare Prophet, spiritual leader of the Summit Lighthouse. During the course of her lifetime Prophet delivered over 2,000 remarkable dictations from various members of God's hierarchy in the higher realms.

Through studying nature, Saint Francis, a great devotee of Jesus Christ, became aware of the tremendous love of God and the joy it could bring. By focusing on his spiritual path and contemplating the holiness of life, he was able to experience a sacred

Introduction

atmosphere in all his activities. He reports that his goal was to transmit the tenderness of love to all aspects of life, even to every grain of sand he walked upon.

To any readers who might be skeptical about the source teachings of this book being valid, may I say that there is nothing wrong with being an "open-minded skeptic." Once you have a chance to examine these teachings, let your own heart decide their truth. I sincerely predict that what is presented will resonate with your inner sense of what truth is.

Secrets of the Inner Light includes explanations of many spiritual aspects of life, including clarifications of select Bible verses that have often been misunderstood. It presents numerous keys for removing the roadblocks on the path of spiritual seekers.

It is clear that Jesus earnestly wants to help us overcome feelings of inadequacy and shame for our perceived shortcomings and past errors. He desires that the infinite Light that streams from the source of all energy, the Mighty I AM Presence, flows continuously into our individualized heart chalices.

Jesus shares his fondest hopes for us:

No matter how many mistakes you have made in the past, your Presence is standing with outstretched arms, waiting for the moment when your hungry heart will reach up and demand the chalice of your own perfection.
The life which will be poured into the cup of your being shall be everlasting and the illustrious nature of your own God Self shall shine forth as the sun illumining the city set on an hill of discipleship (a pyramid of spiritual attainment) which cannot be hid!...
Look, therefore, for the glorious appearing of the Christ in your own being. He, as your own Holy Christ Self, will guide you into all Truth.[1]

The idea that we are potential gods, that God is within us in

Introduction

the form of a divine Self or Christ Self, is the core of the teachings in this book. The idea of an inner Divinity is no new revelation. The mystical teachings of the world religions have repeatedly revealed that we have unlimited and eternal divine potential. These concepts are clearly set forth in my previous work, *Unifying Truths of the World's Religions*.[2] These teachings from Ascended Masters Jesus and Kuthumi build on these ancient truths and clarify the magnificent benefits that are provided to us by our Creator. These blessings are available to all souls who sincerely seek the divine Presence in their life.

HIDDEN KEYS

During his lifetime on Earth, Jesus gave many instructions only to his disciples. In addition, his public teachings, recorded in the New Testament, were often given in parable form. While the parables are wonderful, memorable stories conveying timeless spiritual truths, they often do not explain the deeper mysteries of the divine Light within us. It is clear from the Gospels that Jesus, in his great wisdom, withheld these advanced lessons from the general public, only to share them with his close disciples—much like an accomplished teacher imparts advanced concepts to the mature students but, when speaking to the young and innocent, teaches much lighter, more "digestible fare." The Bible tells us:

> *But without a parable spake he not unto them: and when they were alone, he expounded all things to his disciples.*[3]

The sayings of Jesus that were recorded two thousand years ago have been readily available to everyone in numerous versions of the Bible. They have continuously been discussed and analyzed, though often with incorrect interpretations. Jesus acknowledges the importance of having a proper understanding of his teachings:

Introduction

> *Spiritual men and women of today recognize that their God-identity is a mighty rushing wind of Power dominated by glowing, infinite Wisdom and saturated with radiant, holy Love without limit. Souls of vision are universally coming to realize the significance in their lives of the mysteries I taught to my apostles and disciples in secret and in parable.*[4]

Clear explanations of the teachings of Jesus enable spiritual seekers to fully complete their passage to a most beautiful, joyful, and eternal life. Although Jesus is considered widely to be a 'Christian' source, these explanations of the spiritual Path fit well with the spiritual journey described in the inner mystical teachings of all world religions.

This science of the spirit is for the raising of our souls—so we may enjoy spiritual experiences and progress higher into the Light. The intent of this science is to raise our consciousness and open our hearts, leading us ever closer to the company of saints and an eternal life of great love and beauty.

Our souls have a natural desire to experience greater beauty, a beauty that is throughout the heaven world. These higher spheres exist, as described by numerous books about the afterlife and summarized in my collection of descriptions in *Our Magnificent Afterlife: Beyond Our Fondest Dreams*. These worlds contain not only environments of great beauty, but contain only goodness, love, peace and fulfillment.

The blessed Master Jesus confirmed the existence of a plurality of heavenly realms in John 14:

> *In my Father's house are many mansions: if it were not so, I would have told you. I go to prepare a place for you.*[5]

Our Loving Creator desires to help all spiritual seekers find their way to His Greater Reality, which is the only safe refuge from the storms of life. We are, and have always been, a part of God, but

Introduction

in order to return to true oneness, we need to transmute and transcend our imperfect past actions that have caused our sense of separateness from the divine.

Entering the kingdom of God, which is synonymous with the divine consciousness, leads to outpourings of divine Light and love that are beyond our fondest dreams. Only then does a soul truly realize its divine identity. All spiritual seekers who absorb and practice these teachings are preparing for the Loving Presence to unite with them, tangibly, inside the temple of their physical body!

CHALLENGES ALONG THE WAY

There may never have been a time on Earth when an accurate understanding of the deepest and most timeless teachings of the Christ has been more urgently needed. The United States and many other parts of the world are terribly divided, largely because forces of darkness sow division between nations, races, political persuasions and religions through godless ideologies. They foster envy and greed between the rich and poor and continually seek to undermine the cultural norms that give a measure of harmony to human societies. Truth is the antidote for these situations.

The healing of these schisms that divide God's children is greatly needed. Misinterpretations of the sacred texts have contributed much to the haze that has clouded righteous thought and living. Healing will come when simple, unadulterated truth prevails in our hearts and minds. When we are able to find truth without misunderstandings and misinterpretations, we can rise above our own internal discords and be restored to wholeness, soul freedom and awareness of our true divinity,

Many who self-identify as spiritual seekers get distracted by world events, as well as by the temptations and indulgences that are all about us in human society. They may be unaware of the fullness of God's divine plan and grand design (Chapter 1). Or, even worse, they may conclude that spiritual pursuits are less valuable than the

Introduction

human pleasures of the hour and end up abandoning even a pretense of spiritual practice. This is a great tragedy because they do not realize how tremendously loving and giving our Creator is. Most people do not understand how much our Creator wants His children to enjoy the greatest goodness, beauty, peace and fulfillment. Instead, many focus solely on material acquisitions, pursuing status and popularity among their peers and disregarding the indwelling Spirit.

Yet, there is a profound yearning within virtually all mankind for a better comprehension of life. One big reason people are searching for answers is because they want to transcend the confusion and negativity that permeates our planet. Unfortunately, there are such tremendous amounts of negative and scandalous attitudes on Earth at this time, that even sincere devotees of the Spirit have difficulty not being influenced by them. This seriously hinders spiritual devotees in manifesting their higher, divine nature.

When we ignore our conscience—our gentle inner voice of wisdom and love—God's Light is clouded, and we tend to misqualify the energy from our Creator that sustains us every moment. Once we realize our dependence on Spirit, we begin to understand that our happiness ultimately depends on attuning with God. With this attunement, the Light can be clearly received to transmute our burdens of uncertainty and fear, for then we are willing to make the necessary changes in our lives and transcend our human consciousness to embrace our higher, divine consciousness. We then become loyal to the Light of God in our life, learn to depend upon it for all our needs, and trust it to lead us to our highest goals!

DIVINE SOLUTIONS

You will discover that God wants us to follow the examples set by the saints and Ascended Masters, who are referred to in some traditions as our elder brothers and sisters. They have lived on Earth like

Introduction

us, in a human body, and have balanced their karma here in the 'denser' material plane. They use God's power for the greater good. Many well-known saints and other great religious leaders and humanitarians throughout history are now Ascended Masters. They assist us by working with our Higher Selves, teaching us, and enabling us to do greater works than we would otherwise do on our own.

The teachings from the Masters Jesus and Kuthumi given in this book show how we can follow this same spiritual route to divine wholeness that was taken by those who are now Ascended Masters. The instructions are so logical and sensible that they are easy to embrace as a definitive pathway that leads to attunement with the Light of God.

Souls will learn to trust and come to a point of conscious desire for and acceptance of their true identity as divine beings. I am reminded of an observation by a fellow seeker who once shared his personal revelation about our life here on Earth: "We are divine beings having a human experience." To which another seeker added: "And our mission is to help one another to find our way back Home." For clearly, an essential part of our spiritual progress is to help others find the way back to a whole and happy life, which can only be found within the arms of God.

Once these essential divine teachings are widely known and taken to heart, this planet has the potential to enter into a Golden Age where lies will not be spoken, and where those who would consider doing evil or causing suffering to others will realize that the laws of karma will direct any negative actions or energy they create back upon themselves, which would quickly erase any negative urges. People will widely understand how divine justice works, and have no desire to stray from a path of harmony, peace, and loving assistance to each other—which, in essence, is the Will of our Loving Creator.

Beloved Jesus shares with us his passion and his goal for each one of us:

Introduction

> *It has ever been my wish to convey to the children of God the nature of their total Being in order to enhance the fulfillment of their hopes, to make possible their union with the allness of God, and to assist them in stretching their identity into areas of greater happiness and wholeness. Verily, to heal that which is lame, to restore crooked limbs, to magnify the sacred fire of perfection within the crucible of man's identity is my passion.[6]*

In addition to the powerful teachings in Part I, Part II contains specific teachings related to most of the dynamic decrees, affirmations and prayers contained within the *Corona Class Lessons*. These use the power of the spoken word, connecting us with the higher realms to accelerate our spiritual evolution. We can harness the spoken word to invoke divine Light and to obtain heavenly assistance from countless Ascended Masters, Angels, and other heavenly beings.

The Appendix is provided for convenience in making daily calls for personal spiritual growth. It contains nearly all of the decrees, affirmations and prayers contained within the *Corona Class Lessons*. It also includes some unique material not found elsewhere in the book.

Every one of us is continually being sent the promptings to come up higher, to realize our eternal destiny. With the correct understanding of the teachings of the Christ and the application of the spirit-lifting practices presented here, I believe anyone can enjoy rapid spiritual growth and deep attunement with that which truly matters: experiencing and magnifying God's Light and love to the world.

So, turn away from the record and memory of strife, division, and intolerance on Earth. Forget, at least in some portion of your daily life, the stress of the Earth. Feel at peace as you assimilate these higher teachings, and experience a deeper, sacred communion with your Divine Self! Here is my prayer:

Introduction

Beloved Heavenly Father/Mother God, may all spiritual seekers who contemplate and apply the following spiritual truths and use these practices, come to realize their tremendous value. May they experience new levels of peace, understanding and loving Light. Let the door of our true and future spiritual nature be opened wide, energizing and uplifting the entire Self!

From Chapter 13, Our Empowering Beautiful Vision:

All life is energy and the source of this energy is Divine Light. The action of Light is fully the consciousness of God. Our task is to attune to this Light, this God consciousness, allowing it to flow through our four lower bodies as much as possible. This Light contains God's highest purpose of goodness, and increases in flow as we outpicture God's will in our mind's eye.

Part One

KEYS TO JOY AND FREEDOM

Chapter 1

God's Grand Design

Many people take the very fact of their life for granted. They may go through life only rarely, if ever, feeling immense gratitude and love for our Creator or for our countless blessings—such as having loving relationships, good health, sunshine, fresh air, being able to walk in nature and innumerable other blessings. The beauty and goodness on Earth are due to the superb and glorious *design* of the physical world we live in.

Most people do not fully realize that our All-Powerful, Wise and Loving Creator manifests ever-expanding benevolence and wonders throughout the Universe. The word "awesome" is overused in our daily lives, but what truly *is* awesome is the beauty, joy, peace, wisdom, and power of Almighty God. Even more incredible is that we each have a most glorious divine potential. We are destined to enjoy countless divine experiences with God. Once people comprehend the enormity of our stupendous blessings and unlimited possibilities and what the grand design of our Creator is, life will be seen and enjoyed with far more hope, anticipation, love and appreciation for the glories that lie ahead.

As we evolve, it's important to be open-minded to extraordinary possibilities, even if they may be initially difficult to believe. As you read through these chapters it will be demonstrated to you that *man is intended to be a manifestation of God.* This is apparent when the inner or mystical traditions of the major world religions are examined. If people understood God's divine plan for each and every soul, realizing with certainty that following His plan would ultimately bring them joy and even bliss beyond measure, they would rejoice and cease any misqualification of God's energy that might cause suffering or detract from their personal spiritual progress.

Not only is there an overall divine design, every individual also has a unique mix of talents and potential, so it is helpful to pray to be shown our particular interests, skills and the most important and fulfilling tasks for our life. Dear Master Kuthumi shares the importance of discovering our true being and identity:

> *Every lifestream has a matrix, or God-design, which he ought to outpicture each day. Unless this is made known to the outer self of the seeker, it is difficult for him to cooperate with the mighty plan of the inner life.*
> *It is most helpful, when, either through prayer or invocation, by decree or earnest effort, students determine to find out everything they can about their great God-design—and then begin to experience elements of that design day by day through a particular plan of action.*
> *It is essential for all who would bring the power of negative conditions under the submission of the Real Self to realize that they have a listening ear in heavenly places awaiting their call for the secrets of their own beings to be revealed— especially the spiritual means to change what must be changed.*[1]

More information about the unique aspects of every soul can be found in Chapter 10: "You Are Unique."

From the progressive revelation given to us by Jesus, we hear of the wonders of God's grand design of love that blesses us with His inner divine Light:

> *The life plan of the Father is like the most beautiful rose in existence, whose unfolding petals (the form) yield to Life's direction and become cups of fragrance offering golden liquid light which can enshrine in each lifestream all the joy and glory of the Masters' unfolding plan of the ages for that one.*
>
> *Life is God, Life is I AM, and it was intended to be beautiful, eternal, powerful, and happy. This can be so only through your outpicturing of all that is the power (will of God), the kingdom (wisdom of God), and the glory (love of God). There is no other way....*
>
> *May the highest sense of the beauty and perfection of the Presence enfold your hearts and lives this season and forever.*[2]

What is so easily forgotten, but is so absolutely important and beautiful, is that the ultimate characteristics of God, Who is in everything and is all-powerful, are goodness and love. This is confirmed in the sacred texts of the world religions.[3]

The Master Jesus also shares with us his promise of peace and our Father's love:

> *When in my luminous Presence I step through the veil into your octave, it will be to say to you as I do today: "Peace, be still!" and "My peace I give unto you." ...*
>
> *The rose, whose petals are so wondrously soft as to exceed the finest velvet, symbolizes the gentle but symmetrically beautiful caress of God's love. The Father would give to every man, woman, and child the embrace of His nearness,*

SECRETS OF THE INNER LIGHT

His encouragement, His Law of Love, and even His very Life every hour.[4]

In our Creator's magnificent design, no favoritism is present, and sooner or later each individual soul recognizes their inherent responsibility to embrace the truth of their own divinity. Each soul will have an equal opportunity. Each soul differs in their unique talents, in what they experience in life, and in how long they will take to return to righteous co-creation with God. By the grace of our loving Father/Mother God, every individual who aspires to spiritually advance will be given divine support. Once embraced, this grace will fully illumine and elevate every determined soul, resulting in the ultimate end of sorrows and stains from past sins.

God expects that when love is given, a degree of interchange will occur—love is returned to the giver. God wants us to create goodness in our world as He has imbedded goodness within us as a part of life itself. We are expected to multiply and share our blessings, and as we do, our understanding of divine truth will increase. This understanding can be greatly enhanced by an accurate understanding of sacred scriptures, uncontaminated by false or misguided interpretations.

The flow of life is a flow of giving and receiving love and goodness—of self-emptying and then being refilled with new and greater capacities for giving more and more love and goodness. And these deeds build a storehouse of treasure for our future benefit in God's kingdom.

Astronomers estimate that just in the *physical* universe, there are billions of galaxies that each contain millions, if not billions, of stars.[5] And, there are other levels, planes, or dimensions of vibration beyond the physical dimension! And in all probability other life forms exist beyond those on Earth, and they will also experience the fruits of their loving or unloving choices, just as we do.

Once people understand how divine justice works within this

grand design, most will desire to refrain from purposeful acts that cause suffering to others, and Earth will be more heaven-like.

One thing that blocks souls from fully allowing the joyous mind of God entry into their consciousness are memories of negative experiences, which include actions and habits that have caused harm. Our saving grace is that we can choose to immerse ourselves in this original pure and grand design. This is the Christ mind. Those who are willing to embrace this divine mind and memory can enter into the perfection of design contained therein. Doing so allows the joy of the Holy Spirit, the divine Light, to flow into and through us. How to do this is addressed throughout this book.

This flow of Light from the heart of our Creator circulates throughout the entire universe. Consider that just physical light vibrates in the range of an incredible 400 *trillion* times a second[6] and divine Light may vibrate even faster. This divine Light contains God's will for goodness in unlimited supply. Great joy comes to all who fully understand and believe that this never-ending stream of goodness is universal, and flows through all creation. What we actually have is a perfect and all-powerful loving parent for every one of us; one that has blessed us with the wonderful endowment of free will.

In other words, we are all "royalty." We can each create, feeling the great joy and energy of God's loving Light flowing through us. All that is required is that our creations are in line with God's will of goodness and love.

Let us consider: "From where does life originate?" From the loving will of God, where directives go forth to all aspects of life. And these concentric circles of direction and identity are released and more easily recognized the closer we get to them.

The Masters inform us that until we can fully identify with this central cause of creation, we will not have complete awareness or totally enlightened consciousness. They teach that once this occurs, then it is possible for the individual to radiate from the Center of

Being outward to the concentric realms of the universe. This process is unending within the divine Spirit.

What is the nature of the Holy Spirit? What comprises the core of our ultimate being in God? The Master Jesus tells us the characteristics of the Holy Spirit:

> *The Holy Spirit must needs [most assuredly has] express qualities of intelligence, qualities of power, and qualities of great love. It is unthinkable that even a little child imbued with the holiness of God should fail to exude the fragrance of a wistful, searching intelligence and a buoyant yet balanced outreaching love—a love extending beyond the borders of persons, places, conditions or things, a love centered in the very heart of Truth and identity complete.*[7]

God's kingdom is His loving consciousness. It consists of the triune aspects of:

1. Divine Love, which is understood as the best way to qualify all thought and feeling. Love is the "highest and best use" of all energy and Light.
2. Divine Wisdom, which knows and desires all goodness/harmony, joy, peace, and happiness for others and self.
3. Divine Power, which is energy, also referred to as divine Light. It is all-powerful and all-knowing.

Increasing one's love and wisdom, so that we become greater forces for good, allows us to receive greater power. Love + Wisdom = Power. For example, wise and loving parents will choose people that demonstrate love and wisdom to care for their children when they are away—empowering them with their authority, and responsibility for their children. Wise parents will *deny* that power, by not choosing anyone to watch over their children who does not demonstrate such wisdom and love.

Thus, when souls stop intentionally or ignorantly misusing their free will, which has resulted in suffering for themselves or others, and instead begin to focus on the Holy Spirit, attuning with the source of life and its perfection, they then receive greater Light/energy/power. Subsequently, they are guided by their Higher Self to focus on taking loving and wise action and to cease acts that cause suffering.

God and His Elohim (the builders of form who are highest in the hierarchy of creation), Angels and Ascended Masters grant this greater Light, this greater authority and responsibility, to those who demonstrate that they will use it to co-create with God's will for greater good, by using that greater energy with love and wisdom.

Not only can the goodness of our Creator be found within the principles repeated in every world religion, but numerous examples of God's blessings of beauty and wisdom can also be found when researching descriptions of the heavenly worlds.

This book contains explanations and techniques provided by our beloved Master Jesus and Master Kuthumi to guide souls on their spiritual path. These help to reduce and eliminate negative habits. They also assist us to focus on and attune with divine Light, which incorporates guidance for righteous living, with all its commensurate feelings of internal joy and bliss. As that loving Light (from its divine source and inexhaustible supply) flows through our being, this flow increases as we radiate that loving and wise Light outward to all others in our world.

We can then live our lives promoting and nurturing greater kindness, goodness, beauty, peace and occasional bliss. This will empower us and increase those joyful qualities as long as we continue to attune to, and thus operate from, our Higher Divine Self. The Higher Self denotes a level of consciousness in man that is elevated beyond the typical state of being in mankind. In this work it is also referred to as the Holy Christ Self, or Christ consciousness. The Christ contains the potential of the personification of God, the Universal One, within each of us. By our desire to be with God and our attunement with Him, we can join with Jesus and other saints and Masters as we pass our initiations which come to every soul on the Homeward path.

Many traditions acknowledge the existence of the Higher Self and associate it with the individual's eternal or divine inner being. Operating from the Higher Self results in an ever-increasing spiral of self-nurturing love, wisdom, and power that has no end. Numerous spiritual sources report that once an individual chooses this route, they begin to enter God's consciousness, which has no limitation.

Though challenges and tests will come along the way, staying focused on and maintaining attunement with one's divine Self enables success through every challenge. These are all opportunities for greater mastery, and though there may be some temporary suffering involved, life with God results in ultimate good.

Master Kuthumi, who was embodied as Saint Francis, shares with us the contrast between lives of stress and hardship on Earth and better possibilities for the future:

> *Know that every day, right while millions live in discord, we [Ascended Masters] continue to have and enjoy harmony and Christ-communion in an atmosphere where the veil is removed and we see clearly the face of our God presence and live.*[8]

The results of our human mistakes and their accompanying bondage block us from knowing the great love and joy of our Creator. There are oceans of love waiting to flood into our consciousness as we transcend our self-imposed limitations and sense of unworthiness.

Ultimately, our Creator's plan or design consists of the organization of His ideas—ideas such as the love between family members and dear friends, the beauties found within nature, the delicate balancing of solar systems, and our entire physical universe. It also includes the system of ultimate karmic justice that provides every soul the opportunity to learn what is required to enter the higher and more loving realms. Many more aspects of this design will be addressed throughout this book.

All the beauty that we can see on Earth is just the hem of the garment of the beauty and love that awaits good and righteous people in the afterlife. It is comforting and beneficial to regularly remind oneself that God's grand design—our dynamic universe—contains immeasurable amounts of good.

We are blessed with a message from God, passed along to us through Jesus, who is fully attuned to the consciousness of God:

Be still and know that I who made thee will walk with thee alway, for I AM the very core of thy design. I AM thy Light and I AM thy Life and I AM thy soul's identification with immortality now and forever!
In the stillness of the dawn of thy immortality, I AM the resurrection of divinely inspired good works within thee.[9]

Again, we see this joyful confirmation that God is always with us, and that His divine and loving Light, purity and perfection are what make up the very core and foundation of who we really are! He is the source of our life and grants us a continual outpouring of His energy. He promises us eternal life as we strive to be like Him. Our future will be joyously spent in the ongoing performance of good and loving works.

Chapter 2

Misunderstandings Concerning Jesus

Some of the writings that come from New Testament scripture have not been properly understood. This misunderstanding extends to other sacred writings such as the Gnostic Gospels, other early Christian writings, and many additional documents which have been discovered in the Holy Land in recent decades. Those who actually put the words on paper are thought to have been sincere in their search for truth, but some of the spiritual concepts they addressed were challenging for contemporary writers to put into words, adding to our difficulty in comprehending them today.

And, even more significantly, theologians and academics who have devoted years to the study of sacred scripture have proven, rather dramatically, that there exist several places in scripture where, in the early centuries after Jesus, words and whole passages were inserted or removed from the Bible as we know it today.

The very process of the formulation of the Bible is still controversial, but there is unquestionable confirmation that a significant amount of its modern makeup is the result of a secular, irreligious Roman emperor. At the Council of Nicaea in 325 A.D., Emperor

Constantine, a military dictator, together with a carefully selected council of religious leaders, decided which books of the Bible would thereafter be included in "official Christianity," and which other numerous texts would be permanently banned. Excluded texts included the Gospel of Thomas, the Gospel of Mary, and the Secret Book of James, despite the fact that they were endorsed by earlier religious leaders and enjoyed widespread popularity in the first and second centuries. These texts assert that any dedicated and diligent individual, male or female, could attain mystical union with God, just as Jesus did. These truths and related doctrines, such as the divine origin of the soul, rather than the concept of being "born in sin," were highly threatening to Roman authorities and would-be church leaders.

Many scholarly analyses have been published regarding the edicts of this Council and their ramifications. Their conclusion is that the excluded books make it clear that extremely controversial concepts were clearly not a part of the true teachings of Jesus. These controversial concepts that were, in fact, inserted into sacred scripture include a fiery "Hell" and "eternal damnation," as well as teachings that women should be excluded from the clergy and that they are "subservient" and "lower" than men.

Before long, this officially recognized version of Christianity even displaced the long-standing pagan beliefs of the time. But it is also important to note that the new official Christianity in the ensuing years became the only recognized religion in the Empire. What followed was that the Gnostics and other earlier Christian-based sects gradually became targets of persecution. In fact, from roughly the year 800 and forward through the Middle Ages, the Catholic Church was the only recognized Christian body in Europe. The Church itself suppressed numerous opposing Christian "heresies" that were deemed to violate Christian beliefs.

One basic concept that is crucial to understand is the incorrect belief that Jesus Christ was the only son of God. Our beloved Master Kuthumi addresses this:

Misunderstandings Concerning Jesus

> *The average Christian is bound to the tradition of the historical Jesus being the chosen, anointed, and "only begotten" heir of the favor of God. He does not seem to realize that God created ONLY favorites in all his children* [as joint heirs in Christ] *and that he expects all of his sons and daughters to strive for the one supreme standard of perfection which is innate within the divine image of each and every one. This is the true image of the Christ out of which all were made as children of the Light.*[1]

The official church proclaimed that Jesus was the only son of God, and that common people outside of the priest class could not communicate directly with God. Their distorted interpretation of scripture was intended to make individuals dependent on the church as an indispensable go-between from man to God.

This did not involve spirituality but a desire for power. The reality in the scriptures is that we are being told that we are expected to grow in the Spirit and to strive to emulate Jesus in his mission of overcoming. When we do this, we can, likewise, inherit God's kingdom.

The interpretation that Jesus was the only son of God hides from us the truth of our birthright—our unlimited divine potential. It is easy for this concept to be misunderstood. What Jesus did was to become One with the only Son of God, which is the Christ.

What is the "Christ?" It is the Universal consciousness of God that went forth as the Word, the Logos that God used to fire the pattern of His divine identity in His sons and daughters and to write His laws in their inward parts. The Christ contains the potential of the personification of God, the Universal One, within each of us. It is the illumined Christ consciousness that Jesus and other saints and Ascended Masters attained through attunement with God, and by passing the initiations which come to every soul on the Homeward path.

We can begin to understand how misleading some church

doctrine has become. After all, we can ask, "Why make the effort to discipline ourselves, to become perfect, when we are taught that we are worthless sinners, incapable of perfecting ourselves?" But this false doctrine is directly opposite of what Jesus actually taught, revealing that we are all "children of the Father."[2] And further, he taught his disciples that their striving and service led him to describe them as "Sons of God,"[3] and "Heirs to His kingdom."[4]

In Matthew 5, Jesus also admonished his disciples:

Be ye therefore perfect, even as your Father which is in heaven is perfect.[5]

These are hardly words reinforcing a false status as "miserable sinners," undeserving of the Father's love and care. In short, we are not supposed to dwell on our mistakes, but rather to learn from them and not repeat them. If the goal of perfection is thought to be unattainable, it will not be pursued.

The reason that Jesus lived such an exemplary spiritual life and was able to perform many miracles was that he had balanced past karma, and passed the initiations given to his soul, thereby becoming completely attuned with "the only begotten Son," the Holy Christ Self.

In John 14, Jesus declared:

I am the way, the truth, and the life: no man cometh unto the Father, but by me.[6]

Jesus was referring to his Christ Self, the true Self that every one of us has, the "Light, which lighteth every man that cometh into the world."[7]

Master Kuthumi explains:

When the Master said, "I AM the Light of the world," he affirmed the Son Presence as that Light. And he promised

> *that as each one would lift up this Son (i.e., Sun or Light) of man within himself, he would also know that Son in Jesus.*[8]

Master Kuthumi then quotes Jesus, who states from a consciousness that is completely attuned to our beloved Creator:

> *Then shall ye know that I am he—and that the I AM in me, as the I AM in you, is the Light of my world and your world and is the All of cosmos....*
> *When ye shall have lifted up the Son of man within your own soul and temple, then shall you also know the Father, as I do, through the Presence and Person of the I AM THAT I AM. And* this is *the Word that is made flesh in me. Hence, I am Jesus* the Christ. *I AM He.*[9]

For those readers who are more oriented to fundamental Christian teachings, please keep in mind that although this interpretation of the Bible may be different from yours, it does not take anything away from our beloved Lord Jesus. It simply removes the unnecessary limitations upon the rest of us, revealing the truth about our identity, and our potential to be fully a Son or Daughter of "Our Father," in the same way Jesus advised us to address God in the beginning of the Lord's Prayer.

God cannot be limited. When we believe that we are *not* a part of God, we limit ourselves. Jesus said, "I Am the Light which lighteth every man that cometh into the world." Jesus never said that he was the only son of God. He was, instead, fully and completely at One with the One Son, the Christ. His perfect Higher Self, just like ours, operates at the level of the Christ—the intermediary between God and man. The mission of Jesus was to show us "the Way," to bring us spiritual renewal, with profound teachings about love and forgiveness, and, finally, to demonstrate the power of God within each one of us to defy death.

The traditional Christian view of Jesus deifies him, making him either God incarnate or the exclusive son of God. Either way, this interpretation precludes the potential of everyone else. This interpretation is inconsistent with many early Christian teachings that were deliberately excluded from the New Testament. If we accept this traditional view we are kept in earthly bondage.

In truth, Jesus taught us to live in the same way as he. To view Jesus as our elder brother and mentor in this way takes away none of our love, respect, gratitude, and honor for him.

In Matthew 12, Jesus asks his disciples rhetorically,

Who is my mother? And who are my brethren?
And he stretched forth his hand toward his disciples, and
said, Behold my mother and my brethren!
For whosoever shall do the will of my Father which is in
heaven, the same is my brother, and sister, and mother.[10]

Jesus, at the Last Supper in the washing of his disciples' feet, demonstrated in dramatic fashion his role as a servant-leader. He never wanted us to worship him, only to worship God our Father. He *did* want and expect, however, respect for the office he had attained, the mantle of the Christ.

The Book of John is one of the most mystical books in the Bible. Mysticism refers to a direct communion with God, an attunement and a Oneness with God. This can be a frightening concept for those afraid of losing their unique individuality, but the beautiful aspect of Oneness with God is that each of us can retain our individuality at the same time that we are attuned in Oneness. From John:

At that day ye shall know that I am in my Father, and ye in me, and I in you.[11]

This is a very concise confirmation of our ability to achieve Oneness with the divine, yet retain our individuality. This

Misunderstandings Concerning Jesus

powerful quotation is yet another confirmation that Jesus is not claiming to be the only son of God.

And again, from the book of John:

> *Jesus answered and said unto him, If a man love me, he will keep my words: and my Father will love him, and we will come unto him, and make our abode with him.*[12]

This tells us that we have the potential to fully attune with God, and fully become a part of God's One divine Family, with all of the good and positive aspects of our unique individuality remaining.

Jesus Christ came to show us the way. Once we reach a point of realization that the carnality (pertaining to the exclusively self-absorbed human ego), the suffering, the lack of love and forgiveness is no longer what we choose to be immersed in, we will want to reach higher. We will want to strive daily to attune to our ultimate, real, Divine Self, our Christ Self, the One Son of God.

God loves His children so much that He would lovingly share His kingdom—literally, His consciousness—with every living soul. It is up to each soul—in each person's own time according to the Law of free will—like the Prodigal Son, to leave off from the byways of life and return Home. For then that joyful soul will be received into the forgiving and welcoming arms of the Father.

We would do well to understand God's loving and total goodness and to focus on the highest of possibilities—the opportunities that come to us daily. The joys of Light permeate our being as we offer them in the form of kind service to all in our world. God wants this for every soul; He does not want us to be enslaved in the dark places of the lower nature. When we persist in the pursuit of the Christ consciousness, we leave behind any sense of separation with the rest of Life.

Master Kuthumi describes the anchors that weigh down humankind, that we can free ourselves from:

> *The human problem of self-love, self-pity, or self-delusion (and this includes every addiction, binding human habit, and predilection to sexual perversion) is no longer of concern to those who abide in the true knowledge of the indwelling Father and Son. No malady of over self-concern exists for them—with its attendant sinful state and sense of struggle—to hinder or further delay their progress or trap their energies while they painfully speculate, and woefully, as to whether or not they have found favor with God and man.*[13]

It's important to note that "self-love" used here is referring to the negative connotations of that term, such as vanity, selfishness, conceit, egotism, and narcissism. But from our Creator's perspective, we are meant to have a high regard for our own well-being and happiness, as our loving Creator wishes all forms of goodness for us.

We are meant to shed any sense of excessive self-importance and to embrace a selflessness, as we joyfully focus on our love for God and the plan for All-Good to be shared with all. Greater love lifts our spirit higher, revealing more and more of our identity in God.

There is a false belief among certain Christians that non-Christians will be missing out on their divine heritage, because they do not know the Lord. God's mercy, however, is universal, for our Creator's highest and most predominate attribute is love. This is abundantly evident when researching the many loving aspects and mystical teachings contained within every world religion.

What really matters is that we honor God and put our faith in God's guidance. We can have "a listening ear" and go about life, as best we can, listening to the still, small voice within, the voice of conscience.

This misunderstanding of scripture comes from such passages as the following:

> *Jesus saith unto him, I am the way, the truth, and the life: no man cometh unto the Father, but by me.*[14]

Traditional Christians believe this means that every person must have Jesus Christ as their Lord and Savior. According to this interpretation, those not exposed to Christianity might never have the chance to attain salvation, never having had the opportunity to hear of Jesus. In fact, Jesus was referring to the One Son, the Christ. No one can come unto the Father except through the same life experiences involving self-purification, mastery over negative emotions, forgiveness, and unconditional love such as Jesus gracefully demonstrated.

In another example that could lead to misunderstanding, we have Jesus in John 14:7-9 telling Philip:

> *If ye had known me, ye should have known my Father also: and from henceforth ye know him, and have seen him.*
> *Philip saith unto him, Lord, shew us the Father, and it sufficeth us.*
> *Jesus saith unto him, Have I been so long time with you, and yet hast thou not known me, Philip? He that hath seen me hath seen the Father; and how sayest thou then, Shew us the Father?*[15]

Contemplate what it was like for Jesus to be at One with God. God, being pure Spirit, manifests Himself on Earth through those who purify themselves as Jesus did. Anyone can strive for and achieve spiritual self-mastery, as Jesus and many other Ascended Masters and saints have done. Only when we comprehend this mystical concept can we cease the limiting of God in our lives.

Once we realize that God is the divine Light within us it is easier to understand the mechanics of how and why our unlimited divine potential is possible. As we purify ourselves to strive to attune to this divine Light we can experience the great joys our Lord makes possible.

The following quote from Jesus in John 14 helps to explain our divine potential:

> *Believest thou not that I am in the Father; and the Father in me? The words that I speak unto you I speak not of myself: but the Father that dwelleth in me, he doeth the works.*
> *Believe me that I am in the Father, and the Father in me: or else believe me for the very works' sake.*
> *Verily, verily, I say unto you, He that believeth on me, the works that I do shall he do also; and greater works than these shall he do; because I go unto my Father.*
> *And whatsoever ye shall ask in my name, that will I do, that the Father may be glorified in the Son.*
> *If ye shall ask any thing in my name, I will do it.*[16]

In their Oneness, what is the difference between Jesus and God, our Father, in their instruction that we can ask anything in their name, and receive it? Jesus asked in his Father's name. We can also ask in the name of the Father, or the One Son, the Christ, for things that are in accordance with the will of God.

Let there be no doubt about our being children of God, with unlimited divine potential. Let us take a closer look at the quote given above, from John 14:12:

> *He that believeth on me, the works that I do shall he do also; and greater works than these shall he do; because I go unto my Father.*

Dear Master Kuthumi reports that what Jesus actually said was:

> *If you believe in the Christ in me, placing therefore your attention on me, you will do greater works even than I did because I go to my Father.* [17]

Here is an explanation from Jesus regarding why we have the potential to do greater works than he did two thousand years ago:

> *As my light-energy/consciousness is accelerated today through my oneness with the Father in heaven, I am able to transmit to you through your loving tie to me greater power than when I was in the unascended state. Inasmuch as you also have access to the Holy Christ Self, as I did two thousand years ago, our combined effort can and shall produce through you greater works than were possible in the previous Piscean dispensation [which encompassed the previous 2,000 years.]* [18]

The crucial points evident in the preceding quotations are that God and Jesus are not separate from us. The divine Light unites us. Jesus is not the only son of God. We are God's sons and daughters too, and with desire, focus, striving and perseverance, we can achieve the fullness of our potential, just as Jesus did.

Jesus demonstrated a state of consciousness which each one of us can achieve. Because of his Oneness with God the Father, there were times when what he spoke was not in any way separate from God speaking. At those times he was completely speaking God's mind. In other words, at times, God was speaking directly through Jesus. Yet Jesus was also able to retain his individuality, even being fully attuned to his Father. This is the deeper teaching of Jesus — that we can achieve this same state of Christhood that embodies freedom, love, wisdom, and power.

For example, Saint Paul, one of the greatest disciples of Jesus, said:

I can do all things through Christ which strengtheneth me.[19]

The Acts of the Apostles document Saint Paul's tremendous mission. They are dramatic accounts of the Christlike qualities he brought forth in the building of the early Church. His energetic and courageous exploits in converting the pagan peoples of Asia Minor and the Mediterranean are brought to life in Taylor Caldwell's epic book on the life and faith of Paul, *Great Lion of God*.[20]

Another error within some traditional Christian beliefs concerns forgiveness of our sins. As will be discussed in Chapter 8, "Freedom from Sin," forgiveness comes from having a loving attitude, as well as repentance and a transmutation or healing of the desire to commit that sin again. Our prayers and calls, using the power of the spoken word are very helpful in accomplishing this. (Part II, "Key Teachings, Calls, Prayers, and Decrees.")

Beloved Master Jesus shares with us the persistent misinterpretation of his teaching on sin:

> *I spoke to many, saying, "Thy sins be forgiven thee," and again, "Go and sin no more"—yet the world's religious delusion to which countless millions pay unfortunate allegiance (believing they do my will and the will of the Father) centers around this false idea that propitiation [appeasement] in the form of a painful punishment is required by a vengeful Deity. These see my crucifixion as sacrificial, my mission as unique, and my Sonship as greater than all, whereas to God every son is already one with the Father.*[21]

Jesus wants us to know that when misinterpretations of his teachings exist, they create a flaw in the foundation upon which we develop our individual Christhood and build our spiritual temple. This can significantly mislead us. He tells us that his crucifixion (which was made easier by his foregoing Transfiguration on the Mount) was more of a sacrament than a sacrifice:

> *If any sacrifice be required for man to return to his natural, spiritual Sonship, it is the sacrifice of wayward and willful human qualities. As beloved Kuthumi and I have stated before, the path to God is never so much a sacrifice as it is a sacrament, never so much sacrificial as sacramental.*[22]

All that needs to be sacrificed are human tendencies that we are best rid of anyway. Compare our worldly human desires with the eternal beauty, goodness and joy of the heaven worlds. We are spiritual beings, whereas human existence is fleeting and our body temples are, compared to all of eternity, short-lived indeed. Let us therefore embrace our true and eternal characteristics!

More insight is shared by Jesus regarding traditional misinterpretations of his crucifixion:

> *Just think of the hundreds of years that Christendom (which means "Christ's kingdom") has contemplated the sacrificial aspects of my crucifixion! But in this case, the truth about sacrifice could not possibly be stranger than the fiction that has been handed down concerning the crucifixion.*
> *Biblical writers, saints, prophets, and holy men have written and taught about the idea of appeasing an angry God through the blood sacrifice of his Son. Although these have acted with great sincerity, they have nevertheless been influenced by the strictly pagan practice handed down from distant days when men departed from the ancient religions of Atlantis wherein true communion with God was taught and experienced as the interchange (sacrificial emission) of light between the soul and the Spirit.*
> *Subsequently, the true art of sacrifice (self-giving unto God) degenerated into the sinister and perverted uses of the sacred fire.*[23]

It is important for us to understand that our Creator simply desires our loving attention in return for His loving Light energy that we constantly receive. This enables the natural process of evolving completely back into our pure spiritual and eternal state—being transformed into "Christ-man" or "Christ-woman." We then join with our Creator to continue divine creation throughout the Cosmos.

A significant error in fundamental Christian thought is that the Bible, a great book, should be the *only* source of spiritual truth. Whenever orthodox religion refuses to acknowledge progressive revelation, it interferes with the clear spiritual insight that is continuously available to spiritual seekers who are advancing on the road to greater enlightenment. Progressive revelation comes from direct attunement with our Creator, Ascended Masters and other high Cosmic beings.

Many have unnecessarily limited themselves and their attunement with God through over-dependence on the Bible. Although the Bible is beautiful and mostly true, it is not infallible and complete. After all, the lives of Jesus and other holy men and women have continued after their embodiment on Earth. Let us be guided not only by sacred scripture but by ongoing progressive revelation whereby not only Jesus, but also the great prophets, saints and holy men and women throughout history still have important information and guidance to share. Discernment is essential, however. As Jesus advised us, it is best to "Believe not every spirit, but try the spirits whether they are of God."[24] We are wise to utilize our inner divine guidance to distinguish what is true from what is not. Another way is by taking a good look at the fruits of various spiritual teachers to see if their students are truly benefiting from those teachings.

From the *Corona Class Lessons,* Jesus wants us to know:

> *Progress as progressive revelation is the law of spiritual evolution. For with each new level of attainment, even after the ascension, vistas of knowledge transcending the old open*

before the soul. And some of this knowledge will even seem to contradict one's former understanding or prophetic insights, even as a child grows into new truths and discards the outworn mode of expression.

Thus, I admonish patience with the Word, with its exponents, and with oneself. My disciples through the ages have done the best they knew how at their level of perception; and when they knew better, having transcended a few veils, they brought forth from the next level of their comprehension revelations which exalted all who were moving up the mountain with them.

Thus, do not shun the prophet in your midst, nor judge him too harshly.[25]

Beloved Master Jesus explains that we need to apply our own spiritual discernment, no matter what the source is:

Unfortunately, many who have been influenced by the best of men and women who set such devout examples as to be considered almost infallible have gotten stuck in doctrinal error. Out of a false sense of loyalty to the saints and the Holy Church (for one's true loyalty ought to remain tethered to Truth as to the water of Life—uncircumscribed by the vessel), these students have not kept up with the spiritual strides of their teachers.[26]

Spiritual writers quite often evolve beyond what they have written, rendering their written word less than complete or in places inaccurate, for there are many layers of spiritual knowledge unfolding.

Today, many students of religion, as well as many academics, believe we are entering a new age of enlightenment—and this despite all the chaos being caused by those who live in darkness, amassing great power, false prestige and even obscene wealth, and who use their status to wreak havoc in society. But despite this darkness, we are also witnessing astounding breakthroughs in all of the material sciences, and the unveiling of greater truths about our spiritual nature. It is important to not be so distracted by the mundane necessities of daily life nor the ample bad news that we face in the world that we miss out on the wonderful insights and revelations of our divine identity being revealed.

Thanks to the love and dedication of Jesus Christ, he has been able to speak to us not only from his unique perspective as the man Jesus, but as the fully realized Son of God, enabled by his pure and perfect attunement with our Creator.

Jesus shares with us the following powerful message directly from the I AM to us:

Be still and know that I who made thee will walk with thee alway, for I AM the very core of thy design. I AM thy Light and I AM thy Life and I AM thy soul's identification with immortality now and forever!
In the stillness of the dawn of thy immortality, I AM the resurrection of divinely inspired good works within thee.[27]

Here, we have a joyful confirmation that God is always with us, and that His divine and loving Light, purity and perfection are what make up the very core and foundation of who we really are! He is the source of our life and grants us a continual outpouring of His energy. He promises us eternal life as we strive to be like Him. Our future will be joyously spent in the ongoing performance of good and loving works. Praise be to Him!

Chapter 3

Losing All Fears

It is recorded in the Books of the Bible authored by John and Matthew that Jesus spoke to the scribes and the Pharisees, saying:

Ye are of your father the devil, and the lusts of your father ye will do...Ye serpents, ye generation of vipers, how can ye escape the damnation of hell?[1]

This statement has caused some people to fear and shudder even unto the present day. It refers to the Great Law in action, the Law of karma, the fact that "like attracts like." This law acts as an automatic judgment upon every person based upon their actions, words, thoughts, intentions and feelings, which indicate whether their will aligns with the good and loving will of God or the lower carnal nature in the consciousness of many people in embodiment.

Consider those whose pride speaks of doing great things, yet their actions are not righteous. Compare them with those who say less but act with loving kindness and thereby seek to heal and illumine everyone who comes into their world. Either an individual condemns himself by unrighteousness and unfulfilling imperfection, or they identify in their heart and soul with the perfect, loving goodness of God. Certainly, the best choice is to radiate vibrationally by one's thoughts, words and deeds that which lifts up one's brothers and sisters as well as oneself.

Jesus shares with us his teaching on righteousness:

As the earth shall be full of my knowledge, so the Law of Righteousness shall follow those who pursue it. Men are not here to judge or to criticize one another, but to judge (ascertain) that they themselves do not cast a stumbling block in another's pathway. This they may forestall by recognizing the perfection of their own Being and giving preeminence to its expression while extolling the same possibility for their fellow creatures. By so teaching and imbibing this cup of Life which is God, my disciples shall commune forever with the kingdom of our Father.
Lovingly, I AM your elder brother, Jesus[2]

Jesus refers to utilizing our innate ability to recognize those aspects within us that are divine, good and perfect—the essential contents of the cup of Life. We can contrast this with the following Old Testament verse that has been commonly misunderstood, causing unnecessary fear in the hearts of many who are prone to guilt over their own past misqualifications of God's Light.

Vengeance is mine; I will repay, saith the Lord.[3]

Despite the fact that theologians affirm the mercy of God, some have mistakenly attributed to God the characteristic of *human* vengeance, based on the above passage. The Master Jesus explains that in the above Bible quote, "vengeance" refers to "divine justice." This justice needs to be viewed in the context of the numerous biblical passages alluding to God's love for His children as well as

Losing All Fears

His mercy for us. There is nothing to fear if we strive to make amends as best we can for past shortcomings and failures, and to embrace righteousness and be merciful by not condemning others. After all, wouldn't we want others to be judged in the same manner as we ourselves would like to be mercifully judged?

Everyone reading this is probably aware of times in their life of doing the wrong thing. Feelings of guilt then result. I can recall numerous instances in my life. One of the earliest was when my dear grandmother was babysitting me when I was quite young, and I snuck into her bedroom, and stole a dollar out of her purse. That was a lot of money back in the 1950's, especially for a little boy—it could buy a lot of penny candy! I have felt the guilt of that action far beyond that day.

Guilt is very "soul-corrosive" if we ignore it. A person riddled with guilt has a self-imposed barrier from the Holy Spirit. We pay a big price by allowing the source of guilt to linger. The refreshing relief that comes upon us when we act to absolve our guilt through honest, positive initiative is a clear sign that the Holy Spirit blesses our efforts!

It bears repeating that God desires nothing but what is best for us. This is again in spite of seemingly contrary passages in scripture, such as references to Hell. Our loving Creator would never allow His children to suffer everlasting pain. A dramatic example is the reference to a lake of fire in Revelation.

And whosoever was not found written in the book of life was cast into the lake of fire.[4]

References to fire in the Bible refer to the process of transmutation and change, which sets all Life free from the painful memories and regrets relating to past sins. We are told that souls who have a heavy load of karma from their misuse of free will, resulting in the wrong use of divine energy, will need to spend some time on an astral plane after they leave embodiment, where they will learn to empathize through understanding and feeling the pain they have caused others. They will experience and sense the same negative feelings and thoughts that others felt because of them, so they can benefit from the value of the lesson. Never are these experiences for the purpose of punishment. They are only for instruction and to nourish the desire to be loving and to be loved. In this way, souls are taught by their own karma, which is a better teacher than anything or anyone else!

Our Creator gives us countless chances to seek forgiveness for our wrongdoings. It is important to remember that God always forgives us. Then we need to strive to sin no more and to replace our sin with good works.

We also need to embrace the spirit of forgiving others as Jesus admonished when he said we need to forgive "seventy times seven."[5] When we forgive others, we release the shackles that were binding us to everyone we are forgiving.

It is important to note, however, that there are rare instances when a particular soul, over many lifetimes, continually opposes and attacks God and leads other souls into purgatory. These souls reach a point where they amass so great a mountain of karma that they would be eternally transmuting it and suffering in that process. Therefore—in ultimate and final divine mercy—these few souls have their energies returned to the source of all Life, and do experience a "second death." This very infrequent occurrence is addressed in more detail in my previous book, *Our Magnificent Afterlife: Beyond Our Fondest Dreams*.[6]

Today, we are aware of countless sufferings among mankind. Thanks to extensive coverage from the media, we learn of miseries throughout the world, and our minds sense the vibrations of hatred, terror and violence—all of which create fear. The Masters emphatically tell us to not dwell on such things, for focusing on those areas does not lead to salvation. Instead, our beloved Master Jesus points us in a higher direction:

> *There are other vibrations far, far above man's poor power of perception in his present state which stem from the living fount of God's merciful heart. These speak of infinite mercy, of infinite beauty, of infinite compassion—of the dawn of a mighty civilization when the golden age shall have fully manifested.*[7]

What frequently happens is that those who strive for greater attunement with the goodness of life become discouraged because they judge themselves to be inadequate due to their awareness of their flawed human personalities. We are, however, advised to leave all judgments to God, even judgments of our own selves. We are to focus on God and the godly attributes of the Ascended Masters and saints with a greater love, which brings great Light and love into our lives. We are urged to definitely not conjure up and dwell upon thoughtforms of imperfection, for doing so can lead us far astray.

Beloved Master Kuthumi describes for us what the Masters want us to know:

> *It is not our intention to destroy aught else but illusion itself through the conception (and reception) in man of self-governed perfection and holiness. Only thus is the curtain of mayic [illusory, misleading] mist drawn back and the bright reality of truth seen to be shining in pristine purity. When you perceive the truth concerning your own life, it cannot help but quicken your spiritual pulse. Mounting hope leads to enthusiasm for the divine plan. And the inrushing power of the Holy Spirit as a joyous anticipation calms and claims the heart in the noble interest of exalting the whole consciousness into a more radiant, divine manifestation.*[8]

The greatest fear and illusion is that all that we know will end in death. Once that illusion is transcended, the purpose of life is viewed as stretching far beyond our limited human lifespan. Self-awareness is expanded, and we sense the immortality of our soul. Through the process of transcending and transmuting all illusion, any fears located in the conscious as well as the subconscious mind are eliminated.

The key is self-mastery. We are advised to develop our mastery and control over our four lower bodies (the interpenetrating energy fields of our physical, mental, emotional, and etheric [memory] bodies). As we learn and apply these teachings from Jesus and Kuthumi, we will develop the courage, by leaving behind all fear, to live in a new way, within the consciousness of God and His son, the Christ.

Chapter 4

Faith Rules

If thou canst believe, all things are possible to him that believeth.
Mark 9:23

From the very core of our being, as our faith in the presence of God in all things expands, we move closer to our ultimate victory over all that is unreal, including our own mortality. When souls believe they are able to have the positive and loving qualities of God, they are not blocked by doubt which would prevent these qualities from being recognized.

People who are doubters often demand to be shown miracles before they will accept spiritual truths. Yet those who are spiritually developed can use their "spiritual eyes" to recognize the spirit behind the physical. They do not demand physical evidence to prove spiritual reality.

When Thomas touched the wounds of Jesus' hands and the wound in his side, he professed his belief. Yet Jesus said:

SECRETS OF THE INNER LIGHT

Because thou hast seen me, thou hast believed: blessed are they who have not seen, and yet have believed.[1]

Those who have great faith are able to magnetize the perfection of their Higher, Divine Self, without the need to demand demonstrations from Heaven for physical miracles. These souls are said to be more "advanced" on the Path. They understand and know the reality of God intuitively.

The dominant divine Law is, "Because Thou art, I AM." Souls benefit from remembering this most basic truth. Without God, life would cease, for God is the animating principle of Life. When souls use their free will to make choices not aligned with God's will of goodness for all life, significant problems manifest.

Ultimate salvation can only occur when an individual determines with his or her own free will to believe in their true identity, the Higher Self, which is an aspect of God. If, instead, a person loses interest or commitment to this divine potential and returns to the weary ways of the mundane world, they cannot then expect to be blessed by God's grace. This is because, *more than anything else,* grace is given to those who seek and earnestly desire to attain the kingdom, which is Christ consciousness. Souls need to reach the stage of living righteously according to the laws of Creation. Living according to God's laws brings one peace, fulfillment, sought-after life experiences and even blissful experiences. This is the pathway that our Creator has provided for us to advance step-by-step along the way.

Beloved Masters Jesus and Kuthumi have blessed us with keys to the many mysteries of spiritual life that are "pillars of truth," providing the answers spiritual seekers need. The true spiritual nature of man is indeed holy and of God, and can only be understood by the higher, spiritual divine mind, the higher aspect of our consciousness.

The lower, or "carnal" mind of man, which is also described as the exclusively self-absorbed human ego, is unalterably opposed to and unable to comprehend these truths. The carnal mind of man will rationalize and do its best to preserve the status quo, using lies and misconceptions. What is required is for spiritual seekers to use their "spiritual eye" to confirm and know spiritual truths, instead of their "material eye" to prove spiritual truths. The penalty for non-belief in God's laws is an illusory sense of life that is centered upon mortality, toil and darkness.

Inner peace blesses devoted souls with direction, comfort and inspiration from on high. We can experience heavenly joy in this lifetime if we use our free will to accept direction from God. We can receive His grace and increase in the bliss of divine Light, unless we abuse the Law of free will by allowing thoughts, words and deeds that we know and sense deep down are *not* in accord with God's will.

Beloved Master Jesus tells us of God's beautiful purpose in wanting every soul to believe in and embrace a divine consciousness, or Christ consciousness.

> *The Godhead desires only to DEIFY man ("to glorify as of supreme worth," i.e., to make man Godlike by his complete soul-identification with the Spirit of Deity) by giving him his full release and freedom from oppressing circumstances (of karmic retribution).*[2]

On a mass scale, ongoing misuses of free will by numerous souls on Earth have led to enormous human suffering and significant weakening of faith in God. A large percentage of humanity on Earth have allowed numerous ideas spawned by the devious logic and rationalizations of the lower self to result in great losses of love as well as frightful diseases, suffering, and a world full of fear. This is a product of incorrect thinking and feeling. Jesus tells us:

> *Unfortunately, those who most need the assurance of this comforting knowledge are just the ones who find the divine ideas least comprehensible. The people of earth have absorbed much of the pseudoculture of the Cain civilization...seeking material success without the Spirit and popularity without Truth.*[3]

As a result, long-standing hatreds and abuses among mankind have hidden the framework for the urgently needed divine direction in the world. The Masters have told us that the hope for Earth lies in those relatively few spiritual seekers, compared to Earth's total population, who strive for their victory in their personal Christhood. To do this a strong faith is essential. Without embracing the truths that lead to spiritual self-mastery, the soul is really just wandering in a human wilderness. Because of God's unlimited love for His children the Path exists for us to achieve immortal victory. Divine guidance is imperative for all to achieve basic spiritual mastery and self-control.

Achieving a faith-filled consciousness has the wonderful effect of making life more worthwhile, where spiritual success and love grow. We can all enjoy continually exploring God's love. This is done by welcoming the divine spirit within, which expands the sense of divine love, of hope, and of creative ways to overcome debilitating emotions like doubt and despair.

It is by the power of faith that a person can trust in God and allow themselves to spiritually advance. This power of faith enables a soul to foresee and be a magnet for the manifestation of God's good intentions. Faith empowers an individual to not be held back by timidity, but rather to confidently expect God's goodness to grow. God's gift of free will to each of us requires that we consciously desire, call for and accept His heavenly gifts. This is, in fact, how God enjoys and shares in His holy kingdom.

Why is faith required? Because it is difficult, with our restricted consciousness (restricted by not only our habit-patterns of imperfection and ignorance, but by the limitations of our brain while in physical embodiment) to know the whole picture. It is best to think twice before rejecting spiritual concepts just because they are not completely understood. One pattern that needs to be changed occurs when we have those who claim absolute certainty about things they know little about. These individuals may have difficulty comprehending certain concepts that can be understood without difficulty by those who keep an open heart and mind.

All souls living on Earth encounter human misqualifications of fear, sorrow and hatred. The Masters advise us to minimize time spent with these feelings as they do not help our attempts to rise up higher in the Light. Instead, they recommend that every person attune through faith, prayer and meditation to focus on the *highest spiritual principles conceivable*. These emanate from the great loving heart of our Creator, and consist of limitless beauty, compassion and mercy—the foundations for a great civilization coming forth!

You can kindle your faith with these spiritual potentials and enjoy the energies they provide. You can perceive the attributes of Heaven while still on Earth. As it states in the Lord's Prayer:

Thy kingdom come. Thy will be done in earth, as it is in heaven.[4]

Are there *any* limits to the right application of this power of faith? Jesus tells us "no!" though the exercise of it needs to be within the confines of God's will rather than our own human desires.

Verily I say unto you, If ye have faith as a grain of mustard seed, ye shall say unto this mountain, Remove hence to yonder place; and it shall remove; and nothing shall be impossible unto you.[5]

Although perfect faith does have the power to move a mountain, it would have to be for a good purpose and in accord with God's will. Figuratively speaking, some of these "mountains" are man's negative habit-patterns (Chapter 11, "The Power of Habits").

The *enemy* of faith is doubt, which weakens and blocks the creation of God-inspired and focused goals. The *expansion* of faith is a key ingredient in an evolving spiritual consciousness.

Becoming closer to God requires the belief that He is, and the belief that God in you, right where you now are, can declare, as He did on the mountain top to Moses, "I AM THAT I AM."[6] This passage from Exodus, where God reveals His name "for all generations," is one of His greatest revelations to His children, affirming as it does our direct and inherent connection with our Creator.

To attain a knowledge of God demands a willingness to try to see "inwardly," that is, beyond appearances. Effort is needed to discern the divine Light that is not normally visible in the physical world. This Light is referred to in the Bible as the Light of Life.

In him [God] was life; and the life was the light of men....That was the true Light, which lighteth every man that cometh into the world.[7]

The implications of this investment of God's Light are exceedingly profound. Stated in simple terms:

We are permanent spiritual beings having a temporary human experience!

Such is the generous and loving gift bestowed by our God upon each and every one of us. We can consider this greatest of gifts, this most profound of mysteries, every morning upon arising from our bed, every evening when retiring and whenever we pause in our busy day: Permanently vested within each one of us, is the very Light of our Creator, the Light of Life itself! Unfortunately, so many do not recognize or comprehend this Light that shines in the darkness, which is the current, sorrowful state of many souls on Earth.

Faith is the essential ingredient for the transcending of our human consciousness into God's consciousness. People will believe in what is logically clear, which is why it is so important for souls to understand the science of spiritual reality. This science of the spirit graces us with a permanent foundation for joyous, spiritual living. This is the true reality of things, as opposed to experiencing life in a limited way with only the five physical senses. This permanent foundation makes living a spiritual life possible, with its daily wondrous newness. Jesus sums it up for us in the following:

> *Cosmic freedom is imbued with cosmic stability—with power, with graciousness, with creativity, and with the divine expression. It is a tangible flame all about you which can be contacted to elevate you to our standard of perfection and beauty.*[8]

It is helpful to offset any fear of change with the knowledge that any progression closer to God results in greater peace, joy and fulfillment.

Understand that we will be totally forgiven for all we have done that was less than perfect. Yes, we may have to offer prayers or give some form of penance, and, if possible, make amends to others we may have harmed, but our Creator, being a most loving parent, wants none of His children to feel alienated from His Glory by a sense of unworthiness, or a feeling that they are not forgiven. An understanding of this point is vital to the nurturing and growth of our faith. This subject of sin and forgiveness is thoroughly addressed in Chapter 8, "Freedom from Sin."

Nurturing our faith and expanding our spiritual vision is the key to opening ourselves to a complete and full sense of God reality and Christ consciousness.

Chapter 5

We Are God's Children With Unlimited Potential

Many Christians mistakenly believe that Jesus Christ is the "only begotten" son of God. Two Bible quotes that have contributed to that belief are:

Jesus saith unto him, I am the way, the truth, and the life: no man cometh unto the Father, but by me.[1]

He saith unto them, But whom say ye that I am? And Simon Peter answered and said, Thou art the Christ, the Son of the living God.[2]

These quotes are referring to the Christ consciousness that Jesus had attained, a Christ consciousness that all, with adequate preparation, may achieve. There are *numerous* verses in the Bible that make clear we are all sons and daughters of God, with unlimited divine potential. Several are listed in my previous work, *Unifying Truths of the World's Religions,* along with quotes from the sacred texts of the other world religions that affirm this fact.

Some of the most straightforward scriptural statements confirming our individual, divine potential are located in 1 John 3:

Behold, what manner of love the Father hath bestowed upon us, that we should be called the sons of God: therefore the world knoweth us not, because it knew him not.
Beloved, now are we the sons of God, and it doth not yet appear what we shall be: but we know that, when he shall appear, we shall be like him; for we shall see him as he is. And every man that hath this hope in him purifieth himself, even as he is pure.[3]

God desires *every one* of His children to strive for the highest levels of perfection. We can tap into this perfection as we attune to our Higher Divine Self, which is also known as our Holy Christ Self, our higher consciousness, or the Christ consciousness. Realize how much we are loved! God does not want us to experience continued suffering on Earth. We are not meant to always be in delusion and certainly not continuously beset by unfortunate circumstances.

Time is on our side. One lifetime is not enough time to evolve to the level of purity, love and divine attunement to make our Ascension and enter the higher realms of Heaven. We have all lived before. We need to know that the concept of reincarnation is real. The belief in reincarnation is evident through many of the world religions. There are numerous books on the subject that present overwhelming proof of it.

Within Christianity, the Dead Sea Scrolls and Gnostics texts offer persuasive evidence for reincarnation. So-called heretics who taught reincarnation were persecuted and the concept of previous lives was declared false after the Fifth General Council of the Church, formed by Emperor Justinian I, in 553 AD.[4] A wonderful book containing well-documented facts about the church's suppression of reincarnation and our divine potential is *Reincarnation: The Missing Link in Christianity.*[5]

Our beloved Jesus had this to say about the refusal of Christian church leadership to acknowledge reincarnation:

> *One example of a major loss which occurred through...a refusal of the clergy to move forward with Holy Truth is the present denial of or utter silence on the doctrine of reincarnation and the preexistence of the soul, taught both by me and my disciples and by Origen of Alexandria, which has been confirmed many times over in the direct experiences of the saints and just ordinary people.*[6]

As we attune to our Christ consciousness, we are blessed with the potential to forever lose any sense of loneliness or separation. We can also lose any feelings of struggle that would ensnare us and sidetrack us from the noble and righteous goals of our Higher Self. We can transcend to a level beyond being primarily about one's self and instead be immersed in the fulfillment of God's will and His loving plan.

When we are receptive, our Christ consciousness gradually reveals our role in this divine process. This results in becoming closer to God, loving Him and all in our world, and feeling divine Joy as we increase the flow of love to others. This process is the pathway of the Ascended Masters, saints, mystics and successful spiritual seekers throughout the ages.

This Path, which all need to follow eventually to return to our true home, will inevitably include having to deal with individuals who will find fault with, and perhaps even ridicule, our spiritual journey.

There can be many reasons why an individual will criticize another as that person strives to advance on his or her spiritual path:

1. The individual may be in a dark state of consciousness (immersed in the material world) and literally opposes any expression of higher spirituality.
2. The individual may be ideologically confirmed in a religious doctrine that denies another's individual Christ development—a belief that Jesus Christ is the *only* son of God.
3. Perhaps, at a subconscious level the individual is threatened by the sacrifice and striving that is required to achieve the blessing of spiritual self-improvement.

Some of these individuals can be recognized by how they will easily point out petty imperfections in others while ignoring their own.

Jesus himself experienced all of these forms of opposition as did his disciples—as have all the true saints through the ages. This, in more mystical terms, is referred to as the Path of Initiation. If we work hard and are dedicated to the Light, we will be blessed by God for our efforts, and assisted in overcoming all challenges along the way. Just as any real achievement requires dedication and hard work, including spiritual development, so are there wonderful rewards and blessings for the efforts expended!

Many Ascended Masters and saints feel that there is nothing more important than to spread this news of the upliftment and joy that is available when one is in this flow of loving Light that accompanies all good works of altruistic kindness—the eternal Cause.

Therefore, we are prompted to be a facet of the perfect and divine prism through which the immense shower of Light flows as part of our loving Creator's divine plan. We cannot allow thoughts of past errors to interfere with this possibility and best-chosen path. Just because we cannot go back in time and redo our past mistakes doesn't mean that our Creator will not forgive us, as He expects us to forgive others and ourselves. Master Kuthumi wants us to know that everyone can do this, and reap the resulting love and Light as we share it with others.

> *It matters not that you have made mistakes in the past. This is quite common on Earth today. What really counts is that you are willing to become the purity of your own Godly nature. As you sustain this God nature, being "good-natured" with the constancy of a saint, meeting every trial and temptation with equanimity of heart, the love and pristine wholeness of your own I AM life-currents descending through your crystal cord [aka "silver cord," the thread of Light and contact with God] will pass through the matrix of your Godly nature.*[7]

There is a grand sense of freedom achieved when souls have transcended the level of the human ego. I recall a time when I was young and eagerly searching for spiritual answers. I joined a "spiritual" organization as a staff member to attend their very expensive "deprogramming" courses for free. I realized that these courses, being so ridiculously expensive to the general public, bothered me. I was also soon bothered that at the end of every day, we basically sang our praises, looking up at a giant picture of the founder, and so in essence, worshipped only the founder of the organization. After two weeks of being on "staff," I realized that these practices were not in line with what I felt would be a proper spiritual path for me, since I felt strongly that spiritual teachings and courses should be low cost so everyone could afford them. I also didn't like basically worshipping the founder of the organization. So, I left and instantly felt free to pursue my spiritual search within other organizations that would resonate within my heart.

Evolving in this positive direction gets easier with the help of more and more attunement and love with God and His hierarchy. Leaving behind much human nonsense, we can instead live a life of good works. Due to the Law of karma and attraction, if we rise up to this level of living, it will result in a joyful return to the sender as well as amassing divine treasure. Sincere and persistent disciples on this path will know when their victory is close at hand. This comes about when their attunement is constant and they are no longer sidetracked by the distractions of stressful situations. For then the power of our Creator's wisdom and goodness manifests through the soul.

Master Kuthumi affirms this in his teaching:

Faint heart never won fair victory. Remember, the Life (God-force) in you is omnipotent....
God is the eternal Father of all that is good...God in you declares, "I AM"—and this Life can never cease to be! This is your hope and eternal substance. This is your faith become a tangible reality.[8]

We are blessed with descriptions of this most worthwhile and eternal goal which provides powerful motivation to achieve it. To that end, we will be inspired to ensure that what we do is done carefully with pure love for God, the divine hierarchy and all in our world. This is our path to self-mastery and freedom. We can pursue this path, developing our expertise along the way. We can co-create with God to manifest God's works—and not for personal celebrity.

In this process, we can enjoy being like Santa Claus 365 days a year, giving our presents of love and service! We can be generous with our praise of others' good qualities and works to nurture and encourage them. Yet at the same time, there will be no need to seek praise for ourselves—the reward is in the giving. The love we give is returned to us and helps everyone to better realize the love that God has for His children—and we return that love to our Creator.

Beloved Master Jesus wants us to know this Christ consciousness. He tells us:

We Are God's Children With Unlimited Potential

By allowing the Presence to take full dominion in your life, you will experience an expansion of Christ consciousness equal to (and I hope greater than) that which manifested in me during my 33 years (and more) of focusing the sacred fire in the temple of my then un-ascended body.[9]

Chapter 6

The Christ Consciousness

Today, millions of souls have succumbed to the nefarious habits of recreational drugs and lifestyles that lack righteousness. As these souls pursue freedom without the guidance of spiritual law, they do extensive harm to themselves—not only to their physical forms but by disrespecting their sacred energies. Our physical bodies, on loan to us while on Earth, are holy temples of God, and are not supposed to be defiled. When this is done, individuals will feel, down deep at a soul level, self-condemnation and guilt, which leads to feeling apart from God.

Often these same people proclaim how very free they are, yet they are blind to their self-imposed prison, and the wonderful truths of God they find so difficult to believe—that we are far more than these physical bodies we inhabit. Only when they realize how cut off they are from the purity of divine love will they begin to nurture their attunement with their Higher Self and call to God for help.

Freedom is won for all souls who realize that *God is right within the very center of their being* and who decide to *fully love God*. It is won for all who hold and strengthen this belief *regardless of what is going on around them.* To these souls, by the grace of our Lord, His power of salvation will be realized. This is the Path of wisdom—*believing and knowing God within.*

The Christ consciousness is the potential within every one of us. It is like a newborn baby, delivered into the world and into our hearts. This infant grows and matures so it may fulfill its life's purpose and divine destiny. Beloved Master Kuthumi has expressed this idea most eloquently:

> *It is invaluable for the chela [student] to pause and consider some of the wonderful yet basic seed ideas of Truth. These you will prove with ease to be God-ideas that can be expanded until the whole self, rising with them, is exalted into the all-knowing, comfortable Mind of Christ....*
> *The universe, like a sheltering mother, holds in contemplative wonder his own blessed being. Her boundless love desires to see the living Christ stretch his tiny limbs within the manger crib of limited human consciousness and expand to reach for the skies at last, beaming as the star of Bethlehem with peace and good will to every divine manifestation, saying with the angelic hosts in tones of purest love: "Glory to God in the highest, and on earth peace, good will toward men!"* [1]

It is helpful to remember that the Universal Christ is always by our side, ever ready to fill our lives with greater loving Light. As Jesus said:

Lo, I am with you alway. [2]

The only way that we can have God's kingdom here on Earth is when enough people understand and accept, on an individual level, the potential of the Christ Self within them.

The Christ Self of every individual is the sinless concept of perfection within that soul. It exists even if that soul doesn't desire it. When, however, a soul believes in and aspires to perfect attunement with the Holy Christ Self, significant assistance can be given by the Ascended Masters. This divine nature cannot be controlled or influenced by human, inharmonious or impure energies. Although all human thoughts and deeds utilize God's energies, only righteous actions are in tune with God's will for goodness. It is up to each individual to strive to attune with the love and wisdom of their Christ Self, which adds to the goodness of the world.

Dear Master Jesus tells us of his request to our Father for us to share in this great blessing of Christ consciousness:

> *Long ago, as I expanded my soul into the essence of communion with the Holy Christ Self of all through the universal Christ, I sent forth the call on wings of light to the eternal Father, to His heart of creation and being, to flood the essence and consciousness of Himself into the hearts of His children so that all who did hunger and thirst after righteousness might drink of the water of Life freely.*
> *Blessed ones, the water of Life flows freely from your I AM Presence charged with the feeling of the unlimited and unmeasured current of God's being, imparted unto each son and daughter in accordance with his capacity to receive. It is this full quality and power of God's immortality and intelligence in the very 'water' (energy) of Life which quickens in every son and daughter of Life the sense of the soul's eternal mission.*[3]

Thus, focus on God, visualize all aspects of the divine nature, what it feels like and how living in that state of consciousness would affect your response to every situation. This Christ consciousness is ever close at hand, therefore be vigilant to receive its guidance and assistance. Jesus continues:

This unifying, intelligent current from the heart of the Creator flows into the hearts of his offspring, enabling the alert and perceptive to imbibe the fullness of their inherent potential, regardless of how far short of the mark of Christhood they may be. The Father is ever a fount of hope!
Were it possible at this very moment for every seeker of oneness with God to outpicture the fullness of the divine nature, there would be no continuing need for greater effort; for the reality of Life would have dawned. Alas, such is not the case, for lesser aims have consumed men.[4]

Misqualified energy coming through impure thoughts and actions will cause that energy to return back to the individual in a form that will provide opportunities to learn necessary lessons. It has been reported that these karmic "re-actions" are overseen by a Karmic Board of high Masters who have the wisdom to determine what specific "karmic experiences" will offer the greatest lessons for the advancement of the soul.

Therefore, it is the highest wisdom to hold in mind the idea of divine perfection—the original vison of our Creator—for perfection in life. This is God's manifestation of His own life within us. The book of John tells us of the adulterous woman brought to Jesus, who told her to "Go, and sin no more."[5] Jesus forgave her and then held in his mind the vision of perfection for the woman. His act, whereby he honored her soul and extended forgiveness in front of all her accusers, was such a blessing for her that, as some Apocryphal (not included in the Bible) accounts disclose, she reformed her life and became one of the early and devoted Christians.

Whenever a soul chooses to allow a pattern of imperfection in their world of thought and action, they will be stuck in the mud of confusion—this being the result of carnal (pertaining to a self-absorbed human ego) and disordered thinking. Instead, salvation comes to those who hold God's vision in mind. This acts as a strong magnet that attracts the Christ consciousness and sweeps aside all that is less than perfection.

This is the original God design! The experience and attainment of reaching the continuous state of Christ consciousness is reported to be so magnificent, so indescribably delightful and exhilarating, that all who have attained this level invariably express great enthusiasm, concluding that no matter how long it takes, or how difficult the journey, it is well worth the effort. Once achieved, the return of all of the soul's loving actions occurs, sweeping in joyful energies so that the bliss of Heaven's love is realized in the heart of being. Souls can then perceive and experience the glorious radiance of Christ's illumination and comforting Presence.

There are probably times in life when you have provided a loving service, really helped someone, and then felt a great level of inner peace and joy. Remember those times, and seek to multiply them going forward. For this selfless action unblocks the flow of divine and loving Light.

Behold, the kingdom of God is within you.[6]

As long as a soul persists in allowing immorality and other imperfections and unrighteous acts, that soul will continue to be deceived and under delusion and will live separated from their divine identity in God. This experience of life's carnality never fulfills the desires of the soul, blocking any sense of true fulfillment and happiness.

The portion of a soul that is eternal is that portion that embraces the sinless Holy Christ Self. The soul knows, at a soul level, that the Christ consciousness is essential and foundational to all life. Once attained, a soul proceeds from success to success. This Christ consciousness beckons each one of us to engage in loving service to all in our world. This Christ is God's creation and is the true son of God.

The Holy Christ Self mediates between God's perfection and

the soul in embodiment on Earth that is in a state of spiritual becoming but often still is wallowing in imperfection and error. Such a soul, like the majority of us on Earth, has acquired the habit-pattern of unrighteous and imperfect acts by not knowing and embracing God's Higher Way. We remain bound in lower levels of vibration, destined to repeat these imperfect and unfulfilling acts until we design our activities to reflect a new focus upon the ideal of goodness that our Creator nurtures within us.

If attuning to the Holy Christ Self sounds too difficult, take heart, as there are suggested calls, affirmations and prayers presented later in the book that will significantly help any sincere seeker to achieve this most worthwhile goal. (Part II, "Working with the Light.") These calls invoke divine Light and intensify it around and through the four lower bodies (the interpenetrating energy fields of the physical, mental, emotional, and etheric [memory] bodies).

In addition, it is quite helpful to not dwell on the past. In my own life, I experienced the sadness and a degree of guilt over a failed first marriage. These feelings were difficult to let go, and until I released them, they held me back from going forward in life. What is past is past and cannot be undone. The Masters remind us that to look back, like Lot's wife,[7] can have serious consequences, significantly delaying our progress.

It is essential to forgive oneself for all past errors. This is a complex topic, and it is addressed in detail in Chapter 8, "Freedom from Sin."

We are also advised to not compare ourselves to anyone else. We are each a unique child of God. Do not be dismayed at the sight of another who has attained much in mastery, in wealth, in appearance, in popularity. Also, do not settle at any given level when viewing another who you may have surpassed. Rather, help them along, while continuing to hold fast to the divine vision of perfection in intent and achievement.

Consider and contemplate how all of life is holy. Be willing to embrace your divine truth, your foundational nature of purity.

We are urged to not allow ourselves to be troubled, despite all the tragic suffering on Earth at this time. It is good to empathize with those in need, but we need not become stuck in a state of emotional insecurity. Instead, be sensitive to the gentle presence from on high, which always wants to help in any action for the good.

A great Christian teacher, mystic and saint of the twentieth century, Padre Pio, advised his students to "Pray, hope and don't worry!" No matter what human calamities are occurring, we can be attuned to the loving Light from God. This enables the building up of divine Light and power in the four lower bodies and their chakra centers[8] for use as needed. All who want to be comforters or healers are empowered by maintaining their sensitivity and listening grace to divine Light. Daily loving meditation nurtures this attunement.

It is also important to remain humble despite the knowledge that we are sons and daughters of God, destined for divine perfection in the glorious Light. Embrace the attitude of the Ascended Masters, who remain humble throughout their joy-filled service to life.

All souls need to know who they really are. We need to know that God is so very real, and that our own reality is based on being a part of that divine reality. We are sons and daughters of God!

All that a person creates on Earth is far less than what they ultimately are, for their higher, divine Self is at-one with God, and God cannot be contained within any creation. God's creation is forever expanding, and as God's children we are destined to as well.

Chapter 7
Empowering Humility

How can humility empower us? It is helpful to have a more complete understanding of it. In the Bible, the quality of humility sounds like a definite requirement if a person envisions a future in God's kingdom:

> *Verily I say unto you, except ye be converted, and become as little children, ye shall not enter into the kingdom of heaven. Whosoever therefore shall humble himself as this little child, the same is greatest in the kingdom of heaven.*[1]

We can learn from the Ascended Masters' teachings why humility is so important and how it works. Humility involves leaving the human ego behind and losing any former sense of separation from Life. It embraces the idea of continuously experiencing the joy of giving wise and loving kindness to all. The Master Jesus shares an insightful description of how Ascended Masters view themselves and their role in life:

> *The Ascended Masters hold in common a sense of humility in recognizing themselves as omnipresent facets of the Godhead dedicated as One to the service of the All. As such they are always obedient to the cosmic intelligence of the Mighty I AM Presence in the Great Central Sun [the Godhead], yet humble and compassionate enough to respond to the heart calls of the most discordant or intemperate human on Earth.*[2]

Ascended Masters enjoy beautiful relationships with each other, exhibiting the same kindness, respect and humility to their compatriots that they grant to all who struggle at lesser levels of attainment. The Master Jesus tells us that it is best to *not* use the expression "We're only human." Despite the fact that we on Earth are presently wearing bodies of flesh, this does not eclipse our greater reality that we are Spirit, temporarily inhabiting human form. What should be said, we are told, is "We're really divine!" Let us not hold a self-image of being bodies with "unappeasable longings" and cravings. Rather, it is best to view ourselves as "sparks of the Infinite, longing for reunion with the glory of the cosmic fires [divine Light] of Home."[3]

Furthermore, the Master Jesus shares with us his profound description of what will take place as we act with humility, while we live with determined passion to rise up into our full divine potential.

> *All mysteries shall be revealed unto the humble who are truly meek, who fear not, knowing they shall inherit not only the Earth but also the kingdom of spiritual power to exercise dominion over all the creation. You see, when the Father calls, "Come up higher"; when the Father beholds your true inner compassion, your longing which is only for God-victory over human causes and effects; when the Father sees the vital, absolutely determined intent of your heart to be*

one with your Holy Christ Self and Mighty God Presence I AM, then I do not think it shall be long in coming![4]

During this process, we may sometimes benefit from "divine feedback." This comes in the form of a sense of humiliation or other negative feedback regarding a situation that can be viewed as a "course correction" to get us back on the right track. We are blessed to have this guidance, and it demonstrates a loving parent gingerly guiding his child. It is never imposed in too great an amount, as it is always tempered and not to be more than the soul can bear.

Regarding humility, Jesus is quoted in the Bible as saying:

Whosoever will be great among you, let him be your minister;
And whosoever will be chief among you, let him be your servant.[5]

Jesus was truly a "servant leader." There are many examples of this in the New Testament. None were more poignant than his final act with his disciples in the hours before his trial and crucifixion. He, the Master, in a remarkable demonstration of humility and love, knelt down and washed the feet of each of his followers.

A leader only places himself first when it comes to bearing responsibility. For when a soul reflects the true nature of God, which is love, then the joy of lovingly helping and serving others becomes paramount. Furthermore, as history proclaims and likely as our own personal experience confirms, the honored and respected leaders among us truly serve their constituency by modeling in their own everyday behavior that which they expect and request from their followers—as opposed to leaders that are followed because of intimidation and fear.

Another aspect of humility is not to engage in the condemnation of others. The Masters warn us of this because condemnation is in opposition to the Christ consciousness. This can be a challenging concept on Earth due to the number of people who cause unnecessary suffering by not practicing the Golden Rule. This rule states "Do unto others as you would have them do unto you." A wonderful precept of that rule is "Do unto yourself as you would do unto others—for you surely shall."[6] This is worthy of contemplation.

The act of condemnation inhibits a developing soul from rising up to the purity of motive within that perfect consciousness, which was demonstrated by Jesus throughout his earthly mission.

For God sent not his Son into the world to condemn the world; but that the world through him might be saved.[7]

When a person condemns others, they often wind up condemning themselves. Additionally, there can be times when we condemn ourselves after making a mistake and then we project that condemnation onto others. We are limiting ourselves when we do this, for we cannot love our Creator or the worlds of His creation when we are sorely lacking in self-esteem. In other words, if we do not love ourselves in the higher (divine) sense, we are likewise incapable of fully loving others.

In the case of those who clearly cause the suffering of others, we need to remember that most, but not all, people who cause suffering do so out of ignorance and especially ignorance of the law. For if they knew or believed in karmic Law, it would remind them that what they choose to do to others will return to them.

Humility does not prevent us from taking a strong stand against evil-doers. Love dictates action to protect the innocent. Although we are taught not to condemn evil-doers with feelings of hatred or dislike, if they can be stopped in the act of harming others, then stopping them is a righteous thing to do. The chief point to remember is the spiritual origin of life, which naturally embodies the Golden Rule. After all, those purposely harming others should be treated in the same way we would expect ourselves to be treated if we were ignorant enough to perform such acts. However, we need to ensure we do not wander into the realm of revenge.

Yes, there are those rare instances when a particular soul has long been dedicated to opposing God's will of goodness for all creation. These souls have amassed so much negative karma that it cannot realistically be overcome. Through divine mercy, these souls may have their energies returned to the source of all Life. This outcome is determined by the wisdom of God; it is not by our judgment or our decision.

God sent us into the world to help raise it up. It is essential to strive to be generous and noble in our relationships, and to avoid rigidity and narrow-mindedness. All that is good originates from our Creator, and we can gain a closer and more joyful relationship with God and all of life by striving for two goals:

1. Lead a life filled with good works, faith and love.
2. Reach for and maintain continual attunement with the divine.

Beloved Master Jesus graces us with an overview of how to make progress in living a good, yet humble, life:

By humility and steadfastness of purpose, through thinking faith, hope, love, and God (Good), you will soon begin to outpicture in greater measure the things of the Spirit upon which your heart meditates and dwells. You will not long remain a helpless introvert dwelling in a world withdrawn from reality; neither will you be a callous, selfish extrovert dwelling in the surface foam of life. Instead, you will be balanced, capable of reaching up mind and heart to God and yet with love and tenderness able to reach down with helping hands, free of pride, to your brothers and sisters yet in a state of bondage.[8]

Jesus points out that we need to be humble to avoid pride. Pride reinforces the ego, and we need to transcend the human ego, giving all credit and glory to our Creator for every good thing. As we do so, we lovingly attune with God, allowing greater blessings of Light to infill us. We are then more able to manifest the balanced action in our lives as Jesus has described—reaching up to God with a pure and receptive heart and then blessing those less fortunate with our help.

In the Bible, the dangers of pride are given:

Pride goeth before destruction, and an haughty spirit before a fall.[9]

In our efforts to escape the clutches of pride, we also have to watch out for false humility. Some people are "proud that they are not proud." Some people feign humility to look better in others' eyes—but eventually the truth is revealed, that they have kept their own high opinion of themselves, absent any acknowledgement of the truth—whether they realize it or not—namely, their total dependence on God.

Genuine humility, versus false humility or fawning, is a wonderful and endearing trait. Although it is certainly true that we are not greater than our loving Creator, the truth is that we *are* made in the divine image, and that we are destined by God's grace to become as great as our Creator wants us to be. The divine intent is that we evolve to the point in our humility where we have total identification and attunement with our Mighty I AM God Presence.

Chapter 8

Freedom From Sin

A common error committed by sincere lovers of Spirit is dwelling on their numerous past errors, and then allowing their beliefs and feelings to lead to conclusions of gross imperfection. This sense of regret, or even stronger self-loathing, holds a soul back from advancing on the spiritual Path.

Sin is such an important subject because countless millions of souls on Earth are laboring under an enormous sense of blame and self-condemnation due to real or imagined past sins. Yet the reality is that our Creator is not interested in condemning His children, any more than loving parents on Earth desire to condemn their children. Fortunately, a correct understanding of sin will eliminate the stress and pain involved—after which peace and better attunement with God is possible, accompanied by the power to do greater good.

This is *not* a simple subject because it involves subtleties within spiritual law and the karma of each individual. Sober study and reflection is important. It is helpful to maintain an open mind and a loving heart while considering the validity of these teachings. Every soul needs to discover for themselves the freedom contained in the truth of these principles and to confirm them in their own heart.

Critical to this examination is the knowledge that the "old law" of "an eye for an eye and a tooth for a tooth"[1] was set aside with the coming of Jesus as the Wayshower.[2]

Scripture reveals that in the era of the Old Testament prophets, mankind lived under a different spiritual dispensation. Human civilization was largely degenerate and most rulers were often harsh and cruel in the measures used to subjugate their subject peoples.

In these earlier times, life was rougher, great discipline may have been needed, and stricter laws may have been required. Due to this "eye for an eye" teaching in the Old Testament, many people are afraid of divine justice and also do not feel worthy enough to be heard in prayer. God as lawgiver and also as Spirit is viewed by many as primarily focusing on rigid precepts and harsh condemnation of human wrongdoing.

People can be weighed down by strong feelings of hopelessness whenever they focus on their "sins." After which, they falsely believe that they will never be able to comply with the perfection of the Law. They perceive that the Law is inflexible, and nearly impossible to comply with, so they simply continue on in life without making the effort to discontinue thoughts, words and deeds that they know deep down are wrong. It is really a shame, and a tragic waste of time—simply because they falsely believe that it is impossible to comply with God's laws.

The human, or carnal, mind promotes an inaccurate vision of God. Many people think of God as being like them, regarding God as being susceptible to the same angers and other negative emotions they feel. The Creator is seen by some as judging them harshly, viewing them as guilty of many sins and deserving of punishment. They may even falsely believe that God has human reactions that would include being unfair or having unbridled anger. And, they may view this as "natural" and an understandable reaction. They may be afraid of spiritual law, or they feel that they do not deserve to benefit from studying spiritual law. They may feel that it is not worth the bother to be loving and kind. Instead, they merely focus on basic human activities and avoid all things spiritual.

We know from the New Testament that our Father, the I AM THAT I AM, sent His son Jesus "to change the hearts of men" by teaching a new standard of human interaction, to return fallen mankind to our true, ordained status as sons and daughters of our Father in Heaven. This dispensation was based upon the Golden Rule and upon the great Christian hallmark of forgiveness.

Our Creator is highly interested in *freeing all souls from ignorance regarding what sin is*. This includes being truly free through learning spiritual principles, which empower us to be less apt to succumb to the myriad temptations we are faced with while on Earth.

Although God cannot allow His Law to be less than perfect, much forgiveness and grace occurs during the lengthy process of a soul overcoming their past incorrect uses of free will—decisions that were made that did *not* expand the growth of goodness in life. God is merciful, understanding of His children, and grants nearly unlimited patience as they progress spiritually.

What is often not considered is the divine Love that God bestows upon us, His children. Our souls know deep inside (though for many this is completely obscured) that our Creator is truly all-loving and omniscient. Once free from false beliefs regarding a vengeful God, souls can join in feeling and acting in the same all-loving and understanding manner. In some souls with deep-seated anger issues, psychological counseling can also be of assistance.

Much of the karmic stress and pain that souls experience daily is caused by this misunderstanding of sin and the unnecessary condemnation of self and others taking place on Earth. The confusion encountered by the soul is often a result of remembering past acts that are simply the result of ignorance and not the result of a purposeful intent to cause harm as "sinful acts." These unfortunate "memories of sin" inevitably cause self-condemnation. The truth is that it is the relative few who commit intentional acts of harm to others. It is crucial for souls to stop harboring incorrect views and to no longer make burdensome, false conclusions about their past shortcomings.

We do not have to always be perfect and never make mistakes, but perfection can be our goal and our intent. For our intent is what makes up our true character, and that is what is important to God. All we need to do is the very best we can, and not be stressed in the doing. The key point we have been given is that as we build upon our spiritual attunement and knowledge, it's important to not allow it to be compromised by condemning anyone, including ourselves. The easiest way to avoid this is to be in a state of loving forgiveness towards all persons. This will result, over time, in an increasing flow of God's loving Light through us.

Our beloved Master Kuthumi has told us that God's loving Law is often misunderstood as too inflexible. This misunderstanding can feed a sense of sin:

The blessed Law is in reality neither weak nor rigid....
The Law is the greatest security in the universe, protecting the righteous and commanding the unrighteous to forsake the sinful unreality of their ways and come up higher. While affording ample opportunity for all to mercifully dismiss sin and the law of sin from their worlds, the Great Law also promises absolute God-justice to evildoers who persist in their evildoings, blasphemous toward Christ and his Call.... Your freedom from sin and the sense of sinfulness should liberate your soul from an oppressive apprehension of the hurdles of the Law—and what has seemed to be your own limitation in jumping over those hurdles.[3]

It is interesting to note that some people can enjoy condemning others for the same faults and misbehaviors that they themselves have and commit, turning a blind eye to their own similar acts and traits.

The physical senses tend to keep us focused in the physical and not looking beyond at the intentions of the Spirit—which provides loving assistance to all who ask. Setting our goals high to embrace spiritual reality with its beauty and love will free souls from this ceaseless round of condemnation and the tragic wasting of divine energy in self-pity. If we allow ourselves to return to states of apathy and lethargy, we cannot then expect God's grace to automatically be granted. Our beloved Master Jesus describes the penalty for "falling back" to a former lower state:

> *The penalty for unbelief or inattention to the laws of God is a false sense of existence, entertaining drudgery, mortality, oppression, and darkness—quite the reverse of the God-intent of the soul's exaltation unto the glory of eternal Life!*[4]

Through recognition and repentance of sins and through reducing and eliminating future misbehavior, the obstructive sense of sin can be transcended by God's grace.

Our beloved Master Jesus clearly advises us that we need to rid ourselves of any sense of guilt:

> *To the blessed who have suffered guilt too long:*
> *The power men have given, inadvisedly, to the whole idea of sin must be broken ere the full perfection of God can be fully known. Humanity through force of habit continually re-creates feelings of guilt which mar the soul, shading the brilliant stream of divine illumination passing through, as it were, a pane of glass and depriving the 'lightstream' (lifestream) of the wondrous luminescence of God....*
> *For far too long the race has continued in a round of ceaseless condemnation of themselves and others, resulting in a habitual misqualification of energy. This has caused a false*

conscience to be created within the subconscious, inculcating feelings of guilt and unworthiness in self and others. These feelings reinforce in turn the false conscience which then overrides the inner voice of the divine One, who is the only true and reliable conscience.[5]

To break free from this "false conscience," we need to raise our sights to the greater spiritual reality. Whenever a soul determines to make spiritual progress and to free itself from the weight of carnality and karma, divine Light will illumine that soul's pathway. Though significant work and surrender may be required to transmute and transcend one's karmic weight, setting that goal and focusing on righteous living places a soul on the path of freedom.

Our sense of sin strongly relates to our state of conscience. Our conscience is highly attuned with the divine. It is sensitive to receiving guidance from our Holy Christ Self. Conscience is composed of memory, as well as our feelings and thoughts. When rightly oriented, it is the teacher of each soul, receiving promptings from our Holy Christ Self, and storing this guidance for our present and future direction.

Our conscience has to contend with the influences of the mass consciousness on Earth. This worldly consciousness is a morass of artificial standards and values based on all forms of human interaction and on mass media that, if not identified and dealt with, block any spiritual progression. Much self-condemnation and judgment, as well as misguided error, can be avoided when the spiritual practitioner identifies the assaults brought on by the mass consciousness and deploys the tried and true spiritual techniques and disciplines in Part II to shield oneself from them.

Master Kuthumi describes how to nurture one's conscience:

Your God Self has given you the power of free will so that you will lovingly, joyously choose to meditate on your own life plan—to think about it, to invoke it, to pursue it, and to

> *will it into manifestation. This process is intended to stimulate your own realization of and respect for divine values and enable you to more effectively establish in consciousness that conscience which is a truly sensitive instrument. This inner voice does not induce self-torture and anquish but offers guidance and comfort that enables you to decipher the true will of the Father and the Son always with you in your own I AM Presence and Holy Christ Self.*
> *Out of consciousness attuned to Divinity arises the right idea which transmutes the wrong idea, supplanting erring thought and emotions with the eternal banner of Truth, Light, and Right. This triple reinforcement of your Christ Self frees the soul from all past mistakes based on ignorance, dogma, doctrinal controversy, ecclesiasticism [excessive attention to details of church practice], 'situation ethics', the woeful misunderstanding of the life and mission of beloved Jesus, and all so-called evil vibrations.*[6]

Master Kuthumi addresses the aspects of God that involve each person's conscience and mind. This teaching, rightly understood and taken to heart, can be extraordinarily liberating:

> *This Mind who is universal consciousness embodies the Law and the Truth of being for every manifestation of Himself—made in his image and likeness. As the center of all Self-awareness, including that of his offspring, this Mind, then, is also the divine Conscience—the discriminating intelligence of good and evil, right and wrong, Himself exercising (and enabling man to exercise) free will.*
> *Now, these thoughts are the correct thoughts about God. Going one step further, we see that the correct thought of God in man (i.e., the thoughts God thinks in and through man) is, then, man's only true or necessary conscience. And this divine Conscience is God! With this understanding*

which thou shalt surely gain through oneness with the universal Mind, the first and only commandment the disciple would ever need is "Thou shalt have no other Conscience before me!"[7]

It is vital to be able to discriminate between a false conscience that justifies and condemns oneself, and divine conscience which provides inspiration, wisdom, love and guidance toward the fulfillment of a soul's divine mission in life.

Due to the purity of our Creator, sin plays no part within Him. And, sin can play no part within us unless we practice acts outside the Law, or continue to dwell upon past sins which keep alive an artificial sense of sin. Doing so would only feed the "false conscience" with false ideas.

Forgiveness will be complete as soon as it is sincerely sought (along with appropriate restitution if that is possible). Although feelings of guilt and shame provide a motivation for people to confess and become penitent, guilt and shame which endures never allows anyone to be free, for they contain the frequency of condemnation—both toward others and oneself.

It is possible to transcend the level where one has to meticulously abide by "do's and don'ts." We can arrive at a level of simply attuning to God's love which provides a steady guidance through divine consciousness of living in harmony and loving kindness. At this level, souls usually instinctively obey the Ten Commandments while feeling new levels of freedom and happiness.

The benefits of living within the Law include the protection of the Law. Beloved Master Jesus tells us:

The spiritual senses are best quickened by a pure spirit free from feelings of condemnation and guilt. To all sincere chelas [students] of the Great Law, I AM therefore saying, Thy sins be forgiven thee![8]

Freedom From Sin

Our Creator's love and mercy for His children make it easier to repent and make amends for our sins than most realize. As we free ourselves from unnecessary and unhelpful feelings of guilt and instead practice fully loving and forgiving others and ourselves, we can rapidly free ourselves from the karma of our sins.

This relates to the story of the prodigal son in the Bible, *which is more about the forgiving father than the son.* In the story, the son asks for his inheritance early, and the father gives it to him. The son goes off into the world and spends all the money foolishly. After suffering and starving for a while from being broke, the son decides to return to his father. To his credit, the son plans to confess to his father that he has sinned, not only against his father, but against Heaven. And he plans to tell him that he is no longer worthy to be his son, and to request to be just his servant.

But when the son returns, his father, seeing him at a distance, runs to embrace him. The son tells his father of his unrighteousness, and that he is not worthy to be his son. But the father is so delighted, he calls for a celebration with a great feast, and proclaims that although his son had been dead, he is now alive again—he was lost and is found.[9]

This story illustrates how forgiving and understanding our loving Father is towards His children. Our loving Creator is eager to forgive us for our sins. He, even more than you, understands your lesson and is glad that you have learned it. What is so important to remember is that *God is not angry with you!*

That being said, His Lords of Karma will not allow deliberate malicious acts against others to not be answered by returning karma. The Lords of Karma are High Masters who are truly compassionate and who creatively assign karmic conditions based on their great wisdom and total understanding of what is best for each soul.

Beloved Jesus describes how the Karmic Board serves to grace us with what our souls require:

> *Let judgment remain the prerogative of the Karmic Board;*
> *they render it with good qualifications and compassion.*
> *They seal each judgment with the power of opportunity,*
> *they are ever mindful that God chastens those whom he*
> *loves, and their mercy droppeth as the gentle rain upon the*
> *souls of all who suffer the necessity of karmic judgment.*[10]

Masters Jesus and Kuthumi want us to not be discouraged by the "high hurdles" of the Law. We are encouraged to reach for goals that may not always be met, but to reach for them anyway, to strive for living a more righteous life.

We are reminded that every victory, no matter how small, takes us a step or two closer to our ultimate victory in the Light. And each success increases our capacity to receive more of that Light, which blesses us with healing and illumination. Each step in the right direction takes us closer to the full manifestation of the Law of Love as it moves all of creation higher in its spiritual Ascension. God's grace multiplies our elevated words and honorable deeds in this direction.

The reality contained within man's love of God, and within God's love for man contains no sin. From the viewpoint that is held by one's Holy Christ Self, where the standard of the immaculate concept is paramount, sin has no reality. This is so, despite numerous but largely misunderstood references to sin within the sacred texts. The time is long overdue to focus our collective energies on the reality of the divine virtue within God's children. This is experienced at the level of the Christ Self, where regardless of the outer form and state of being, the potential of the individual to attain divinity is held fast. Applying the Christ standard would surely result in a drastic reduction in the incidence of "sin" on Earth.

It is simply not possible for a soul to hold a vision of overcoming and spiritual progress for themselves *if they retain an attitude of condemnation and non-forgiveness.* By God's grace, the impetus to make progress in this comes through the Holy Spirit and a soul's sense of joy as the blessings of progress become ever more apparent.

This understanding is given to us so that we may avoid despairing over past misdeeds. Our God has a merciful heart. The kingdom of God, His consciousness, is total perfection and Light. We can conclude that our loving Father is not at all fixated on any particular misdeed. He is, rather, seeking to draw from us what is in His very own nature: a loving forgiving contrition to quickly disavow what is wrong and to go forward with a purified heart, in spiritual dignity.

And this brings us a wonderful dispensation. Even though no one escapes divine justice by evading any part of the Law, it is possible to accelerate freedom through the invocation of the merciful flame of forgiveness, with intense love for God and others. (Part II, "Working with the Light."[11])

The Masters inform us that what is required to overcome our karmic burdens is the building of the kingdom of God's consciousness within us—the concept embodied in Christ of *total good*. It is essential to transmute all imperfect aspects within our worldly consciousness. Doing so, along with the purification of our four lower bodies (the interpenetrating energy fields of the physical, mental, emotional and etheric [memory] bodies) allows the unrestricted flow of pure Light. This Light, which carries eternal happiness, is then magnified by the Christ Mind. When we make the necessary efforts by a consistent assertion of our will power to purify and bring these four lower bodies into harmony, God's grace and mercy can then enter and assist in furthering this process. We experience the transmutation of former thought and feeling patterns. All of this enables our loving Creator to fully live in the hearts of His obedient children, where the Light of greatest joy can flow forth to bless all.

Grace is granted to those who set their focus on reaching God's kingdom, meaning His consciousness, and living by His righteous and just laws.

We have previously read that our Beloved Jesus has granted forgiveness of sins to all "sincere chelas (students) of the Great Law." It is fitting now, at the end of this chapter on sin, to read his follow-up statement concerning this grace:

> *Greater peace in the feeling world and an intense desire to be in attunement with the omnipresence of God will be the first signs following your acceptance of this intercession of my grace. From the center of Christ-forgiveness, there blazes forth a delightful inner confidence that God's abundance is all around you—a feeling that God's love in you is so magnificent that sin and the record of sin are completely swallowed up by it! Thus are death and the "wages of sin" swallowed up in total victory.*[12]

Let us all strive to raise our spiritual sight and focus on doing everything that is required to embrace this higher loving and joy-filled level of consciousness.

Chapter 9

The Perfect You

To the degree that we have been pummeled by negative experiences (and we all have been) our senses can be clouded rendering it difficult to conceive of or know the realities of Heaven's perfection.

Such adverse experiences can leave scars that make it difficult to visualize and strive toward living in attunement with divine perfection. Those most badly hurt by past trauma would significantly benefit from working with a counselor or psychologist.

In addition, how can mankind be expected to be perfect, when we are trapped in significant amounts of negative karma, ignorant of spiritual Law, and filled with habits and desires that hinder our spiritual evolution? It seems quite unlikely that appeals for perfection that come from on High will be heard by the "outer man." However, these divine supplications are, in fact, heard by those who have invested time in nurturing or developing their inner spiritual being—that is, attunement with their Higher Self. God and His hierarchy urge us to strive to be perfect because:

1. It is possible, as many who have gone before have demonstrated.
2. The rewards which come from this spiritual self-improvement are, indeed, "heavenly!"

Our beloved Master Jesus tells us that godlike perfection is possible:

The outer form is only Godly, then, when it expresses divine qualities: man himself is only a manifestation of God when he is expressing Godly attributes. His identity is God's only when he self-identifies with God through words and works identical to God's. And this is possible, else I would not have commanded my own:[1]

Be ye therefore perfect, even as your Father which is in heaven is perfect.[2]

The idea of attaining perfection is mentioned dozens of times, in both the Old and New Testaments. Other world religions also acknowledge that attunement with our Creator and emulation of His divine qualities is the goal for every soul (even if a soul does not consciously know this in their "outer mind," they sense it deep within).[3]

Because our planet currently has tremendous negativity and suffering, it is crucial to remember the path to our salvation. Jesus shares with us an expansion of the beloved Psalm of David:

I know that the whole world is aware of the so-called shadow of death, yet most all seem to find comfort in the Psalm of David, "Yea, though I walk through the valley of the shadow of death, I will fear no evil: for Thou art with me." Blessed ones, to live daily in the Thou-art-with-me consciousness is to live in the certain knowledge that your own Mighty I AM

Presence is walking right within you and helping you to do the perfect thing always.[4]

Many great Masters who have gone before us and climbed the steps of their spiritual evolution are standing by, ready to show us the way to come up higher! These advanced beings are eager to assist, for love is the byword of all true hearts of Light. Nothing pleases them more than to help us when we allow it and call for it. Part II provides suggestions for these calls.

Beloved Master Kuthumi also urges us to renew our closeness with our Creator by perfecting ourselves:

Hold fast the hands of Love that have borne you thus far; for he who fashioned thee of old, fashioned also the Christ! The Light that shines beyond the years overcomes all fear and clothes thee now with the auric radiance of God's own love —the magic circle of Christ's family unity. Let them TRY to shut thee out—GOD HAS TAKEN THEE IN!
Be filled with God and all else shall be overcome, for the Most High shall overcome all imperfections in thee by his gift of Light, Love, and Life, which remain to this day unbroken by any or all patterns less than perfection![5]

Until we have reached a level of perfection through a strong and continuous connection with our Christ Self, we need courage to think, speak and act in the very best way we know how, despite knowing that mistakes may be made. We cannot allow others who would point out our faults to distract or deter us. When we strive for perfection and our motive is good, our release from bondage to freedom will arrive more quickly.

More than once, prophets and saints who have gone before on the path of overcoming have begun their life's spiritual mission when they were seemingly not up to the task. When Moses came upon the burning bush and doubted himself and resisted the Lord

God, He made it clear that Moses' imperfections did not matter. It was rather his trust in God and his willingness to strive that would allow him to succeed in leading the Israelites to the Promised Land.[6]

There are countless examples of "imperfect" yet contrite and loving souls who responded to their inner calling and, through great striving, achieved their life's mission. When Mark Prophet (now the Ascended Master Lanello) was a young man, he doubted himself because of his human shortcomings. His wife, Elizabeth, has shared with us that while he was meditating on his calling to the ministry, he heard the inner voice of Jesus proclaiming:

My Son, if we were to wait for people to become perfect, we would never have any teachers on Earth.[7]

To experience the great joys inherent in perfecting ourselves, we will need God's help, and we will receive it! Although we can see in nature how outside forces create change, dramatic changes are also possible from within the very depths of our soul. More will be presented in the following chapters on the process of achieving perfection.

We are told by the Masters that we can realize and attain the power of God that stems from the cosmic fire that burns deep within each one of us. Since this incredible concept may be difficult for some to believe, let us hear what our beloved Master Jesus says about it:

The creative fires are at the very core of being, and the ancient memory scored in electronic life is that the spirit of man was born out of the very sacred fires by which Elohim gave birth to cosmos. The sons of God simply cannot forget that they came forth from the Great Central Sun to sow the fires of the Christic seed everywhere in the matter worlds— and to endow their Father's creation with the light of Life.[8]

This is a tremendous statement concerning our unlimited divine potential and the nature of life. Here, Jesus refers to the "Elohim," who are the highest in the hierarchy of creation, and the builders of form—Masters of Light and creation, in perfect oneness with God.

Actions that are not in alignment with God's will—that which does not originate in God—things that are not inherently "good," cannot be a permanent part of God. Even though the imperfection that we witness on Earth may be what we regard as "reality," such imperfection does not have permanence from the eternal, heavenly perspective. Things that are less than perfect cannot be eternal.

In addition, we know that our physical bodies are temporary vehicles we inhabit while in our earthly existence. They are not designed to last forever. Our higher celestial bodies, however, which interpenetrate our physical bodies, can exist forever in the eternal heaven worlds.[9]

Mixed in with all the imperfection on Earth, however, is much perfection and beauty. This includes beauty in nature and the love shared by all good people who follow the Golden Rule and experience the joy of selfless service to one another. This perfect beauty and love represents a small portion of the totality of goodness, Light and love found in the heavenly realms.

The earth plane is the school room that the soul is visiting on its journey to its true home in eternity. Ultimately, it is only the soul, confirmed in God, that moves on into eternity. All of our material possessions, and any of the material world's imperfections will not accompany us.

Beloved Master Jesus shares with us the profound and glorious changes that some people experience when they are graced by God's loving Light:

Countless individuals visiting the religious shrines of the world, such as Lourdes, Fatima, and others (many of which were established by my blessed mother, Mary, for the hope and healing of men's hearts), have realized for the first time the awesome futility of life without God. The great influx of the magnetic attraction of the divine has thrilled their souls with such an outpouring of Light, such a sense of nearness to the Presence, as to flush out of the electronic structure of their flesh all the inharmonious patterns they had previously established through the misuse of free will. This has produced what mankind calls a miracle but which I declare again to be simply the reestablishment of the Father's love—which never should have been usurped by human discord in the first place![10]

As we strive for perfection, our good intention, along with our prayers for guidance and assistance, is noticed, which results in the assistance of Angels and Ascended Masters. Over time, we will be able to attain higher levels of perfection. This process is of great benefit and provides a loving service to all on Earth, for it magnifies the message of Christ—for good will and living in harmony with our brothers and sisters.

Beloved Master Kuthumi shares with us his vision of peace and perfection in the future:

And God's peace settles over cities, towns, and villages covering all with a gleaming mantle of splendid and holy light whose weaving waxes stronger with each passing year unto that perfect day when the perfection of Christ shall rule in every human heart.

This can be a reality when trust in God (as freedom's motto states, "In God We Trust") becomes the watchword of every man and woman who will firmly, wisely, lovingly reach out through the dense fog of human calamities toward the peace of spiritual calm. When called into action, this calm produces hallowed feelings of unity and the sweet whisper of Life's ever-new opportunities.[11]

We are guided to trust in God, so we can live with a peaceful heart. For then, our Creator's love for His children can freely flow without being blocked by inharmonious stress and concerns about the future. God's loving Light can enter in and cleanse every cell of our being, so we may transcend past mistakes and any negative situations we find ourselves in. We can be healed in the comfort of His loving arms.

Our dear brother Kuthumi gives his description of the love and the peace we can look forward to:

I am certain that when men fully enter into the kingdom (consciousness) of God, they no longer have tears or a sorrowful heart but dwell continually in a state of listening grace where the positive love of the Holy Spirit for all creation is the only music heard in the heart or mind. In this great spiritual sensing, death is swallowed up in victory. On such as these does the complete meaning of GOD as synonymous with GOOD dawn as reality.[12]

For readers with legitimate concerns about the future due to current chaos on Earth caused by entrenched anger and opposing views, remember that security rests in God. Both material and spiritual security become more available to souls who choose to serve and work with God's Light. Ultimately, all who work with the Light come to realize that it is Light that truly serves them!

Our complete and total fulfillment and joy in Life comes from our very own Mighty I AM God Presence, that perfect and eternal part of us that is most real and all-powerful. This perfect, divine Self naturally desires that we create goodness in life, and that everything we do is done masterfully or perfectly. This Presence is available to guide and assist us in all our endeavors that are for the good, aligning them with God's will.

Master Kuthumi tells us how our I AM Presence can assist us as we evolve, just as this has been achieved by all past saints.

It directs you through your Christ Self to silence mere human qualities and to develop that vital quality of listening grace where, in love's meditation upon God, you diligently seek to know and be His will and wisdom in action.

Precious ones, if you would overcome as the saints have done, not vain effort or undue strain but the practice of a gentle submission is the requirement whereby you welcome the gift of heavenly virtue--responding always to the heavenly constraint of the gentle Presence, whose guidance is unfailing when your desire for Truth is uncompromising.[13]

This "gentle Presence" requires our attentive listening ear. It is our divine conscience, and as we daily tune into it, we will be able to hear it more clearly. This is an important aspect of daily spiritual life, and we benefit from its guidance to the degree that we can lovingly and peacefully perceive and heed it.

Others will come to notice the goodness that you bring into the world. Some sensitive people may even be able to sense your benevolence in the loving Light radiating from your aura, to the degree that you choose to direct your divine Light without limitation to all in your world.

Our loving I AM Presence showers us regularly with our Creator's consciousness. We receive the many blessings of wisdom's loving Light through the "silver cord" connecting our chakra centers and heart to our Higher Self.

Beloved Master Jesus shares his description of his attunement with our Creator.

No matter how engrossed I was in the action of mind and hands, how delighted my eye with the creation unfolding before me, I was always able to listen and to hear the hum of the universe and my heavenly Father's heartbeat, to feel the waves of His love sweeping into my being and then flooding back on the return current like the ebb and flow of the tide.[14]

Jesus wants us to know that this Light energy can be built up within, and can be used when there is a need to assist others. For example, it was used when the woman touched his garment and received the healing that she could not find elsewhere. This was described in Mark 5:25-34. Jesus explains the importance of his continual attunement with God in enabling him to provide healing blessings to others.

> *You see, the sensitivity of my soul was the means to keep me in tune with the Father's heart and to build up the charge of his great love and power in my body and sacred centers. So must all do who would be healers and comforters to Life— keep sensitive to God and oblivious to human hurt, and hold a sense of God's omnipresence as the only reality, when all around are concerned with the baubles and glitter of mere mortal intelligence, popular opinions, human feelings that wax hot and cold.*[15]

When Jesus says to keep "oblivious to human hurt," he most certainly doesn't mean that we can be callous, unaware or uninterested in the sufferings of others. He means to not allow oneself to get pulled down and encumbered by those sufferings, which could neutralize us and disable our ability to stay peaceful, keep attuned to the divine, and provide assistance when possible.

The Masters desire that we improve our ability to always choose the wisest and best course of action available when working for the highest good. They want us to have this knowledge, not by experimenting through long decades of trial and error, but through our direct (even in some cases instantaneous) link to the wisdom and love of God.

They teach us that our problems began long ago, when souls

began to focus not solely on what was good, but instead on negative, harmful possibilities not in accord with God's will. In essence, long ago "Pandora's box" was opened, so that our consciousness was filled with negative possibilities alongside positive ones. This idea of dualism, of the temporal reality of evil as well as good, stole our childlike innocence and made suffering a common feature in human life.

Jesus touches on this concept of innocence:

Holy innocence, dear hearts, was never the state of being naïve or gullible; otherwise, God himself would be considered to be so. Rather, holy innocence is and always will be the outpicturing of the Christ Mind in the soul's search for the fullest expansion of the infinite mind of God. This is the rapture of real Being! Innocence is the inner sense of the little child, one with the Spirit of God.[16]

What is this "outpicturing of the Christ Mind?" It is full awareness concerning any situation focused on—literally connecting with the omniscience of God. This enables the highest and best solution for every challenging situation. This "outpicturing of the Christ Mind in the soul's search for the fullest expansion of the infinite mind of God," from the above quote, is worthy of contemplation. Jesus reports experiencing rapture doing this. It conveys total trust in our Creator, as we strive to be fully attuned to the perfection of the Christ Mind.

This Christ Mind, from the One Son of God which all souls receive as a divine birthright, contains all Wisdom, all Love, and all Power. Every situation we find ourselves in calls for the manifestation, through us, of this Christ Mind. This is easier said than done, but this goal is presented to us in great love, for our own joyous rapture! For this is how it feels when our Creator's divine Light flows through us as we radiate it outward to others in our world. Indeed, this may sound difficult to achieve, but the goal is defined, and it is clearly a goal accomplished by many souls in human history.

Personally, I am frequently distracted by worldly things, resulting in not yet achieving the fullness of this ongoing state. But I ponder my individual path daily and for the most part I manage to avoid the trap of self-condemnation when I fail to quite measure up. In fact, I frequently use these occasions as sources of insight and even inspiration.

I know and take great comfort in the advice of the Masters. Namely, that it is the *process of striving*, the exercise of an inner resolve to be more Christlike, to live the Golden Rule and do one's part "to love life free" that receives the attention and the blessings of Heaven.

When we are able to diligently practice this attunement with our I AM God Presence we then experience an acceleration of knowing God's will and what is the correct course of action for the greatest good. Our Creator's goal is for each one to be a vehicle to bring greater joy and goodness into our world, reduce suffering and offer wise advice and a cheerful and kind disposition where it is strongly needed.

The Ascended Masters are a great source of assistance, for they have also been in embodiment on Earth and have faced similar tests and trials. They urge us to not just read about these things, but to put this information into practice as they did while on Earth, for this is the essential route to winning our freedom.

It is difficult to gauge the level of progress a soul has attained using worldly standards. Those who successfully reach attunement with their Christ consciousness go about their business filled with a divine enthusiasm or zeal that is beyond this world. And many people caught in the stresses of their everyday lives miss examples of such progress.

When considering the many different aspects of God's Law, Beloved Master Kuthumi reminds us of its basic foundation—Love!

> *The kingdom of God, the kingdom of His image and His consciousness called forth through His qualities, is the one true expression that shall win man's permanent victory for him.*
>
> *Blessed hearts, there are so many aspects to the Law, and yet in practice the Law is quite plain. As it is written: "Love is the fulfilling of the Law"—the whole Law of man's being. Therefore, we would not complicate man's pathway toward salvation; neither would we oversimplify spiritual matters.*[17]

With these teachings we are more able to make our decision to become enthusiastic builders of a better world, to be a fellow member in the Fellowship of Light. My dear wife puts it this way: we are sacrificing the human ego and joining the Divine Ego. This is not a huge sacrifice, though some may see it that way; rather, it is the wise choice that leads back Home!

Chapter 10

You Are Unique

Every one of us has a unique identity, which in a sense may only be fully known by our Creator. But we need to learn how to recognize as much of it as possible, by identifying with our divine and perfect Higher Self. The reason that it is so important for us to comprehend who we are from the divine perspective is that it will give us a heaven-oriented road map! We can come gradually to understand our personality in God, what errors we have entered into, what karma (good and bad) we have accumulated, what life skills we have garnered over the course of our lifetimes, and other aspects of our unique identity. All of this can yield a clear picture of our way forward in Spirit.

We have diverse and complex pasts, due to the eternality of life and the reincarnation of our souls living different lives on Earth—until we make our Ascension and are free from the "cycle of rebirth."

For many, Heaven may seem unattainable. For those who are young, the higher realms may not be viewed as important, due to believing they will be in embodiment for a long time. But greater knowledge of our true Self in God can spur us along. Many highly developed souls have testified throughout history about the profound and joyous adventure of pursuing their path of spiritual self-discovery. Although the following two examples portray lives of poverty, many souls can be of greatest service and achieve their freedom through the proper use of wealth, when used in accordance with God's will.

Prince Siddhartha Gautama was shielded by order of his father, the King, from seeing the outside world while growing up. He was deliberately kept unaware of suffering, including disease and poverty, so common in human existence. When he eventually ventured forth to explore his neighborhood, he was surprised and shocked to see people who were old and diseased. Most shocking to him was seeing a dead body being burned on the steps by the river, as was the custom then. But he was inspired during his outing when he encountered an ascetic—one who spends his life in prayer and fasting—abstaining from worldly indulgences.

Since Gautama felt he was living an unrealistic and spoiled life within his family's royal palace, he left his family and young wife to become an ascetic. He learned and practiced various forms of meditation. Taking fasting to its limit, he grew weak and emaciated, and along this journey, he discovered the "Middle Way," or the noble Eightfold Path, leading him to avoid the extremes of self-mortification. This process, coupled with his meditations, led him to become the "Awakened One," also known as the Buddha. He spent the rest of his life teaching others how to achieve this awakening, which sages came to describe as "nirvana," a state whereby one can live in God-consciousness while still on Earth.

Saint Francis of Assisi (in his life on Earth before becoming our beloved Master Kuthumi) was also born into wealthy circumstances. As a young man, he enjoyed living fashionably in society. While serving in the military, he was taken prisoner and held captive for a year. During that year he contracted an illness and endured a feverish convalescence. It was then that he experienced a profound spiritual awakening, while evaluating his goals in life.

This led him from then on to shun material pleasures and devote himself to serving humankind. Subsequently, when selling cloth and velvet in the market for his father's business, he gave all the proceeds to a beggar. This caused his enraged father to disown him. Francis went off on his own, with no resources but a deep faith that his heavenly Father would meet his needs. Soon, a vision from Jesus led him to rebuild the Chapel of Damiano. He went begging for stones to build with, and along with a small number of followers rebuilt the chapel. They went on to build other chapels in the neighborhood of Assisi. Saint Francis also cared for lepers and preached brotherly love and peace to those in the countryside.

Many young people were inspired by the incredible love and self-sacrifice shown by Francis and came to support him in his work. Francis eventually founded the Franciscan order and received the blessing of the Pope. He subsequently went on to establish other orders. Francis was known for his great love of nature, and for calling all creatures "brother" and "sister." We are blessed to have his loving wisdom shared with us. Once again, here is what Master Kuthumi conveyed to us in Chapter 1, concerning the importance of discovering our true being and identity:

> *Every lifestream has a matrix, or God-design, which he ought to outpicture each day. Unless this is made known to the outer self of the seeker, it is difficult for him to cooperate with the mighty plan of the inner life.*
> *It is most helpful, when, either through prayer or invocation, by decree or earnest effort, students determine to find out everything they can about their great God-design—and then begin to experience elements of that design day by day through a particular plan of action.*
> *It is essential for all who would bring the power of negative conditions under the submission of the Real Self to realize that they have a listening ear in heavenly places awaiting their call for the secrets of their own beings to be revealed—*

especially the spiritual means to change what must be changed.[1]

Master Kuthumi explains that we can learn more about who we really are, our unique qualifications, talents and interests by invoking guidance from above. As this is accomplished we can move forward and bring about our "particular plan of action." Our calls for divine guidance can sometimes tell us *how* necessary change can be implemented, so that we can fully achieve our purpose. Asking for this guidance will help us to contribute the greatest good in our lifetimes.

Life can be an ongoing struggle if we don't understand the best methods for our energies to be synchronized with those of our Christ Self. Many spiritual seekers do remember at least a glimmer, and often much more, of their original divine plan. Others, who have no remembrance of their divine plan, may have ongoing difficulties in life, not enjoying any sense of the fulfillment and success that they witness in others. It is so helpful to know that our Creator and His loving hierarchy of more advanced souls are ready and most willing to guide and assist us. And, as our faith grows in our divine Self, we begin to grow in virtue, love and wisdom.

Patience is required, for the process of soul evolution can take longer than eager souls would like. There are certain cycles of time required to manifest our personal transformation and growth. Making the active effort to add positive divine qualities to our consciousness opens the door for further spiritual evolution. There are many layers in our consciousness, and some of them, such as bad habits and other self-defeating behaviors, require persistent attention. Of great assistance are prayers and more advanced decrees for mercy's transmuting flame. (Part II, "Working with the Light.")

It is essential to remember that we are not rejected by our Loving God for temporarily becoming absorbed in unrighteous living, or "sin." As our love for God and our brethren is developed by application of these principles, we are able to more easily be forgiven through the grace of God.

If more time is given to focusing on Godly attributes and appealing for divine guidance, and less on finding fault with ourselves or with others, our masterful personalities would be realized more quickly. Beloved Kuthumi urges us to:

> *Bid welcome to the corrective influences of heaven—ever pure, constant, loving, instructive, and eternally useful— transmitted by angels who are thy teachers and the guardians of thy victory. (Sent from our retreats, they know exactly your need, if you will only listen—and develop the habit of good listening.)*[2]

What we are familiar with in ourselves is generally something we are comfortable with, or at least something we tolerate. However, remaining solely with what is familiar does not further our spiritual evolution. We cannot be complacent with regard to our environment, as well as our consciousness. Willingness to enjoy the adventure of new challenges, of higher states of consciousness as well as different environments, is necessary to make progress.

We are encouraged to embrace the purity and reality of greater love and goodness that exceeds our past experience. Master Kuthumi puts it this way:

> *The contemplation of the Fatherhood of God is an invaluable safeguard when journeying in consciousness from the familiar world of day-to-day routine into the vast and infinite reaches of God's immortal love and loveliness.*[3]

Many are simply not willing to expand their limited awareness through effort. If such lethargy remains, it is a major roadblock to further progress. In this state of inertia (and illusory feelings of satisfaction or a form of tolerance with the status quo), it becomes difficult to mount the energy required to focus on higher development and more virtuous living.

Master Kuthumi expresses the divine desire for every soul:

All admonishments spoken herewith concerning the nature of man's being are given not to condemn but to spur our readers onward and upward into Life and real living by transporting you from the mundane to those immediate areas of Self, just beyond the fringe of present attainment, and thence safely forward on a journey into Being which will expand not only your intellectual capacities but also your awareness of that other self, the inner self, or soul.[4]

For some, one form of resistance to any divine prodding to come up higher has been living a life entirely focused on the everyday mundane aspects of life and denying any degree of spiritual awareness or experience—anything that cannot be physically seen, explained or "verified" by the five senses. This perspective is naturally doomed once an individual makes their transition out of the material world. After all, we are all going to leave behind our physical vehicle when we "die." As time inevitably marches on, this is going to occur for all of us in the not-too-distant future, so it is the better part of wisdom to take these teachings on the true nature of our being—our divine spirit—seriously.

Another extreme that is chosen by some people is to become an ascetic, living a life of extreme denial or a life dwelling on spiritual and psychic phenomena, in short, in a very different way than most people. But we are reminded of the "Middle Way" espoused by Gautama Buddha. Dear Master Kuthumi addresses the required balance:

By striking a balance in the nature of his being, man can experience the spiritual world yet remain tethered to the schoolrooms of earth, mastering the required lessons,

> *enjoying life to the fullest from the inner vantage, not neglecting his duty to family and friends, and ultimately achieve his victory over his outer self and its outer conditionings.*[5]

It is unwise to not properly nurture and take care of our spiritual nature just as much as it would be unwise to overlook the care of our physical bodies. Kuthumi confirms our potential for realizing the joys of divine consciousness:

> *When the shell of materiality is outgrown by the victorious spirit, man rises to a dominion of crowning glory greater than that of the angels.*
> *The proper use of free will makes man God-like by choice. His restoration to the God-estate releases his Adamic nature from the fetters of earth and enables him to righteously regain entrée into that paradise of consciousness from which, through inversion of Principle, he fell.*[6]

Beloved Master Jesus acknowledges our unique individuality in his description of our life's dual mission:

> *The mission of every life is twofold. First there is the universal purpose in which God intends all his creation to share; then there is the unique contribution of each lifestream based on those special inner qualities which only the individual can give.*[7]

And, the Master Jesus also describes how we are shaped over time into our unique character, especially the amazing and complex role our divine memory plays in this process:

> *Out of the divine memory of continuous self-conscious awareness throughout all previous existence there is*

impressed upon the mental body, the desire body, and the physical body the attributes (spiritual 'genes') of the soul personality. These cycle into manifestation not all at once but little by little as the child develops into an adult and throughout life.

Thus, through schooling and the disciplines of the Brotherhood[8], the outer mind must frequent the spiral stairway to the inner memory, thereby establishing the channel for the descent of higher powers and the release of genius attained in previous lives—also recorded in the blessed memory body, truly the archives of the soul's history.

The blessed vehicle of the memory was created to record the divine pattern for each lifestream as well as the truth of his experiences on the etheric plane and his soul awareness in the higher octaves of being. Throughout man's evolution in human form, there has been impressed upon it, however, those discordant thoughtforms, misqualified energies of the mass consciousness, and everyday trivia which crowd out the crystal purity and simplicity of God's continual self-revelation to man, abundant in variety and rich in blessing.[9]

Our loving Master Kuthumi addresses us:

Blessed Ones Growing Up to Be King of Your Own Domain...
The gift of absolute dominion belongs to men and women with the faith, the will, and the wisdom to accept and externalize this God-given right—this choice to individualize the God flame uniquely, to shape one's destiny according to Life's profound purpose.[10]

Here we can see how wonderful, merciful and full of hope life can be. Our Creator loves beauty and art, among all good things, and this is evident in the artistry of Life. As we spiritual seekers develop our attunement with our Holy Christ Self, our potential becomes truly unlimited. We are wise to not allow ourselves to become diverted by the harsh or confusing conditions we encounter in the world. Rather, we need to remember the omniscience of our Creator guiding us through the intermediary of His Son, the Christ. We need to remember that it is our Father's earnest desire to share His kingdom, His consciousness with us.

> *And seek not ye what ye shall eat, or what ye shall drink, neither be ye of doubtful mind.*
> *For all these things do the nations of the world seek after: and your Father knoweth that ye have need of these things.*
> *But rather seek ye the kingdom of God; and all these things shall be added unto you.*
> *Fear not, little flock; for it is your Father's good pleasure to give you the kingdom.* Luke 12:29-32

It is truly not a burden to research and absorb divine wisdom or to nurture and grow one's holy love. Doing so can grace us with God-given Light and energy to build greater good on Earth. Even if our planet were to someday cease to exist, the spiritual realities will endure. And, the records of every soul's noble thoughts and deeds are securely kept.

In this regard, beloved Master Jesus issues to us his great wish:

> *O Being of Man: With all thy getting, get understanding of the eternal principles!*
> *As your precious Kuthumi and I stand before the record of this age and ask ourselves the question, "How can we best relieve human suffering and reestablish mighty principles that will enable man, the instrument, to endure?" we recognize that in the final analysis it is the recognition and self-determination by man himself, as an individual, that sets him apart from his fellows and makes him God's man.*[11]

Those individuals who do not embrace divine truths have common similarities. They may show poor control over their feelings and fail to deal fairly and justly with others. They are often self-centered and try to manipulate others according to their whims and desires.

On the other hand, many souls have mightily evolved and are viewed by our Creator as true blessings to life. These righteous figures include such leaders as the Prophets Elijah, Samuel, and Daniel, and Masters and saints such as Gautama Buddha, Krishna, Saint Patrick, Mother Teresa, Saint Padre Pio and Saint Therese of Lisieux, to name a few of the countless other saints throughout distant and recent history.

What they have all held in common is their knowledge and faith concerning God, and the virtues of right living. They have striven to maximize their practice of love, of being a selfless servant, and garnering continually greater wisdom of what the Masters call "the eternal verities." This combination has resulted in their achieving success and great influence among other people, who at a soul level, recognize their good and godly traits. These great souls perceived virtue as the most logical offering to our life-giving Creator.

Our dear Master Jesus describes these virtuous souls in the following passage:

> *We see no arrogant demanding for deference or favor that would set them apart from others or exalt them in their person, but only a firm, unyielding devotion to be a vessel in the hands of the Infinite One in order to convey unlimited blessing to others. The patrimony [property inherited from one's father] of heaven is given to such souls as these, whether you believe in them or not. Myriad angels stand before them and bow in adoration to the God flame veiled in flesh.*[12]

Jesus has revealed that those who inherit the greatest blessings from our Creator are those who hold to the highest standards of loving wisdom, which create the most good. As recorded in the Bible, Jesus, in teaching us how to live righteously said, "Go, and sin no more."[13] And he asks each of us to emulate his own spiritual journey when he said, "Go, and do thou likewise."[14] These commands were given to awaken the divine aspect within us. He urges every one of us to strive mightily toward greater good:

Today I say to all: Let all proneness to human error cease! Go and sin no more! Let all virtue and wisdom and loveliness; all beauty, all courage, faith, and determination; all consecration, invocation, and adoration be raised on high in the citadel of your own Being...and go and do thou likewise! Keep thou the faith, keep thou the courage, keep thou the determination, keep thou the holy precepts, keep thou the balance!...
Truly the Lord thy God is my God. Truly he is in me and in thee. Truly in this interchange of oneness and unity there is hope that the Holy Spirit of prophecy may fashion in newness a new generation![15]

It is best to not yield to any temptations that would distract us from our chosen path leading to ultimate spiritual freedom. This is not always easy, as it means that we need to rise above the hypnotic spell of the many carnal (pertaining to the flesh, not spiritual, but worldly) offerings within the mass media. Today's world-wide communications network often carries information that is misleading or simply untrue. It is so important to develop one's ability to discriminate what truth is and to follow inner intuition when choosing what to believe. For tyranny and evil have been on Earth during much of its history and are still widespread today, hiding behind all manner of lies and deception.

We will function at our best when we don't allow ourselves to be troubled. Whether we are stressed by a situation that is personal or by something in the community where we live or by an event anywhere on Earth—no matter if it is a health, relationship, financial or other type, it helps to understand the exact cause and to then ask for divine assistance. You can also say to yourself:

The Peace of God, which passeth all understanding.[16]

It is important, especially for those who are often controlled by their emotions or easily stressed, to always remember our true identity. Remember that we are sons and daughters of God with unlimited divine potential. This is our most valuable heritage. Always listen for the divine "gentle presence," allowing our divine conscience to be our guide.

Adding to this guidance, Master Kuthumi wants us to know:

The divine whisper will softly speak your name as God's identification of your Spirit, "I AM," and the meaning thereof will be apparent to you as the soundless Sound, the guiding Light, the presence of Reality manifesting in you, free from the façade of human [worldly] vice or virtue and all pride in self. Then shall you rejoice in the creation of your own immortal consciousness: "The LORD God saw the creation which he had made and, behold, it was very good!"[17]

Although we are in the process of creating an immortal consciousness, we need not carry any fear of losing our individuality. Our unique consciousness, once it consists solely of the good, loving and positive, will ultimately merge with God's consciousness. Nothing is lost, only gained. How can we rationally fear returning to our Source, bearing the fruit of our many successes and the knowledge we have gained?

As we become more God-like, we will desire even more of God.

This is a never-ending and joyous quest due to the nature of the expanding and self-transcending divine Mind. The entire process of the development of our soul personality is permeated with divine love—there is nothing gentler—or more powerful.

Beloved Kuthumi summarizes the beauty of the entire process of soul development:

> *Your self-chosen yet God-appointed mission unfolds as an ongoing service of the ages; the purpose of your life is no longer isolated in a finite segment of experience called a lifetime. Expansion of Spirit's expression and an infinite self-awareness occurs; immortality is understood and magnetized in the unity of your own God flame.*[18]

Chapter 11

The Power Of Habits

Harmful habits of thought and behavior seem to be a part of the human condition, and have plagued mankind for millennia. Their continual repetition creates massive suffering and motivates each of us, at a soul level, to turn to our loving Creator for the best solutions to what can often be a very damaging human momentum. Psychologists advise that wrong habits often lead to self-defeating behavior, poor health practices, and if unchecked, a poor self-image. This can also lead to emotional distress, depression, mental problems and even worse habits, such as drug and alcohol misuse. Finally, such poor habits can result in homelessness or even suicide. It is not an exaggeration to say that bad habits are a plague on society.

In my own life, I had a challenge to overcome a persistent smoking habit. I discovered what an addiction it is, as it wound up taking me about twenty attempts to quit before I had my last cigarette. I knew that smoking was bad for my lungs and overall health, so I made up my mind to make my first attempt to stop three days later. When the day arrived, I went for as long as I could before lighting up—it was less than a day the first couple of times, then the intervals got longer. Unlike what some others do, I did not give myself a hard time when I reverted back to the habit; I simply set a new date a couple of days ahead, with the intention of going longer.

I started giving myself rewards once I was able to abstain for three days or longer. Yet what helped me the most was asking God for guidance and assistance to permanently stop. I got to the point when I absolutely knew I'd soon succeed with God's help, and finally was completely cut free from ever wanting to smoke again. I am so grateful, and much healthier, for eliminating that habit. When we focus our attention more on loving God than on our poor habits, the Holy Spirit can swiftly come to the rescue.

It is essential for spiritual seekers to harness the power of good habits to assist them in drawing closer to the consciousness of God. This chapter explains how to fight and win over the density of flawed thought patterns that keep people psychologically imprisoned, preventing them from reaching their true potential. These poor habits are the products of past incorrect decisions, which are the result of mortal ideas and the mistake of focusing solely on materiality to the exclusion of spirit.

Master Kuthumi sheds light on the value of good habits:

> *When good habits are established and erroneous ones transmuted, a more Godlike nature is evolved whereby the living Christ once again appears and is honored "in the flesh." The cause of heaven is served best by making man the master of his own household (his four lower bodies as well as the members of his immediate family), thus enabling him to take his rightful God-intended dominion over the citadels of his domain, as ever-widening spirals (good habits) of responsibility make him the logical steward of the Good on behalf of communities and nations.*[1]

It is worth noting from this that as our good habits increase, we will be granted greater responsibilities in service to larger segments of society. There is an ongoing need for wise and loving ministering servants.

The Law of individual free will decrees that we are all on our own when it comes to habits. No one but ourselves can change any bad habit that we may have. It was, after all, only our own free will that allowed the bad habit to be formed in the first place. And, once we exercise our free will and shed any particular pattern of wrong thinking or behavior, the energy that is freed up needs to be employed in the practice of a positive habit that will carry the seeker one or more rungs higher on the ladder of Mastery.

In other words, we need to substitute good and divine habits as guided by our Higher Christ Self for those we want to eliminate, and, ideally, this process of exchange is done simultaneously. This is the scientific way, wherein each person attunes with heart and mind to the higher vibrations of the Christ consciousness.

It is helpful to understand the way in which habits are formed. It is similar to electricity running through wires wound around a coil creating magnetic force—the more times the wire circles the coil, the greater the magnetism created. As our habits are practiced and repeated, we more easily and automatically repeat the thought or action. The habit becomes more powerful, whether it is a good or a bad one. It is actually an electromagnetic force which magnetizes other good or bad forces either into the Higher Divine Self or the lower human self. This is basic and essential law that needs to be understood by all who want to take control of who they are and what they want to become.

Habits that are not in accord with God's will are destructive thoughts and actions that flow out into the world at large and create strong negative patterns that cause much suffering to other parts of life. At some point, these harmful patterns are judged by our Higher Self, our individualized Christ, and gradually, or even swiftly, weakened by no longer receiving our focus or energy. This can be accomplished by will power accompanied by visualization and the power of the spoken word, which draws to us divine assistance and guidance for our righteous endeavors. In this way, positive habits can be purposefully created to replace those being abandoned.

In contrast to a gradual substitution of good habits for bad, we have the example of the dynamic, near-instant conversion of Saul of Tarsus, who was passionately persecuting members of the early Christian movement. While on the road from Jerusalem to Damascus to arrest more believers, Jesus appeared to him, from his ascended state, as a great Light. Saul fell from his horse and was struck blind for three days. In those three days, Saul did not eat or drink, spending his time in intense prayer to God.

Jesus then sent a holy man, Ananias, to Saul to restore his sight and fill him with the Holy Spirit. Ananias told Saul:

Brother Saul, the Lord, even Jesus, that appeared unto thee in the way as thou camest, hath sent me, that thou mightest receive thy sight, and be filled with the Holy Ghost.[2]

From the day his sight returned, Saul realized that he was indeed filled with the Holy Spirit, and he spent the rest of his life speaking, writing and demonstrating the teachings of Jesus. Saul became known by his Latin name Paul, whose work spreading the teachings of Jesus included the authorship of nearly half of all the books in the New Testament. Paul's tireless ministry and inspired writings demonstrate his strong, steady attunement with Jesus throughout the remainder of his fruitful life.

The Masters instruct us that once an individual ceases to engage in negative thought patterns, the veil of illusion is gradually cleared and love, peace and bliss can freely flow into that soul's thought and feeling experience.

Jesus addresses us most encouragingly as: *Engravers of Self-Luminous Intelligent Substance*—and shares his great longing for us:

Immortal energy patterns are being woven continuously by the children of God, both ascended and unascended. Whether they are formed carelessly or lovingly, these engravings are cast in the die of self-luminous intelligent substance, ever flowing from the heart of the Presence of God. Once established, they become like tablets of law—commandments which, from the level of the subconscious, exercise authority in the world of the creator and sustainer of the original pattern....

The wondrous power of the Spirit of God must be allowed to prevail if men are to become and remain free from each and every snare, whether self-woven or the unwanted handiwork of another.

Earnestly and lovingly, all heaven yearns to set free from imprisonment in egocentric ideas all captive minds and hearts and souls. How we long to see the auric forcefield of every child of God charged with the pure and radiant energies of our spheres!

There are many good habits which should be further developed and retained. Good habits are conducive to amplifying the power of the higher octaves and harnessing the light of higher dimensions to do the bidding of the seeker for the Christ consciousness here below in the physical plane.[3]

Jesus confirms for us the clinging influence that every thought creates. Thoughts are not merely here one moment and gone the next. They have lasting influence. If in doubt, simply google "thoughtforms." Another powerful reason to assert greater control over our thoughts is because once we enter the afterlife, our thoughts are our basic mode of communication, and they can be read by others, unless an effort is made to block a particular thought.[4]

One modern-day Master, Mark Prophet, lightheartedly shared with his students that a bird might, on occasion, land on our head with a temptation or bad thought, adding "Just don't let it build a nest."[5]

It is not enough to have intense wishes to attune to one's higher Christ consciousness. Unless, after establishing the peace of God within his consciousness, an individual proactively seeks his Christ Self, he will not accomplish it. Still, there is always, at minimum, at least a thread of connection with the individual divine Self in all souls. True spiritual seekers need to be willing, with reverence and the joy of anticipation, to engage the Holy Spirit. This Spirit can actively flood divine Light into our four lower bodies, bringing the soul up to a level of heavenly comfort and peace. It can also bring to the soul a more complete sense of their divine mission in life. Thus, it is most beneficial to focus on God, to visualize as best we can all aspects of the divine nature, and to meditate upon what it will feel like to have the Holy Spirit grace us and come actively into our temple.

Unfortunately, selfish and ignorant goals have been the focus of many. For that reason, these individuals will benefit from going back and refocusing their sights on righteous action, abandoning wrong behavior and re-opening themselves to divine guidance. It is simply a fundamental fact that we are all operating daily within the framework of our established habits, whether good or bad.

The Christ Mind is a part of God, and is not influenced by man's carnal or earthly nature. For that reason, Truth is not subject to various opinions. In higher realms, a soul's consciousness can directly perceive the wisdom emanating from God's omniscient consciousness. In addition, it is also reported that the complete collection of contemplations of saints are within the universal causal (memory) body of God, enhancing and blessing all of life.

It is best to not struggle against any yearning to engage in a bad habit. When the focus is unnecessarily on the unwanted habit, by fighting against it, our emotions are engaged which keeps the bad habit in our focus. Allow your attention to be elevated higher, for this allows the easiest elimination of it. This method reduces the influences of the subconscious mind to further engage in that habit. This also applies to wisely avoiding focusing one's attention more than necessary on any situation we do not want.

What is very helpful is to instead attune to the great Light of God's omniscience which contains all good and loving qualities. Focus on the good and divine aspects of life. Whatever appears in our world to test us, whether it be discordant situations or a great tragedy, such as a loved one's earthly departure, can be more peacefully faced when one's consciousness is saturated with our Creator's loving Light and consciousness, which is always victorious over darkness. While in that loving Light and consciousness, the desire to turn to false comfort, including the distraction of alcohol, drugs, unhealthy diet, lashing out against others and other forms of negative habits, cannot exist.

Here again, we can see the wisdom of modern psychology, which, for example, emphasizes focusing on seeing and feeling yourself ten years younger, rather than dwelling on temporary dietary/deprivation. Or, to visualize yourself in your exciting, and wonderful new career of service rather than picturing the hours of hard study and testing that will take you there.

We are warned by the Masters that there is one exception to this recommended practice of focusing on the positive rather than the negative. Occasionally, a soul may be attacked by the direct negative thought projections of another. The danger from this is its intense and invisible nature. Therefore, it is essential for individuals to learn to identify this form of direct attack, and when alerted to it then take direct action. The action taken should, in both thought and spoken word, consist of an absolute denial of the attacking force's power—of this negative energy being projected against us, by utilizing fiats, prayers and repeated decrees, as may be necessary.

The awareness in mind and spoken word of the all-power, the omnipotence of God's all-goodness should accompany this action, which can totally transmute and vanquish any such direct attack.

This form of attack must be resisted until it is overcome, after which it will return to its source as karmic energy. We are advised that care needs to be taken so that we do not direct the return of negative energy to a source unless there is absolutely no doubt concerning the source. Directing negative energy to another is not recommended unless undertaken by those who have sufficient spiritual development to be able to discern what they are doing and why.

Releasing torrents of anger at any time is harmful to those releasing such energy. Far better to maintain a foundation of God-mastery and control. In this way, the tests in life are passed and divine progress is assured.

Related to this subject, the Bible contains two apparently contradictory quotations:

But I say unto you, that ye resist not evil: but whosoever shall smite thee on thy right cheek, turn to him the other also.
—Matt.5:39.

What appears as an apparent contrary teaching is also present:

Submit yourselves therefore to God. Resist the devil, and he will flee from you. —James 4:7.

It is clear that we need to be able to discriminate as to when resistance is essential and when yielding is called for. On the one hand, others may wrong us, even commit evil acts against us—just as we on occasion may act out of anger or jealousy or some other human emotion in wronging another. It is essential to cultivate a forgiving heart. This means to go to our brother when we have wronged him and, through sincere contrition, ask to be forgiven and even to make amends as may be appropriate. And by the same token, be ready and willing to forgive another who commits wrongs against you, "turning the cheek" as silent though powerful testimony that you honor the Lord's prescription for living a successful spiritual life.

On the other hand, the above passage from the Book of James, as well as other biblical teachings, make clear that as we mature on the Path, it is essential that we do not yield to but rather resist real evil. On occasion, when a disciple spoke out from a wrong or carnal perspective, Jesus rebuked him, saying for example, to Simon Peter:

Get thee behind me, Satan: thou art an offence unto me: for thou savourest not the things that be of God, but those that be of men.[6]

And Jesus publicly rebuked the deceitful and wicked practices of the Sanhedrin in the strongest terms, calling them to their face, "Ye generation of vipers."[7] Regardless of the circumstance, however, it remains true that it is best to retain our God harmony and a sense of divine peace when confronting these various types of situations.

It is best to withdraw from any habit-patterns that are not in accordance with God's will, and to resist reverting back to them in moments of weakness, for they are the open doorway to forces of antiChrist. It is helpful to understand the unpleasant consequences of becoming "re-enslaved" to our former bad habits. Yet, at times this can happen because reverting back to them can provide a false sense of familiarity and comfort.

When we are centered with a strong foundation of good habits that contain God's great love for us, we will no longer even consider allowing bad habits back into our lives. Then, we are protected from the power that any undesirable habits might have over us, and any urgings to engage in them will rapidly dissipate. We are reminded from Chapter 7 that one of the worst habits is when we condemn, judge and criticize our brothers and sisters who are making their best efforts toward their own spiritual evolution.

Our beloved Jesus shares his wisdom about habits and what he considers to be most important:

> *While I am aware that many admire me as Jesus the Christ, I consider that the highest honor anyone can pay me is to give his allegiance to the source of the all-power of God and its foundation in my life: obedience to the precepts of God—a mind dwelling in the constancy of his love and dedicated first and foremost to him, and thence directed as a beam of light to all creation. Do thou likewise and attain within thine own being the victory of Love. This is true worship and perfect adoration of the Father.*
>
> *Remember always: To establish heavenly habits enables the disciple to evolve to a higher state of Christ-illumination—a state which overcomes the world, casts out every unwanted thought (or feeling) of human creation, and attains its cherished victory.*
>
> *We unite our consciousness with every sincere follower of Truth and offer here and now our most powerful assistance in overcoming undesirable habits and replacing them by a mighty fountain of Christ-virtue.*[8]

When we strive to attune to the Christ consciousness and its accompanying love, wisdom and power, we fill our treasure chest with divine riches.

The best way to think about improving our habits is to realize that as we do so we accelerate our soul's growth. We create more good works with God's inspiration—we are then co-creating with God, for whenever we do good works it is God in action working through us. As we increase our good habits, we are blessed by greater guidance about our unique mission in life, as seen in Chapter 10.

Because there is an abundance of excellent habits to cultivate, one may choose to focus on acquiring those that are easiest first.

Remember that every new good habit developed takes us another step closer to our goal. As we establish the correct thoughts regarding a new habit and combine it with repetition of the correct action, we will enjoy a feeling of becoming a force for greater love to all.

When we choose this routine, it completes the circle of love. Our Creator has granted us much life and loving energy, and, happily, we cannot help but return it! And so, a wonderful, "upward spiral" unfolds. As we focus on and commit to developing these elevated divine habits we in turn receive greater portions of grace and blessings from on high.

Chapter 12

Discipleship And Mastery

A disciple is a soul who has cultivated the powerful habit of being self-disciplined. Such souls realize that the way to achieve their independence is through discipline—with discipline comes freedom! They understand that they need to transcend the restless energies that distract them from their chosen path. Disciples realize the cravings and whims they have are serious hindrances that will atrophy and completely fade away as they are ignored—while they simultaneously come to appreciate and enjoy the rewards of their grace-filled, disciplined lifestyle.

In our earnest spiritual seeking, we soon realize that greater amounts of divine Light and power can be bequeathed to us only after we shed all desire to harm life in any form. Entry into the kingdom—the consciousness of God—is only extended to souls who have cultivated the discipline to free themselves from all harmful human emotions and habits.

For these reasons, souls ascending on the Path need to be tested. If a person, for example, has a drug problem they are striving to free themselves from, they may be tested by situations that contain circumstances similar to those that caused them to initially begin that deadly habit. Such tests need to be welcomed, despite being difficult, for they provide the soul the opportunity to affirm mastery over, and freedom from, a harmful practice.

These tests come through our spiritual guides and teachers, inspired by pure and loving intent, for they desire only a soul's victory in the Light. Therefore, be forewarned—the Path to freedom (from all that would keep us from obtaining that freedom) contains challenging tests along the way—all for the greater good! We can be consoled, as well as inspired, that the entire spiritual hierarchy is cheering us on to victorious freedom.

In my own life, my discipleship began during a time of disappointment in relationships, which led me to the conclusion that only God could consistently be relied on. I began to read one spiritual book after another and attended spiritual conferences and retreats. As I continued my deep dive into various religious and spiritual teachings and increased my level of meditation and prayer, I began to experience the power of divine Light and peace in my world. By God's grace, I have successfully overcome several bad habits that kept me mired in the mud, which then helped me overcome several health and financial challenges.

My path of discipleship includes listening to the gentle voice of Spirit, as well as gradually improving my habits for maximum health, and to lend a kind and listening ear to all in my world, ready to provide assistance whenever possible. Daily spiritual calls, prayer and meditation help me to stay attuned to divine guidance and assistance, providing the Light-energy I need, by God's grace, for my remaining time on Earth.

The challenges I faced seemed very difficult to me, and other souls undoubtedly feel their challenges are as well. But in most cases, they are tame compared to the adversity faced by Saint Josephine Bakhita. Born in Sudan in 1869, she lived a happy life until she was seven or eight years old, when she was seized by Arab slave traders and forced to walk 600 miles. Josephine was then sold numerous times over the next twelve years. One of her owners was so cruel that Bakhita said, "During all the years I stayed in that house, I do not recall a day that passed without some wound or other. When a wound from the whip began to heal, other blows would pour down on me." She also received forced scarification and tattooing—over one hundred intricate patterns were cut into her arm, stomach and breasts. These cuts were filled with salt to create permanent scarring.

During the latter stages of her enslavement, Josephine was again sold and taken on a dangerous 400-mile camel trip to the largest port in Sudan, where she was put on a ship to Genoa, Italy. There, under yet another owner, she was temporarily left in the care of the Canossian Sisters in Venice, who introduced her to Christianity. When her owner returned to take her, Josephine refused to go. Her owner appealed to the king's attorney general, but an Italian court ruled that due to Italy not recognizing slavery, Bakhita was a free woman. She stayed with the Canossian Sisters and in 1896 took her vows. In 1902 she was assigned to a convent in northern Italy, where she lived for the remaining forty-five years of her life. She was known for her calming voice, her smile, her gentleness, and was considered a saint by the townspeople. Bakhita was once asked what she would do if she ever met her former captors. She replied, "If I were to meet those who kidnapped me, and even those who tortured me, I would kneel and kiss their hands. For, if these things had not happened, I would not have been a Christian."[1]

A disciple needs to be dedicated to honorable, moral ideals, while rising above discordant situations in daily life. When first starting on the path of discipleship and aiming for attainment in the Christ consciousness, a soul that is used to their former lifestyle may find things strange and problematic. Our beloved Jesus shared these encouraging words concerning discipleship:

> *Those whose hearts have burned within them to know the nearness of God will find the road less difficult and certainly*

less cumbersome than the broad way of materialism. If they stick with it, I guarantee all will find the reward at journey's end to be beyond compare.[2]

For we are not just men and women with physical bodies. We are divine beings made in God's image. We simply need to systematically shed the negative, limiting and unloving habits that remain in our thoughts, feelings and actions. Simultaneously, the joyous Light of love will increasingly flow through us as we experience the deep joy and satisfaction that comes with sharing this love with others in our world.

Master Kuthumi refers to the path of returning to who we really are in this way:

To wear your seamless robe of white light, you must daily open your heart and mind to the communion of heaven. This must be valued above earthly matters. People will not willingly be denied food. Let them refuse to be denied spiritual food!
This is practical, unvarnished Truth, beloved ones. Let them wear robes of Christlike discipline with the same honor that we [the Ascended Masters] feel. Let not the children of human creation or human mockery affect your love for God, the Mighty I AM Presence! The hosts of the Lord actually outnumber the children of mammon as the stars of the heaven and as the sand upon the sea shore innumerable![3]

Would-be disciples need to have, as their first priority, a receptivity to the "gentle presence" of divine guidance. This is further enabled by daily meditation as well as prayers, affirmations and decrees. (Part II, "Working with the Light.") This spiritual work increases a disciple's capacity to receive more Light, which produces an increased power, wisdom and love to know and understand God. This process comprises a significant aspect of our current stage of discipleship—discipleship being an ongoing process without end. As the disciple progresses, he or she is blessed and shepherded by one Master until graduating to yet another level guided by another Master, and so on through the wondrous and unlimited "mansions" and dimensions of eternity.

We are told that even the most advanced Masters think of themselves as being ongoing disciples, since they understand that in this universe, God is the only totality, and as such, can only be totally comprehended by Himself and not completely by His parts. His creation holds numerous octaves of Light which are continuously expanding into new dimensions of the Infinite Being of God.

Beloved Master Kuthumi discusses these points:

The way of discipleship never ends. The absorption of this idea is imperative if you would advance to the heights to which the very soul of God inspires you! Explore the idea of the unceasing Wisdom, the ever-flowing River of Life, and the infinite Mind, and you will discover why this is so. Blessed ones, are not all things relative? Your relation to your Mighty I AM Presence is so intimate and lovely, and yet it is relative to your capacity to absorb and retain the beauty of God. Now, if you increase your capacity to assimilate Light, as the Christ consciousness, will not your relationship to the Master also change?[4]

Being a devoted and persevering disciple will inevitably lead to becoming a Master who has flawless vision. Disciples can always strive to emulate the ideal characteristics of a Master, or their Holy Christ Self or their beloved God Presence. However, disciples are sometimes distracted by other ideas rather than the ideas that God envisions would be for their greatest happiness and success. Keep in mind that God has a wonderful and endlessly fulfilling divine plan (yielding great blessings, joys and beauty) for every one of His children. In this regard, Jesus instructs us about the relative importance of the human personality versus our true divine image:

> *First and foremost, the would-be disciple must learn to forget the importance of his own personality and to remember that God's thought about him is greatly to be esteemed. How wasteful is the daily dissipation of energies expended in defense of the personal self with all its whimsical characterizations.*[5]

Because many former concepts must be given up to make room for more exalted and challenging concepts, a disciple's path can develop into something different than what the disciple may have first imagined—being open to refining their understanding as they evolve. And, there may come a point when the steepness of the chosen path includes leaving behind many human aspects that are comfortably familiar. For some, this could be temporarily frightening if the replacement of divine vision has not yet arrived. It could also be confusing and cause a soul to abandon their goal and revert back to their former state. It is essential to have something better to look forward to, literally a replacement for what is left behind—to envision the divine goal and maintain that vision consistently to avoid returning to the previously rejected lifestyle.

A disciple's first love is loving God—seeking God's love and loving God with a burning desire. Yet, despite the best of intentions, sometimes disciples base their actions on incorrect premises. Over the passage of time, it will be clear who has lived righteously and which projects will succeed in adding to the further manifestation of God's plan.

In this current period on Earth, we are experiencing a tremendous degree of returning karma. This calls for each one of us to cultivate a steady vigilance to numerous dangers, which include any kind of desecrations of God's divine truths. The best protection and security lie in ongoing service to the Light.

Jesus reminds us of the importance of feeling *worthy* of our calling, and sheds Light on the attitude he held to attain his victory:

The concept of man as a son of God and divine manifestation is a part of the high calling extended to every soul who cometh into the world—but few there be that have found it. And so, each disciple must esteem himself to be worthy of God in order that he might anchor himself in the great law which will then walk the earth through him in the pure person of his own beloved Christ Self. Through realizing that man made in God's image is not a sinful creature but a divine being, he is able to discern the Lord's Body.[6]

In this teaching, Jesus says that few have found their high calling. Yet previously, Master Kuthumi described for us the vast numbers of the hosts of the Lord. It is my belief that the vast numbers referred to by Kuthumi take into account the previous "root races" (stages of evolution) that have dwelt on the Earth. They also probably include beings from other worlds throughout the universe as well as spiritual beings who have never physically embodied. There is much information about root races on the internet for those interested in further research.

Jesus also states that we are divine beings, "able to discern the Lord's Body." The "Lord's Body" refers to the *grace* of God, which is His Love, Wisdom, Forgiveness and Power, and God's *glory* which is God's awesome beauty. That glorious beauty exceeds, of course, what we can currently comprehend.

Jesus shares his description of our divine destiny:

You are not intended merely to be guests, but sons and joint-heirs with the unfailing Light of God, clothed with the wedding garment of immortality, the joy of angels, and the all-knowing peace of the inner heart of God's Presence. In the present-day turmoil, I am confident that the sincere

> *student will perceive the disciplines of the Spirit as the sure means of keeping the soul expanding into its mighty matrix of perfection....*
>
> *In the cultivation of the perfection of God's thought, in the harmonizing of the consciousness with the all-knowing wisdom of God, in the supreme oneness of spiritual unity, all else is swept away. All human error and disappointment are forever inundated by a flood of loving purpose, whose end is but a door ajar into the eternal cycles of the rolling spheres, visible and invisible.*[7]

Aspiring disciples will greatly benefit from a regular practice of meditation, as well as contemplation, focusing on developing a *sense* of what their advancing spiritual progression will feel like. This perception is also developed by daily prayer, making calls for the Light to descend and for guidance, assistance and energy, not only for ourselves but for the benefit of friends or other individuals in need and extending to our community, our nation and beyond.

The Master Jesus describes the Christic Path for spiritual evolution and reveals how intimately our own personal journey of overcoming parallels his own:

> *Initially, you must establish a hallowed sense of the reality and the tangibility of the blessing you can obtain and bestow on others as a true disciple of God's great Brotherhood of Light. Let your hearts be humble yet unafraid, desiring to perceive your errors only enough to correct them and your virtues only enough to express gratitude for them. Then I am certain you will find the grossness of the human condition giving way to the refinement of eternal values within you— and as your views change to those of heaven, the reality of the kingdom shall enfold you as a mantle of power.*
>
> *A disciple is one who is disciplined and whose course is parallel to my own. Each such a one I lovingly call brother-*

sister. Welcome into the family of those who consciously present themselves to the eternal Will and Purpose, saying with Isaiah, "Here I AM, send me!"

May the light of heaven bestow its shining reality upon all the earth through you, thereby blessing every heart each day. I AM lovingly offering the mantle of my own Christ-perfection to lives as much beloved by God as my own.[8]

One way to describe the relationship between Master and disciple is that the Master has greater receptivity to God, due to his greater divine attunement and tenure in the Higher Realms. The ideal perspective for a disciple to envision is that divine guidance can be received directly from God, or from God through the Holy Christ Self which acts as mediator between God and man, or any Masters who can transmit to us the Father's Light of wisdom and love.

Beloved Kuthumi shares a joyful proclamation of divine bliss that is received directly from the Godhead:

But beyond this [help from the Masters], the disciple's mind obtains directly from the Father a perennial ecstasy in the flow of knowledge, power, and love and transcends itself in the orderly, everlasting consciousness of God.[9]

Masters always remember, as should disciples or chelas, that regardless of how high a level of attainment is reached, they are forever serving God. All Masters are disciples on the unending Path of the one son—the Christ.

A true Master joyously leads his disciples to higher levels, pleased to be able to shepherd them on the Path, to "watch their back," and provide the security of his love. Within the organization of Masters, the rule is followed that the level of advancement of each initiate is not normally discussed with other disciples-in-training as it might impede their progress.

True disciples continually seek answers to their questions, having a consciousness to focus on genuine spiritual progress. They undertake an ongoing search for the answers to life's mysteries. Each disciple has unique needs as they move forward because each already has their own specific karma and life experiences. One size certainly does not fit all. Thus, different disciples require different guidance and illumination as they face unique initiations.

It is important for disciples to be able to control their energies, so they do not erupt in detrimental emotional discharges. When a soul allows that to occur, it creates new downward pressures, which inhibit a soul's progress and creates new karma.

Master Kuthumi offers us his description of the blessings of choosing discipleship:

A disciple is one who practices the disciplines of the God Self, ruling over and disciplining the outer personality and his own ideational patterns, having the God-awareness of himself as an individualized manifestation of the I AM THAT I AM.

Those so fortunate as to have chosen discipleship as a way of life have thereby chosen to serve the Light. By always placing the Light first, these will find that one day the Light will place them first—at the very center of God's will. Then nothing will be impossible to the disciple, for it is not difficult for the Master.[10]

The commitment we make when we freely choose discipleship sets us on a course of divine direction. Rather than simply maintaining a rudimentary life support, Our I AM Presence becomes our cosmic energy source, a virtual beacon of the Light of God as we move through the initiations to come. As disciples, we become "special agents"—fully utilizing this precious energy, rather than squandering it on purely mundane habits and fleeting involvements. To accomplish this, a constant vigilance is needed requiring us to step in and put a halt to any "human impulses" that would not be approved by our Higher Self. Whenever this occurs, it is necessary to replace that human impulse with a divine impulse.

Developing this habit will lead to full attunement with the Christ consciousness that will forever abide within—always for the greater good. In this way, God's grand design for another dedicated and loving soul will be made manifest, and that soul will rejoice in God's beautiful and exhilarating Light. Once upon this Path of eternal progression, there is no limit to the joy, fulfillment and blessings of divine evolution.

Mankind is in the interesting position of being juxtaposed between their relationship with God and their relationship with their fellow man, created in God's image, which contains unlimited divine potential. Master Kuthumi urges us to not lose sight of the glories that await all who embrace the reality of God's inherent goodness:

> *We strongly advise shunning the wrong idea that Life is formidable or austere and advocate replacing it with the right idea that Life is a marvelous divine opportunity. Blessed ones, Life is full of perfect hope, glorious love, and an ultimate destiny which transcends all mortal dreams. It is essential that the true disciple master the means of transmuting whatever outer condition seeks to corrupt the Life principle. The idea that each life is a manifestation of God must become permanent in the heart of every disciple.*[11]

And Master Kuthumi also delivers to us one of his most convincing reasons for finally taking up the mantle of discipleship:

> *We, the Ascended Masters, are more alive, more charged and infilled with the life-energy of the Great Central Sun than any unascended being. We truly live in the fullness of that Life which is undiluted God, for we have transmuted our*

entire human creation. Therefore our capacity to receive and retain Light's limitless energy is greater in the ascended state than yours is in the less-accelerated earthly state.[12]

If these promptings for greatness elicit any fear or doubt, pause and reflect that the Masters of today were just like us, dealing with stresses, challenges, tests and disappointments similar to those we face. From the *Corona Class Lessons*, we are told:

Then and now all disciples following in the footsteps of the immortals must realize that the prophets and the saints were people like ourselves who had human frailties and burdens and fears, yet whom God called and empowered with his Spirit.[13]

If disciples come up against fear or doubt, it's helpful to remember that persevering and moving forward with loving action will bring former fears and doubts to an end.

There is no fear in love; but perfect love casteth out fear: because fear hath torment. He that feareth is not made perfect in love.[14]

Discipleship is our opportunity to show our gratitude by developing greater empathy for the plight of others while they struggle to deal with the demands of life. Souls who need help are greatly comforted when they have our compassion and understanding, listening ear, in addition to our calls and prayers for their benefit. I know of one spiritual community that displays a placard mounted in the entranceway to one of their retreats, that states: "Cheerfulness is Charity." This is, after all, the way of the Christ—being a ministering servant, being at the ready to extend aid and comfort to troubled souls you may encounter along your way.

Note that from the standpoint of the Masters, there is a distinction between compassion and sympathy. Being compassionate with another is essentially uplifting for both parties, whereas sympathy is, in essence, standing at a higher position and looking down, which is reported to be self-centered and only superficially helpful to another, if at all. Readers are encouraged to research the different meanings of these words.

The Bible contains many examples of selfless service that we can emulate. In Luke, Chapter 10, the Samaritan exercised great compassion in lifting a grievously injured person out of a ditch, cleaning his wounds, putting him on a donkey and taking him to a roadside inn.[15] Instead of doing that, he might have decided to simply pass by, as other travelers had done, perhaps harboring some private remorse and even shedding some tears, but rationalizing in some manner that stopping to help would not be in his, or even the victim's, "best interests."

In comprehending and showing compassion for the plight of others, we are showing our love for God.

Verily I say unto you, Inasmuch as ye have done it unto one of the least of these my brethren, ye have done it unto me.[16]

Even when we are confronted with people who are most obnoxious and argumentative, we are advised that God's grace will guide and sustain us to include them, as much as possible, in our compassionate service. This is the way of the Christ. We are encouraged, as disciples, to take on the disciplines of a Christ and deliver to others the example and frequency of love and understanding—in short, to truly live the Golden Rule. Every time we do this with sincerity and love, we build our "service muscles," and we expand our capacity to be a vehicle for greater outpourings of Christ-like behavior.

To be a disciple helps others make progress in their spiritual evolution—for their observation of how a disciple lives often proves to be an inspiration. Being a good example gives others the living proof they need to visualize what higher, divine, and righteous living is like and to more easily know that it is possible. It is a serious responsibility. As Jesus came to show the way, so may we. And, this is the most joyous way to demonstrate our special talents.

This loving action provides the way for all to return to the one fold, with one Shepherd—the Holy Christ Self—God's One Son—the real self of every soul. This is exemplified in the Bible by the testimony of Jesus:

> *I AM the good shepherd, and know my sheep, and am known of mine.*
> *As the Father knoweth me, even so know I the Father: and I lay down my life for the sheep.*
> *And other sheep I have, which are not of this fold: them also I must bring, and they shall hear my voice; and there shall be one fold, and one shepherd.*
> *Therefore doth my Father love me, because I lay down my life, that I might take it again.*
> *No man taketh it from me, but I lay it down of myself. I have power to lay it down, and I have power to take it again. This commandment have I received of my Father.*[17]

Now it is easier to understand what Jesus was saying. Through his life of selfless service, he was given new and glorious life. And God directed him in this manner to demonstrate to us all how to truly live and grow in the Light.

We are encouraged to make our prayers and calls for this and more to be accomplished, with the divine intercession that the Masters are able to give when we ask them for help. An encouraging message comes from Master Kuthumi, who dismisses the idea that the mistakes of our past can block our ability to advance on the Path of perfection:

> *Your Mighty I AM Presence is able to answer your every*

call made in order that you might fulfill my calling and my teaching. No matter how many mistakes you have made in the past, your Presence is standing with outstretched arms, waiting for the moment when your hungry heart will reach up and demand the chalice of your own perfection.

The Life which will be poured into the cup of your being shall be everlasting and the illustrious nature of your own God Self shall shine forth as the sun illumining the city set on an hill of discipleship (a pyramid of spiritual attainment) which cannot be hid!...

Look, therefore, for the glorious appearing of the Christ in your own being. He, as your own Holy Christ Self, will guide you into all Truth. As your eternal Preceptor, your Holy Christ Self will continually beckon you on the way of living discipleship.[18]

Although these teachings on being a disciple may sound too challenging for some, Master Kuthumi tells us that this avenue, which includes the transmutation of our karma, despite sometimes being arduous, has an end and results in the blessings and greater freedom that lie beyond. For once the power of Christ victory is gained, no limitations remain:

Do not fear to do your part as God wants you to. Accept the rigors of karmic conditions only as a temporary necessity, and realize that you have within your grasp the power of Light to change every wrong condition into Christ-victorious accomplishment![19]

The Ascended Masters can provide us with divine guidance and assistance in passing our tests, learning Cosmic Law, and the daily challenges of life's circumstances. In addition, they can provide help in our own self-understanding. Beloved Master Kuthumi touches upon the continuous discoveries that we will find:

> *The Ascended Masters' guidance is invaluable to all who are striving to increase the scope of their understanding of the self (psyche) in God. We release a continuous stream of divine wisdom to augment the interpretive ability of every seeker that he may cherish the deep things of God. We make the entire concept of Life more beautiful for all children of the Light, simply because its premise is God!*
>
> *Because Life is God, reverence for it will make it more wonderful. Gratitude will expand its blessings and victory will crown its achievements.*
>
> *Disciples, remember: glorious opportunities await your discovery daily!*[20]

Beloved Master Jesus reminds us that true discipleship does not show itself in a mere surface appearance. True discipleship comes from the very core of our being, from our ultimate divine nature—who we really are. And, when we embrace it, we embrace the kingdom of God, and by the grace of God, we shine with an unmistakable Inner Radiance. As Jesus tells us:

> *Disciples are still being born and made and are sorely needed in this hour to carry my word and radiation and the power of the sacred fire to God's children.*
>
> *Heaven will not spurn you! Remember my parable of the lost sheep.*[21] *Let this opportunity for discipleship—learning to teach men the Way—be regarded as the highest and noblest of endeavors, exalting every facet of God's consciousness in your being.... Truly all lesser callings must pale into insignificance before the Truth of the Call of thy Christ....*
>
> *Let this word from our hearts initiate a resurgence of your spiritual aspirations. Know that with God all things are possible.*[22]

Do not forget the tremendous power that Ascended Masters

have, power that they are willing and able to give to any disciple who seeks it and is able to receive *and hold* it. There is a great need for souls on Earth to attune with their inner divine blueprint and to repair all "leaks" in their four lower bodies so that they can retain whatever dispensations of Light that God will bless them with. A disciple needs to be prepared and work diligently to maintain a healthy physical body (as much as possible), healthy and balanced emotions, and be able to focus mentally with clarity and without undue distractions.

Master Kuthumi tells us directly of the power of Ascended Masters to grant to us more Light in this regard:

Our capacity to communicate eternal Life is also greater than your own, and you feel the vibration of our transfer of love and illumination by the extraordinary power available to us. In our presence you experience the heightened sense of our reality, as well as your own, through our ability to sustain in you our energy level as you place your attention on the spoken and written word of our release.
Your attention is the lever that connects your circuit to ours.[23]

Finally, it is worth repeating what was given in Chapter 4, concerning our unlimited divine potential. In the Bible, Jesus makes a statement that, for many, sounds unbelievable:

He that believeth on me, the works that I do shall he do also; and greater works than these shall he do; because I go unto my Father.[24]

The explanation that Jesus gave for this statement is, once again:

As my light-energy/consciousness is accelerated today

through my oneness with the Father in heaven, I am able to transmit to you through your loving tie to me greater power than when I was in the unascended state. Inasmuch as you also have access to the Holy Christ Self, as I did two thousand years ago, our combined effort can and shall produce through you greater works than were possible in the previous Piscean dispensation.[25]

We can also simply remember that:

Where attention goes, energy flows![26]

Chapter 13

Our Empowering Beautiful Vision

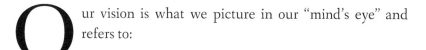

Our vision is what we picture in our "mind's eye" and refers to:

1. What shapes and focuses our thoughts, feelings and actions. It is crucial to always carry the highest and best vision for the greatest good to all.
2. Our level of discernment, which is our ability to distinguish between good and evil.

Our senses, as they are attuned to the Christ consciousness, have the potential to protect us by helping us avoid any situations that do not promote the greater good. Through practice, it is possible to train ourselves to exclude all things that do not belong in our vision. In some traditions, our "mind's eye" is also referred to as the "Eye of God."

One dynamic way to increase our awareness and to purify this blessed spiritual perception is to regularly make the affirmation recommended by beloved Master Jesus:

> *The affirmation "I AM the Resurrection and the Life of my perfect seeing, hearing, feeling, tasting, and smelling now made manifest!" should be repeated often in order to raise the senses to their natural and spiritual perfection—sharper than a two-edged sword when probing the physical dimensions.*
>
> *The purified consciousness when put to its best use is ever so effective in quickly changing the thought from the shadows of error-inducing unhappiness to pure Christ-vision. Thus cleansed, the student observes the Great Law producing eternal joy within his members whenever that Law is called into action.*[1]

Another powerful way to improve our discernment, as well as to create and maintain the highest possible vision, is to make the call for attunement with our loving Creator, whose nature and vision is always of the highest good. Jesus tells us of the affirmation he regularly used that helped him achieve attunement with God and experience the blessings of divine vision:

> *"I AM in the Father and the Father is in me" was the statement which I used often in order to anchor the affirmation of true being within my thinking and feeling worlds. Unlimited good will come to all who faithfully use this statement as a divine decree (mantra) and acknowledge this blessed concept of their cosmic unity with God.*[2]

Regardless of your situation in life, when this affirmation is given, it will help you to rise above any blocks in your perception and see beyond them. And as you do this, the very process of *thinking about God* creates a link that is life-nurturing. This affirmation is helpful in transcending any sense of sin, replacing it with a sense of holiness.

What we hold in our vision has great power. Contemplate and

nurture the vision of loveliness throughout the Earth, and see how God can and does manifest great love. Look at the beauty in nature and the perfect and divine qualities of people and places in your life. Each day we can aim to nurture and amplify the beauty in every person we meet and in every situation. We thereby transcend our former levels of consciousness and rise to higher levels of attunement and spiritual wisdom.

Beloved Jesus confirms for us the rewards awaiting the seeker who strives for divine vision:

> *The clear, calm pool of immortal Love waits to bathe the world, the soul, and all that breathes the essence of eternal Life, with the concepts of God himself....*
> *I AM come to bring peace to the troubled heart and calm repose to the soul in the dignity of life, sustained by the wisdom of iridescent [colorful, shimmering] spheres. Let each one know the Christlike power of dynamic vision, the power within the concept of God's truth in action here. Beloved ones, we won our freedom by the power of Light. Can Light do less for thee? A million concepts of error are as chaff before the winds of God's exalted vision in action.*[3]

All life is energy and the source of this energy is Divine Light. The action of Light is fully the consciousness of God. Our task is to attune to this Light, this God consciousness, allowing it to flow through our four lower bodies as much as possible. This Light contains God's highest purpose of goodness, and increases in flow as we outpicture God's will in our mind's eye.

Blessed Jesus explains the essential nature of our vision.

> *Beloved ones, that which you are outpicturing in your four lower bodies [physical, mental, emotional and etheric] is the index of your present conscious understanding—or your unconscious or subconscious ignorance. What you are and*

what you think can clearly be seen in what is manifesting in those four lower bodies, both from our vantage and by the spiritually attuned and perceptive unascended teachers. The vision of God-identity which you have first beheld and then held in the chalice of your consciousness is that which you are outpicturing, however limited that concept might be. The Law states that unless you are outpicturing in your four lower bodies (the four sides of the great pyramid of self) the fullness of the divine image, you have not accurately perceived that image: As a man seeth in his heart, so is he in outer expression.[4] Conversely, he cannot be or become that which he has not seen.[5]

Our etheric bodies, otherwise called our "memory bodies," interpenetrate our physical bodies, along with our mental and emotional bodies. The vibrational frequency of this etheric vehicle, unless heavily polluted with negativity, is the highest of our four lower bodies, and it conducts both positive and negative energy to our mental, emotional and physical bodies. Throughout our entire existence, and literally in each succeeding moment in time, we either nurture or harm the divine image which it carries.

Jesus continues with his explanation of the etheric/memory body and the importance of its purification:

The etheric body is a chalice for the sacred fire of your I AM Presence, the vessel of the chakras and the temple of your Christ Self—when purified. The soul who has elevated itself vibrationally to a comfortability in this exalted plane wears the etheric garment as a vehicle for so-called out-of-the-body 'soul travel'. Thus we emphasize that upon your deliberate purification and spiritual exercise of the memory body depends your accomplishment of assignments given to you prior to this life as the set goal of this embodiment.[6]

Our Empowering Beautiful Vision

This touches upon our potential ability, once our etheric body is adequately purified, for us to be able to do good works even while we sleep. Our soul takes a journey each night while we sleep. Our finer body, as it is referred to, leaves our sleeping physical form and, in general, either goes into mundane dream or nightmare states or, in the alternative, and depending on our spiritual progress and development, our soul travels to higher realms. Once there, we can actually work with and assist other souls—generally with the assistance of Ascended Masters or Angels—or we can study in any of numerous etheric retreats, again with the assistance of heavenly beings.

Purity of heart is essential to magnetize divine Light, enabling the disciple to experience the vision of our Creator. When the devotee has consecrated his life to God, it is possible to maintain one's perfect vision of being surrounded by divine Light. This practice will significantly increase the flow of Light into our etheric (memory) body which eventually reaches all four bodies, including our physical body. Sooner or later, if the appropriate invocations for Light are given, these calls and prayers bring results. We also need complete faith in the process as well as to be steadily outpicturing the ultimate goal of becoming one with our own I AM Presence.

In other words, divine Light can be magnetized by our steadfast holding of our divine vision. And as we pray for the benefit and forgiveness of others, we may receive the grace of forgiveness for our own past misdeeds. Making amends in all situations where we have harmed another along with prayers for forgiveness helps us to lighten our karmic load. Doing so creates new opportunities for those we have reached out to, and assists our own ongoing service and greater spiritual advancement.

Beloved Master Kuthumi explores how all of creation is sustained by our Creator. Within God's hierarchy, the Elohim are "Builders of Form" at the highest level of creation. They sustain all creation through their perfect and divine vision.

God is not the matter universe, neither is the universe God. It is, however, the vessel into which He pours His Life; and the only Life there is in matter is God. Furthermore, without the divine Being extending a portion of Himself into substance—spiritual or material—the inner structure of that substance would collapse. Likewise, should Elohim withdraw their God consciousness from the embrace and the vision of the physical universes—these, too, and all therein would cease to be.

Beloved, God is not the mind that comprehends and knows in part. But the mind of man that potentially senses the things of the Spirit is connected with and utilizes the one universal intelligence of God. This spiritual intelligence whispers to life, and life obeys the impetus of Love's mandates, hastening joyously to observe the ritual of Life's (God's) perfect plan, amplifying the divine intent to the fullness of its power.

The mind is a tool of wonderful flexibility. When it is set free by the power of imagination (operating through the 'third eye'—the spiritual center located at the brow of the forehead) it can envision a multitude of glorious concepts which range from mere fancy to creative sublimity.[7]

One of the main gifts from our Creator is that of free will. We are able to choose what we think about during the entire course of our life. We either govern ourselves wisely or not. The plain truth is that a consciousness of thoughts and feelings that is not wisely controlled inevitably leads to failure. Our thoughts *must* be governed. And they require the truth of our divinity as a foundation.

Master Kuthumi speaks about this:

The frailty of human reason is ever in its identification with the finite self. A sense of being entangled in the process of

identification with objects and experiences hinders the revelation of mans' true spiritual nature....
Ignorance is the first sin.... If then, it be ignorance which is the first habit to conquer, it can be recognized that by the golden flame of Christ-Illumination the realm of shadow is pushed back....
Ignorance is a habit based on sluggishness of mind and an unwillingness to sharpen and use the tool of thought. Lack of knowledge must be countered by joyful seeking after the glory of God, both below among the learning of men and above in the lofty hills of sacred knowledge and spiritual experience.[8]

In other words, we are intended to not only *not identify* with the limitations and illusions of the physical self, but rather to live as spiritual seekers with discrimination and listening grace, ever aiming higher on our trek through Life. We are encouraged to do this by not only studying and serving life, but by direct spiritual experiences through meditation, prayer, fasting, yoga, sacred music and other means that help us to transcend limitations and grow in spiritual attunement.

Merely being "intellectual," or feeling pride concerning our level of knowledge can block the blessings of our loving divine consciousness. It can block our ability to hear the gentle whispers from on high which provide divine guidance and illumination.

The Masters advise us that it is counter-productive to accept the negativity of the world as ultimately real. Or, to believe the carnal projections and demeaning claims we encounter that say our physical bodies are inherently impure or vile. Any perception of such innate evil or impurity blocks our ability to realize perfection.

Beloved Master Jesus tells us:

The idea that a person, place, or condition is inherently bad —when held in mind—can actually result in a manifestation of imperfection. Only by recognizing, through holding a perfect vision, the perfection of the God Source, can the students of the Light externalize the Father's perfect world— in themselves and in all others.[9]

It is counter-productive to focus one's attention more than necessary on fearful or evil manifestations on television and in the news. It needs to be done only enough to keep abreast of worldly events for the purpose of mitigating wrongdoing and transmuting adverse energies through prayer, meditation and divine decree. Otherwise, our time is best spent holding the "immaculate concept" of all goodness that is ever available to spiritual seekers actively seeking it. Beloved Master Kuthumi tells us:

I am wholly persuaded by the direct vision of divine reality that the Godhead sustains the quality of perfection everywhere and that the immaculate concept is a direct extension of the fullness of immortal Love expanding itself into all manifestation.[10]

There is great beauty to behold when one truly seeks it. The Master confirms this and continues his teaching upon this expansive perspective:

Nowhere in the universe is there a lack of beauty, for God is everywhere. Let none, therefore, fear to expand his consciousness. The exploration of earth, the solar systems, and all of cosmos through the expanding soul consciousness offers far more safety and satisfaction in probing the unknown than mankind are presently realizing through scientific exploration by satellite, rocketry, or spacecraft.[11]

The Masters tell us that we needlessly suffer because we do not hold to a higher vision. One major aspect of this suffering is that students often feel alone—when they are not! It is so supportive, some would say crucial and essential, to feel the company of Ascended Masters with us as we journey along the Path. It is important to know and include in our vision that we are never alone—for feelings of loneliness block our empowerment.

Master Kuthumi shares an inspirational message of support and beauty that can help us banish any sense of loneliness:

> *You know and believe that separation does not exist in God, but because of mortal conflicts and blind spiritual senses, most chelas [disciples] are not able to perceive in its entirety the heavenly grace that always surrounds them or to know when the Ascended Masters are blessing them. If they did, inasmuch as blessings are constantly being poured out, the disciples would never sense anything except the beauty and love of God flooding through them as an ocean of cosmic mercy; and their Christ-image of immortality would soon quicken them above every subdivine stratification.*[12]

Praise be to God! What a wonderful message to contemplate, and to revisit whenever the need arises. Let us ever keep in mind this empowering statement so we may hasten our progress with greater joy and less stress. And let us remember that we can always turn to a fellow disciple for comradeship and for mutual reinforcement.

Finally, we have as our starting point who we are now. For many of us, it incorporates our image, or vision, that is marred by imperfection caused by numerous past errors and by being caught up in a world of suffering and deceit. This imperfect image has been reinforced and continued for generations and lifetimes caused by destructive choices and misused will power, and needs to be cleansed of all impurities—all false beliefs about our limitations and lack of unity with God. Our future vision needs to be patterned after our perfect vision of the Christ.

Every moment, God continues to give us His ongoing gift of Light. We will do well to recognize this gift from our loving God and send our gratitude for this Light of life. Then God and the divine Self within others will receive our heartfelt blessings in return. This Light, before we qualify it, is God in action. When we qualify that energy in line with God's will for greater good, we are ourselves God in action.

It is helpful to remember that God continually radiates perfect love into the universe. As we work to purify our vision and make progress on the Path, our beloved Jesus delivers a message about the most direct and reliable path to true happiness. In his perfect attunement with God, he delivers a message to us from our Creator:

> *I AM the source of all joy, of all abundance, of all! Why then, do men seek to find happiness elsewhere? It is because in their sense of lack they amplify their need to possess that which in reality is already their own. This is a misunderstanding of the divine vision of universal Love which gives without limit to all.*[13]

We are blessed by our Creator's confirmation: that all that is good and joyous is already available for all to share. We are urged to hold the correct and perfect vision of the abundant and joyful life. Such a life is the wonderful reward for following God's laws.

Chapter 14

Jesus Dying For Our Sins

In the New Testament, there is a verse about the shedding of blood which ties in with the idea of Jesus dying on a cross for the sins of mankind.

And almost all things are by the law purged with blood; and without shedding of blood is no remission.[1]

The idea of Jesus dying for our sins, the "vicarious atonement," is essentially the false idea that salvation is available to all simply because Jesus, described as the only Son of God, died for the sins of all human beings. But this is a misinterpretation of the concept of atonement, and originated by way of false doctrines introduced in the very early days of Christianity. It was codified as doctrine at the Council of Nicaea in 325 AD during the reign of Emperor Constantine. At Nicaea, the view asserted by Constantine's allies was that Jesus was the only and exclusive Son of God and, in fact, equally God with the Father.

To numerous, sincere Christians, however, Jesus was not exclusively God's son. Various early Christian movements contained widely-known doctrine that held that Jesus was, in fact, a saint, a prophet and a great soul who lived a life of integrity. It was believed that Jesus, by his holy and virtuous life, showed the Way to return to our place of origin in Heaven. In those early days, they often repeated and recognized Jesus' specific teaching in the Lord's Prayer, where he told all to pray to "Our Father" in Heaven. And, in the Book of 1 John and numerous other New Testament references, we are told that in living as Jesus did, we are rightfully "the sons of God" and heirs "with Jesus" to the kingdom. Every disciple contributes to their divine attunement and their "at-one-ment" when their actions increase the Light of the Christ within themselves, and by demonstrating the way to their brethren.

Sincere saints and biblical scholars have for centuries incorrectly taught the idea that blood sacrifice was necessary to appease God's wrath. These writers were influenced by the long history of this practice in the Fertile Crescent of the Middle East,[2] involving the sacrifice of bodies and blood to God. These actions were perversions of the actual requirements of communion with our Creator that involve the sacrifice of our lower nature being replaced by our striving for the high ideals of our true nature in God.

True sacrifice is self-sacrifice that involves "shedding the snake-skin of the serpent [carnal] mind."[3]

Jesus explains what sacrifice is:

> *The scriptures declare that "without shedding of blood there is no remission" of sins. I am declaring to you and to all men forever the truth concerning this biblical statement, herein quite simply revealed: without the shedding (casting off) of that life, or life force, which has been misqualified with human foolishness, the sins of man can never be remitted (requalified with the love plan of God). Moreover, without the release of the life-essence (i.e., 'blood') of the Lamb who is your Holy Christ Self, you cannot balance your karma. Hence, it is by a continual requalifying, mastering,*

governing and controlling of energy through the Ascended Master Light of the individualized Holy Christ Self that men and women shall rise to the point where their former sins, which are solely error recorded in memory, are blotted out by the Holy Spirit.[4]

Jesus is telling us that we need to shed, or transmute, the energies or Light that we have misqualified in the past through wrong action and the misuse of our free will. Our powerful calls can invoke God-purity and can lead to purification of past errors and wrong behavior. (Part II, "Working with the Light.") In this process of being cut free from the energies of past misdeeds, we can put on our "wedding garment," our new clothing of purity, love, wisdom, peace, and power.

Jesus goes on to address the false notion that God is biased toward some over others:

The idea that God, your beloved I AM Presence, favors one child and rejects another is totally inconsistent with divine Law. My own life was offered to God to epitomize the Cosmic Christ, to prove that man and woman in physical embodiment can ascend out of Matter and remain close by in octaves of Light (invisible, yet co-occupying the physical plane at a higher frequency) to mightily assist the earth and its evolutions in returning to the original divine plan of the abundant Life.[5]

In addition, Jesus states that he continues to be available to help us, as are other Masters, because *every single one of us is destined to rise up to the Christ level*, whether we currently realize this or not. Once we have completed our preparation, we will also be available, being purely guided as Jesus was by God within, to also show our less-evolved brethren the way. Once purified, souls will radiate, or shed, God's loving Light that flows through them to where it is most needed to transmute planetary karma or sin. This activity is the true "shedding of blood."

Many souls fail to comprehend and appreciate the extent of our Creator's outpouring of Light energy to maintain all life, and the ignorance of this is actually an error that creates self-limiting karma. This limitation returns by the Law of the circle. Souls are not able to fully rise up in consciousness until they have transmuted their karma (incurred by their own immaturity, and also by willfully or ignorantly disobeying God's laws).

In general, this process of "returning karma" is an aspect of the mercy of God. The misqualified energy returns so that we have an opportunity to learn through helpful feedback and to transmute, using spiritual practices, harmful karmic patterns we have previously created.

One way we can transmute our karma is by serving life through our service to others, which can itself be a truly joyful "sacrifice." Jesus alludes to this type of joyful service as an integral part of our purpose on Earth:

> *...for this cause you and I came into the world—to take upon the office of our Christhood the burden of world karma so that the lost sheep gone astray from the House of Reality might experience a deferment of their karma and a certain relief from suffering while they learn of me and my true burden, which is Light. This Light, when internalized by themselves, will enable them in their turn to take full responsibility for their own burden of karma as they, too, follow the same path of discipleship you are on: personal transformation through integration with Christ, the Light of your world.*[6]

It makes complete sense that we need to evolve to the point where we can demonstrate that we can be trusted with the Almighty Power of God before it is granted. Therefore, our goal is to purify ourselves to increase the flow of divine Light and love through us. We then have an increase of the energy, love and wisdom contained in this divine Light which we can "shed" or radiate to others in need, enjoying the gift of giving always. We will be guided in the highest and best use and direction for bestowal of this Light for the greatest good. This is all part of God's grand design.

It is helpful and comforting to occasionally focus on the words our Lord gave to Jesus:

And lo a voice from heaven, saying, This is my beloved Son, in whom I am well pleased.[7]

We are told that these same words will apply to each one of us, as sons and daughters of God, when we have passed through our own initiations. It will then be most spiritually gratifying to fully experience the love that our Creator provides to us, as will be seen in the eyes of numerous friends and loved ones with whom we share our time on Earth.

Chapter 15

Transcending Mortality—Being "Born Again"

The Book of John, surely among the most profound of all the Bible's books, has been pondered by scholars, debated between Christian theologians, and inspired mystically-inclined seekers since it was first written down twenty centuries ago by the blessed apostle known to be Jesus' closest confidant.

Here, we explore the concept of human mortality from John 3, wherein the Pharisee Nicodemus has a dialogue with Jesus, exclaiming that no man could be able to do miracles like Jesus unless that man has God within him. Jesus then takes the opportunity to explain the dual nature of human existence, and how it is possible for an individual soul to achieve immortality.

> *Jesus answered and said unto him, Verily, verily, I say unto thee, Except a man be born again, he cannot see the kingdom of God.*
> *Nicodemus saith unto him, How can a man be born when he is old? Can he enter the second time into his mother's womb, and be born?*

> *Jesus answered, Verily, verily, I say unto thee, Except a man be born of water and of the Spirit, he cannot enter into the kingdom of God.*
> *That which is born of the flesh is flesh; and that which is born of the Spirit is spirit.*[1]

Nicodemus was stuck in a literal interpretation of the words Jesus used. Jesus now explains precisely what he meant:

> *But I spake of purification through the rebirth of water (Mother) and through the quickening of the spirit by the sacred fire (Father) as being necessary for the soul to reenter the consciousness of Alpha and Omega (divine Principles of the 'beginning' and the 'ending' personified in the 'Father/Mother Elohim') whence he is come and into whose kingdom he shall go. This rebirth by purification through the 'waters' and the 'fires' of Life is the means to enter in to the Holy of Holies of thy I AM Presence.*[2]

Our indwelling sense of the sacred provides powerful transformational potential. It gives us a fulfilling and strong sense of well-being empowered by the Holy Spirit and furthers our attunement with the consciousness of Christ, the Son of God. Our ability to radiate divine love and wisdom will be magnified as we become more Christ-like. Through this process, souls are indeed "born again."

Our beloved Jesus makes a profound statement summarizing this process that students of world religions will recognize as capturing the essence of our shared mystical Oneness in God:

> *And lo, a universe is born! Man is "born again" in the rebirth of Truth. And the Lord God once again beholds in man the creation of that Good which He made because it is Himself.*[3]

From the words of Jesus, "That which is born of the flesh is flesh; and that which is born of the Spirit is spirit," we discern that the "flesh" refers also to the lower, carnal aspects of life on Earth. The "carnal mind," that which is temporal and passing, simply cannot comprehend the spiritual and, literally, the eternal aspects of life. It is doomed by its own separation from spirit. Those who are attuned with spirit enjoy an inner peace in contrast to those wholly entrenched in the worldly mind, which can never find lasting fulfillment in anything. When we identify with superficial things, we are blocked from realizing our identity in God. When we shift our consciousness toward our Higher Self, an entire universe is opened to us.

One challenge to overcome is that the physical senses needed for life on Earth have been dulled for a variety of reasons (deficiencies in diet, the use of alcohol and drugs, all manner of toxins, the density of television and the entire "entertainment industry," etc). Other contaminants are mistaken beliefs and the accumulation of negative karma from this lifetime and previous ones. Clearly, this entire negative conglomeration presents a great challenge to the evolving soul, making it more difficult for many people to realize what the problem truly is, as well as its spiritual solution.

We can, each one of us, as God's blessed offspring, use the all-powerful source of divine Light burning within the very center of our being. With the Light in our hearts and with God's directives, we can move through, transmute, and overcome all that would deny us the achievement of our individuality as a Son or Daughter of God.

Jesus inspires us with his loving and compassionate heart, to take time in our earthly journey to help free others from their carnal prisons:

Alas, such is the nature of the carnal mind (as it stains the four lower bodies with the dye of nonidentification with the living God), from which the soul must be rescued by the living Christ! O my beloved, do take pity upon the poor souls buried under a heap of carnal illusion spawned by the mass media and the educational systems—saturating the thinking/feeling/memory process of an entire generation.[4]

Indeed, the amount of tragic suffering on Earth today is unimaginable. This is the result of ignorance, as well as that which is put forth intentionally by individuals who are so committed to evil that they are actively and continuously engaged in opposing God's loving will. These are bleak times. Many historians and philosophers, not to mention psychologists and religious leaders, view modern-day society as failing to provide even a rudimentary platform for balanced human development. Increased crime, widespread addiction, higher rates of suicide and rampant mental illness and homelessness bear this out. It is not surprising that we have such a high level of cynicism in many people but perhaps especially in our youth, who find enormous hindrances in their search for righteousness on Earth.

But in the face of all this tragedy (and because of it), humanity is turning back to God in unprecedented numbers. Millions are hearing at a soul level a call to return to God's grand design, whereby each soul who embodies on Earth can make the effort to achieve Christ consciousness in this lifetime; the great key being to love the Lord thy God with all thy heart, and to be grateful for all the blessings in life. Jesus urges us to:

Lift up your eyes to the reality of the Light of God which is everywhere and feel the radiance of the Light enfold you. Feel that Light penetrate your being as immortal Love reaching into the very core of your being—physical, emotional, mental, and etheric.[5]

Engaging in the effort to be "born again" will bless souls with an increase of divine Light/energy in their physical bodies, as well as their thought, feeling and memory worlds. It is important to remember one's true identity as a son or daughter of God. As this process raises the consciousness it results in being less subject to the strife and stress in our physical world. A soul on the Path of Light benefits greatly from firmly establishing this in consciousness.

Beloved Master Jesus shares his prayer for our success in this calling:

O immortal Love, seal them within the fold of Thy heart until they, too, are free, returning with me to that sacred altar of Light exalted where all joy is e'er [ever] in fulfilling Thy holy Will.[6]

Another view of this, our common goal, lies in revisiting the statement by Jesus from the book of John:

Jesus saith unto him, I am the way, the truth, and the life: no man cometh unto the Father, but by me.[7]

Jesus would have us understand that we simply cannot attune with God using our physical senses. We need to utilize our natural, but often unused, spiritual senses that enable us to attune to our Christ consciousness. As we transcend worldly consciousness, becoming "born again," we are creating more and more threads of contact with the divine. As progress is achieved, we receive encouragement from the gradual increase of spiritual blessings, whether they be greater clarity, or a greater sense of the peace of God "that passeth all understanding,"[8] or an easier and more spontaneous ability to share loving words and acts of kindness with others.

The need for those who would "come up higher" is first and foremost to gradually substitute all the various aspects of the carnal mind with the joyous light-filled radiance of the diamond-mind of

God. This process takes time, but every carnal layer shed brings us closer to the purity of God's consciousness.

When speaking of the "carnal mind," we are not referring to what is sometimes thought of as "carnal:" sex. Sex is a blessing and a normal part of being incarnate, especially when it enhances our connection with our intimate partner. When sex is obsessed over, however, being the primary focus of a person's life, this then blocks one's ability to attune with the higher, more righteous and divine aspects of life. Unnatural, perverted or obsessive thinking and actions about sex are indeed an aspect of the carnal mind.

As Saint Paul taught the early Christians, the carnal mind is enmity with God. The carnal mind is a human creation of darkness, caused in large part by mankind's fears and doubts of God's love for us. It is the antithesis of the Christ mind. Paul stated this about our carnality:

For ye are yet carnal: for whereas there is among you envying, and strife, and divisions, are ye not carnal, and walk as men?[9]

If we have sown unto you spiritual things, is it a great thing if we shall reap your carnal things?[10]

Most definitely not! The carnal mind is a deceitful fabrication that needs to be purged from the soul for the soul to have peace. A good prayer for this action comes from the Psalmist David:

Let the words of my mouth, and the meditation of my heart, be acceptable in thy sight, O Lord, my strength, and my redeemer.[11]

Let us not forget that what we learn about our true identity is stated in the very first book of the Bible:

So God created man in his own image, in the image of God created he him.[12]

We have already been urged to be perfect. We have now been shown how to open our spiritual centers. In addition, powerful tools can be used to help us shed our imperfections, so we can be fully within the flow of divine and perfect Light, containing our Creator's love, wisdom, and power. (Part II, "Working with the Light.")

There have been individuals who have chosen to never relinquish their carnality, who convict themselves by holding firm to their self-serving beliefs, continuing in their same pattern, even mocking the will of God as they refuse to repent or acknowledge the harm they have done. For these people, the mercy of God's Law relegates them to their chosen non-identification with God, fulfilling their free-will choice. Their absolute rejection of their divine potential, repeated over innumerable lifetimes and in spite of uncountable opportunities to repent, leads to what is referred to in scripture as "the second death."

This final death of the soul itself ends the opportunity for the individual to seek redemption and return to the Light. These tragic souls do not suffer eternally, but rather come to their end abruptly, as God's final act of mercy. It bears repeating that the second death is not the common destiny of the vast majority of souls. Such a choice is rarely made by any soul and is only possible by continual warring with God and His emissaries! And, it is a foolish and ignorant choice, based on turning one's back on the unlimited potential of beauty, joy and glorious blessings that await us.

Because of our Father's abundant mercy and grace and the many opportunities given to each soul over many lifetimes in the earthly realms, most souls, like the Prodigal Son, return sooner or later to the open, loving arms of God. Devoted spiritual seekers can rest assured that their life experience will eternally expand in the growing love, peace and beauty of God's creation.

As we continue on our journey heavenward, dear Jesus gives us this blessing:

May the Christ consciousness of the Eternal Mind dwelling within you—uniting with the Christ Light of every Ascended Master and cosmic being—express the fullness of God now and forevermore![13]

Chapter 16

Losing Life To Find It

In this chapter we have additional examples and explanations from the Bible and the Masters that explore the concept of being "born again." This re-birth means different things to different denominations, and goes beyond the ritual of baptism or the declaration that several Christian denominations adhere to, namely, that a Christian's rite of passage is to declare that Jesus is one's chosen Lord and Savior. Rather, at the very least, being "born anew" is an ongoing process.

He that loseth his life for my sake shall find it.[1]

I know of one spiritual seeker who, when asked if he had been born again, smiled and responded that, "yes," he had been, in fact, many times. At the time I took his statement to mean that he had on these occasions experienced a spiritual transformation, virtually a life-changing new direction in his life.

Personally, I have also felt born again on numerous occasions. Being raised in the Episcopal church, I always felt that Jesus was my Lord and Savior. I now realize that in addition to my love for

Jesus, I love and have allegiance for the wisdom, love and power of God through Christ, the One Son and intermediator with God. Not only Jesus, but throughout the ages many others have become saints and Ascended Masters after they have "lost their (human) lives" in service to humankind, demonstrating great spiritual attainment. They all have inspiringly demonstrated the beauty of discovering our true, divine nature.

Sometimes a meditation experience has been so profound that I sincerely believe I transcended my old self. Occasionally, a certain teaching enables a new revelation to dawn within me. I remember that after giving a session of "bija mantras"[2] every cell in my body felt saturated with Light, confirming for me the reality of God. There have also been certain days when I was working on my two previous books, and certainly this one, that were so spiritually uplifting that it felt like being born again. On those special days, I have felt so blessed and could see the world with new, "born-again" eyes. As we go forward on our personal life journey, each one of us is best served by being always open to receiving new releases of Light, which can sometimes result in grand new perspectives.

The life of the lower self, so desirous of material things and being "stuck" in the ego-driven worldly consciousness, produces results that are not truly fulfilling. Yet, due to the comforting aspects of its familiarity, as well as the excuses-driven human ego, it can sometimes be a stressful tug-of-war between our lower and higher selves to let go. A popular phrase often used in recovery therapy is "Just let go and let God!"

Once we realize that those portions of this life that were guided by the lower self have misqualified God's Light and at times caused suffering and loss, it becomes easier to let it go. When we understand that we need to gradually replace the carnal mind's attendant darkness and detours with the Christ mind, we liberate ourselves. It is easier to let the carnal mind go when we realize that a carnal life inevitably leads to desolation; whereas a life in Christ leads inevitably to one of the "many mansions" Jesus promised to those who follow in his footsteps. A soul can make rapid progress by choosing to attune to the Christ Self and the lovingly whispered guidance it bestows.

When we are willing to let go of the lower self's endless desires and immerse ourselves in God's Light, we will indeed return to the far more beautiful, peaceful, fulfilling and loving life in God's kingdom. The resulting love and goodness from our divinely-guided actions then return to us. This is the activation of the principle "It is more blessed to give than to receive."

Beloved Jesus touches upon the sense of impoverishment that we feel when we are stuck in a carnal consciousness:

> *Men and women of the carnal sense are always in the process of shedding that sense—the impoverished sense of material life—for the abundant Life of God.*[3]

Caring and comforting servants are required on Earth to tend to the needs of all states of consciousness in all socio-economic classes—to encourage and assist all souls in realizing their unlimited divine potential and identity.

Another way of viewing "losing life to find it" is in terms of carrying a cross. Jesus discusses this as a process we can experience over time:

> *The "way of the cross" pertains to the meeting of God and man. It depicts the manifestation of God in man who is in the process of obtaining the perfection of his own ascension in the Light, even as I did. Eventually this "outer man" will be completely absorbed into his perfect Selfhood, but were he to merge prematurely with his God Self, which is an all-consuming fire, it would destroy the very fabric of his soul-identity.*
>
> *Therefore, it is the mercy of the Great Law, which never lowers its standards or fails in its compassion, to create a*

wide spiral in the eternal cycles of time and space where the becoming God-likeness of man is nurtured by the wisdom-love of God.[4]

Jesus refers to the goal of the "Ascension in the Light,"[5] He also refers to the God Self as an "all-consuming fire," which is not physical fire, but a degree of intensity of divine Light that is far higher in vibration or level of frequency than the current state of our four lower bodies. Exposure to it prematurely would cause damage or destruction. Yet, though it may currently sound somewhat frightening, the idea of our ultimate experience of life or consciousness in this significantly higher level of vibration, Light, or Spirit, can be logically understood and accepted as the key to our eternal existence within its joyful flow. Yes, it is radically different from material living, but it is a freeing, bliss-filled experience that literally "can't be missed" for all souls who love God and evolve in their spiritual destiny.

The wisdom and love of our Creator allows for every individual, in accordance with the gift of free will, to advance on the Path according to one's divine blueprint and timetable. Every one of us, as long as we are "materially bound," has coils of both conscious and subconscious habits that need to be unwound and replaced by new strands of loving devotion to God, others, and all of life. This process can be as long or as short as we desire. It ultimately depends on our will reflected in our striving and commitment to change, based on our love for God and His goodness. This is all made possible by the grace of God!

We have been provided a pathway that will lead to our eternal freedom, when we will fully know how much we are loved by our beloved God. The sacrifice that we make is the giving up of ongoing frustrating and non-fulfilling attempts at finding true and lasting peace, wisdom, love, and joy via the material, worldly, or carnal avenue.

This pathway is not really one of sacrifice, but rather one to surrender all that cannot last, all that can never bring true happiness. It is a sacramental pathway much more than one of sacrifice. Jesus confirms that this process is not sacrificial in this statement:

> *O my beloved, my Galilean life was not sacrificial but sacramental. It was a freewill offering to God which you, too, shall one day make (and some of you have already begun the process) in the course of your journey back to God's heart.*[6]

Our Holy Christ Self, or Christ consciousness, is our teacher, and is available as we attune to it. Earnestly seek and embrace it. Desire it more than anything else. This loving, gentle and sublime Christ presence, when sensed, is best obeyed so that we may be guided by perfect wisdom as we encounter every possible situation and test that life presents. Beloved Master Kuthumi points out the importance of its guidance:

> *Some students do not feel the need or the desire to surrender their will completely to God, thinking to retain, by right, some control. Blessed ones, in examining the cosmic record of centuries, I have never found one case in which human control exceeded or even equaled the wisdom and perfection of God-control and God-guidance. And I do not think I shall!*[7]

It is possible for even those who are enmeshed in a material, temporal state of consciousness to yet observe that certain individuals they encounter radiate "something wonderful" to those in their presence. These individuals may appear quite ordinary and be leading relatively humble and nondescript lives, yet they are noticeably able to maneuver the challenges of life on Earth with a great spiritual composure.

Master Kuthumi continues in his encouragement of aligning

oneself with one's true divine Self, which is God's will, offering us the wisest and most loving guidance:

> *This investment of God (notice, I say "in-VEST-ment") is an act of the supreme guiding intelligence that controls every star in the sky. Here God's investment becomes man's investiture as the Father invests the power of his will in his sons and daughters who surrender their will to him and VESTS them therefore with a mantle of authority and responsibility to expand His kingdom below as above. This precept is still taught by Jesus in his parable of the talents: Thou hast been faithful (i.e., obedient, responsible, trustworthy) over a few things, I will make thee ruler (a co-creator with me) over many things....*
> *Truly you create yourself by allegiance (obedience) to your inner blueprint and the Voice within who so lovingly guides you into all Truth.*[8]

This is a key explanation of why we need to drop our lesser, ego-driven will and allow divine wisdom to guide us to success and freedom in the Light. By doing so, we give our allegiance to our own "inner blueprint"—essentially *becoming true to ourselves.*

During this process, it is helpful to view Light as divine. We are not focusing on physical light, but rather ultra-high divine frequencies. At some point of regular attention to divine Light, it is reported that our own sense of weight will decrease and one will feel lighter. This is due to natural law—what we focus on we become. This enables us to attune to the wisdom and love of God as well as to harmonize our mind with others and all things in creation.

Although most of us can testify to feeling a sense of struggle during our time spent on Earth, Jesus shares with us a most comforting teaching:

To God your life is a life of hope; for he has vested the entire creation, including YOU, with the energy and consciousness of his being. I am confident, then, that patience will show you how to climb graciously, without backtracking....
God has been spoken of as a consuming fire and indeed he is. The sacred fire is the being of God. The flames of God are all flames of freedom; for God is Truth, and the power of Truth does make all free through the fiery baptism of the Holy Spirit. Therefore, fear not, little ones, any man-made doctrine which purports that God desires aught [anything] but what is best for you![9]

Faith in God's love for His children is required. Let us once again be reminded of the fact that God loves us more than the very best mother on Earth loves her children. John, the beloved apostle, addresses what we shall be:

Behold, what manner of love the Father hath bestowed upon us, that we should be called the sons of God: therefore the world knoweth us not, because it knew him not.
Beloved, now are we the sons of God, and it doth not yet appear what we shall be: but we know that, when he shall appear, we shall be like him; for we shall see him as he is. And every man that hath this hope in him purifieth himself, even as he is pure.[10]

As we grow in our attunement with our Christ consciousness and shed the carnal consciousness, we will also grow in our comprehension concerning what is our real nature in Spirit. It is both natural and essential to love the Holy Christ Self when we realize the blessings it brings and the understanding it provides about ourself.

We can use our willpower to silence the lower self, or the carnal mind, which contains pride, opposition to knowing the truth, and an accumulation of mistakes made over time. Prayer is an important way to achieve this. The energies of the carnal mind need to be transcended and transmuted, because they block the Christ consciousness. In essence, the carnal mind is hostile to God.

If left unchecked, the worldly mind would maintain its controlling influence, keeping one's soul in chains of mundane mediocrity and illusion. When the truths of divine life become evident, the soul will no longer accept being dominated by the carnal mind. This will allow that mind to be replaced by the Christ consciousness. Once a soul can silence the confusion of this lower mind it can more readily hear the gentle, loving guidance of the divine Conscience or Christ Mind.

Let this mind be in you, which was also in Christ Jesus.[11]

Master Kuthumi tells us of the steps that are essential to raising our consciousness. The first is obedience to the voice of God. The second is thinking about Light, and the third is thinking about power (not human power, but the omnipotence of God). If we focus on these three things while we repeat the I AM Lord's Prayer, we have a wonderful tool that will, over time, help to free ourselves from what is holding us back.

> *Our Father who art in heaven,*
> *Hallowed be thy name, I AM.*
> *I AM thy kingdom come*
> *I AM thy will being done*
> *I AM on earth even as I AM in heaven*
> *I AM giving this day daily bread to all*
> *I AM forgiving all Life this day even as I AM all Life forgiving me*
> *I AM leading all men away from temptation*
> *I AM delivering all men from every evil condition*
> *I AM the kingdom*

*I AM the power and
I AM the glory of God in eternal, immortal manifestation—
All this I AM.*[12]

Jesus tells us how these factors aid us in our spiritual advancement:

The Light of God within you and the Power of God within you will assist you in expanding the Light (Christos) in every molecule of your being, until your own Presence floods forth its light rays to the center of each cell and to your heart center itself to glorify you as a Sun of God even as was done for me![13]

As we focus our attention on the power of our Creator in its permanence, strength and beauty throughout the universe, our divine desires can be fulfilled by God's grace and all-powerful love. Blessed Master Kuthumi describes the need for all to receive, and to give, more love:

By giving comfort to others you cannot help but receive in return, and the world is so full of need. Immortality is best achieved by service, then; for by doing the Father's business, the stream of divine love is channeled through you, and God will not deny his own channel the boon of the divine interchange.
How necessary are instruments of service, in not one but many fields. Let all serve God as the great light of their divine Self directs. And may all be blessed thereby with the rewards of immortal service so enjoyed by the Ascended Masters![14]

As we choose to follow this path of service that leads to immortality, it is helpful to be reminded that it is a path leading to greater peace and divine love. This choice leads to happiness and fulfillment.

> *Let not your heart be troubled: ye believe in God, believe also in me.*
> *In my Father's house are many mansions: if it were not so, I would have told you. I go to prepare a place for you.*
> *And if I go and prepare a place for you, I will come again, and receive you unto myself; that where I am, there ye may be also.*[15]

Let us trust in our divine Creator, and the teachings of dear Jesus. Let us not allow ourselves to be overwhelmed with all the problems on the Earth. Let us maintain a quiet mind, even when others do not. Be comforted in the presence of the Christ as the mediator between man and God. The peace and the happiness to be found in Heaven is referred to as being in our Father's house. His many wondrous mansions await us.

Beloved Master Kuthumi graces us with his inspirational overview of how to live life, and closes with a prayer of praise for service:

> *Your immortality is attained here and now, blessed ones of the Light. It is won in your joyous use of the shining hours, in your radiant, God-expressed harmony, in paeans of praise released to the heart of God from your own wonderfully charged, beating hearts, swelling with the love-tide of gratitude for life....*

A PRAYER OF PRAISE FOR SERVICE:
O Love of God immortal Love,
Enfold all in thy ray,
Send compassion from Above
To raise them all today!

In the fullness of thy power
Shed thy glorious beams
Upon the earth and all thereon
Where life in shadow seems.
Let the Light of God blaze forth
To cut men free from pain.
Raise them up and clothe them, God,
With thy Mighty I AM Name![16]

Chapter 17

The River Of Life

The divine Presence continually floods us with divine Light, which contains divine Power, Love, and Wisdom. There is no soul on Earth who is denied this flow of Light. Along with the loving energy of this Light is the spiritual wisdom and guidance that can be thought, heard or felt through our still small voice of conscience. Yet there are many who disbelieve in it or actively reject it, which effectively blocks this guidance. Innumerable Ascended Masters and heavenly Emissaries are available when called upon for those who are open to their divine Presence, to provide specific assistance as needed.

On Earth, many people ignore spiritual realities by focusing exclusively on their five physical senses. Master Kuthumi expands on the gift of life that God gives each one of us:

> *The most gracious gift of God to every lifestream is the totality of Being—not a mere fragment but the totality of that blessed Reality. The deceit of the senses has kept men and women from realizing in full potency all that is of the infinite nature within them awaiting holy recognition.*

God abides his eternity, peering through the screen of time and manifesting on the stage of life in various phases of his Reality; and yet, this too is Life. From this dream of partial knowledge men must awaken to behold the splendor of themselves in all things.[1]

Ideally, every individual would recognize and be grateful for this energy flow. We benefit when we are good custodians of this energy, by not allowing emotions to arise outside of our control. Proper self-control is crucial not only in our feelings but in our minds.

In this regard, we profit by not clinging to a perspective that life is against us, that it is grim, harsh or difficult. Instead, we benefit from viewing life as a wonderful experience, filled with opportunity.

It is worth repeating what blessed Kuthumi told us in Chapter 12:

Blessed ones, Life is full of perfect hope, glorious love, and an ultimate destiny which transcends all mortal dreams. It is essential that the true disciple master the means of transmuting whatever outer condition seeks to corrupt the Life principle. The idea that each life is a manifestation of God must become permanent in the heart of every disciple.[2]

We might take a page from the Native American beliefs that all of Creation has a Spirit, for indeed, God's life exists throughout. The Masters tell us that this life energy is active throughout the entire physical universe, not only in the animal kingdom, but in the vegetable and mineral kingdoms, as well as on many higher planes of vibration. Unbeknownst to many, God's energy sustains the invisible world of "mythological" Nature Spirits—the world of "elemental" life including elves, fairies, undines (water spirits] and more.

The River Of Life

We have the ability to assist elemental life, which is sensitive not only to divine guidance, but to lower negative influences from people. We do elemental life a great disservice when we fight amongst ourselves. They are our unseen helpers! These "little brothers and sisters" in the elemental realm make it possible for us to have an ongoing earthly existence.

Human negativity creates a "weight" or darkness that elemental life must shoulder if life forms are to continue to function on Earth. Master Kuthumi explains how our human emotional disharmony creates difficulties for the Nature spirits, or elementals:

> *Under the extreme burden of mankind's imposed discord, the elementals, like children out-of-sorts, do not always obey the hierarchs of their respective domains. Conflicting planetary forces, inharmony among their numbers, and overbearing planetary karma results in natural cataclysms which bring on untold human suffering....*
>
> *Every sincere disciple [should] ponder the example of beloved Jesus' control of the elements and their obedience to him. Each chela can learn to direct natural forces, as greater and more significant spiritual achievement becomes a fait accompli [a thing accomplished] in his life.*
>
> *My brothers and sisters—it cannot be overstated that peace and harmony are the key to your God-control whereby you gain entrée and take dominion in all octaves of natural life. Thus, with all your heart, still the tempestuous emotions, cast anger, revenge, and hatred into the sacred fire forever, and wage the warfare of the Spirit against the ego with its pride, ambition, and cunning.*[3]

The elementals were created to help mankind. As we make progress on our collective spiritual paths, they will be able to gradually establish their god-control in all areas of the four lower kingdoms. As this occurs, souls will be able to collaborate with elementals that have been serving the sons of Light for ages. Although these lower kingdoms were originally given to mankind to manage in a time of stewardship, this ability was gradually lost as the Nature kingdom was forced to absorb ever-greater misqualified energies caused by human ignorance and misbehavior. Elemental life in all its forms has for ages been burdened by the negative energies from mankind. This has also extended into the animal kingdom, which has led to the savagery and violence that certain animals display.

The power of Christ will ultimately replace the tragic and unnecessary "laws of the jungle" with harmony which is the true essence of Life in God. Then, the elementals will be freed, and the Edenic beauty of nature will be restored.

The wolf shall dwell with the lamb, and the leopard shall lie down with the kid; and the calf and the young lion and the fatling together; and a little child shall lead them.[4]

Chapter 18

Sharing The Light

We all know the joy of sharing a new experience, an exciting piece of news, or an inspiring story with friends and acquaintances. At times like this, we feel a special camaraderie. And quite often, we then find that "one good turn brings out another," and others are moved to share similar uplifting comments and insights. Perhaps at no time is this more true than when we share, sincerely and directly from the heart, something spiritual—a profound teaching, a personal awakening, even a sudden inspired realization—that filled us with an inner joy and great gratitude. This is because there is within all of us a deep desire to share the blessings of divine wisdom with others who are open to learning. It is our basic nature to share the love we carry within, and what is more loving than to impart to others joyful Light in true friendship?

Master Kuthumi encourages us:

> *Be ye therefore unafraid to share in holy wisdom, being careful to select from those nuggets of spiritual Truth, stored for safekeeping in your immortal being, special gifts to bless*

> *your brothers and sisters with the illumination that banishes ignorance forever from their spiritual quest.*
>
> *There is a special act of grace given to all who seek to teach men of lesser comprehension concerning the glories of God's kingdom. Spiritual teachers on earth guided wholly by sincerity are, by reason of their stand, angel ministrants in human form....*
>
> *"Fear not, little children, for it is your Father's good pleasure to give you the kingdom" is their message.*[1]

As previously stated, spiritual knowledge is not gained merely through the written or spoken word, but also through various practices such as meditation, prayer, yoga, sacred music, fasting and other means. Of greatest importance are loving kindness and service to all in need, along with maintaining a mindset filled with good and positive spiritual truths. As this occurs, less room is left in consciousness for the lesser aspects of this world. Our interest in mundane things soon fades away. For souls to experience the allness of their divine nature, the "lesser self" needs to be left behind. This process can also be accelerated by invoking the purifying divine Light, which enables the soul to totally identify with being a Son or Daughter of God. (Part II, "Working with the Light.")

Sharing is truly a basic part of our divine nature. Our Creator is magnanimous—the most loving and greatest giver in all of Cosmos! And God shares his entire identity and Self with each one of us when we move to return to and honor our own divine Presence.

Actively sharing insights and the history of our own spiritual journey with kindred souls can be a blessing for all concerned. However, as Jesus and other great souls throughout human history have demonstrated, the preeminent method for showing others the way to overcome is by presenting a living example, by leading a life that demonstrates the wisdom and love that lifts all souls higher. Being that example can be more powerful than sermons or writings, and makes a lasting impact upon all who see it. Words are important, of course, but the power to amplify those words lies in their demonstration through example. This is known by the Ascended Masters as the *living word*.

Remember how supported we are when we endeavor to share and demonstrate divine Truths. Master Kuthumi reminds us that he and other Ascended Masters are available in tangible, practical ways to guide and assist all who are ready:

> *As Life is God, it is continuous. The true Master, whether in the body or out of the body, is he in whom the Word is embodied as the active principle for and on behalf of the Almighty's Law of Life. The power to communicate from the higher to the lower octaves is possessed by every Ascended Master and requires but the pole of a receptive chela to transmit the vibratory action of spiritual assistance, love, and blessing—including fresh solutions to stale problems, nifty ideas and practical inventions that are the gift from the Master's heart to the chela for the whole human race.*[2]

Millions of souls on Earth are seeking and not yet finding. Some do not even realize that they *are* seeking—yet deep down in their soul, they know a far better life awaits. They feel a great need for teachings that raise up their soul. Sons and daughters of God feel profoundly painful yearnings to understand more about life and how to escape the futility and confusion so widespread across the Earth. Although many souls feel strongly committed to leading a more spiritual life, it can be difficult for them to avoid getting caught up in the negative attitudes and behaviors which ensnare so many. Unless we are aware and vigilant, these attitudes can easily remain a part of our conscious and subconscious habits, which would block a greater immersion in a loving consciousness.

Souls who do not appear receptive to a life of greater joy and freedom may have significant anxiety and feel threatened concerning the very subject of the divine. This fear can be incapacitating, even as they are suffering from a lack of fulfillment in their lives. We are all being urged to enter higher realms that require a loving heart. Hopefully the day will soon come when *all* will welcome the manifestation of God's grand and loving design into their lives.

People cannot see their unlimited divine potential unless they are able to perceive God as being truly woven into physical manifestation. It is then that the soul can really begin to cease being ensnared by human illusions. The carnal mind has created strong defense mechanisms to protect itself, and those still under its grip need to be understood with compassion. Appeals to such a soul may not work unless the soul has already begun practicing some degree of love and devotion. Appealing to the Holy Christ Self within the soul will yield the greatest success. Strive to reach the Christ Self of all you meet, so that the individual may be cut free from fear and doubt, for our Christ Self can reach out to any soul on Earth to demonstrate their potential to be consciously united in Christ.

Those who embrace this calling need to know they will invite criticism. Be prepared to be misunderstood and even accused of things you are innocent of doing. People are often threatened by someone who takes a stand on moral principle or offers a spiritual viewpoint that others perceive is contrary to some religious dogma they subscribe to. They may then level accusations or charges of wrongdoing against you. In addition, dark (malicious and aggressive) forces may use such an incident to further persecute you. This may also be for the purpose of dissuading as many as possible from your message and example. Therefore, be wise and be aware whether you, yourself, are compromised by what Blessed Master Kuthumi calls "human willfulness, rebellion, pride, anger, aggressiveness, ambition or any such abuses." Pray for guidance, strive to genuinely serve and do your best to not stray from the Path, and do not be discouraged!

Beloved Master Jesus offers this encouragement for all who would feed his sheep:

If the Ascended Masters and the cosmic hierarchy were to await the full manifestation of absolute perfection before sending out teachers to proclaim the truth of God's light and love, mankind might have to wait a long time to be free! I am grateful, therefore, for those who are both honest and humble enough to admit to mistakes, yet zealous and hardy enough to submit to human criticism by going forth to do the best they can to serve in the Father's vineyard. Many of those who suffer the most severe criticism shall go further to attain their victory than man may think.

Their heart's right motive and prayerful attitude, seen and heard at higher levels, will in due course attract a higher state of perfection until at last they attain the cosmic consciousness of the immortals—though their critics remain sidetracked and bound in limitation and self-created confusion. Yet we would have none thus fail. Let all be vigilant![3]

Master Jesus addresses the task of teaching those whose minds resist or who appear closed to concepts relating to God.

It is... essential that those who are agnostics or atheistically inclined be taught the facts concerning the True Self as one would teach these truths to the little children. We recognize the difficulty in this approach. Nevertheless, we admonish you to press on. Do not prejudge your hearer's capacity to comprehend Truth, neither underestimate the power of Truth to communicate itself through you by the Holy Spirit.[4]

Even if a person appears to be close-minded on spiritual subjects, we are encouraged to speak with them calmly and without prejudgment. In doing this, we provide a pathway for the divine spirit to connect with the individual's Higher Self. Over time, seeds of ideas they have received by the subtle transformative influence of the Holy Spirit, can grow into a strong faith that the individual makes their very own. This is so, even if the individual appears unreceptive at the time. Master Jesus describes why such efforts are beneficial:

Think you that in extending the love of the Father to a cynical or scornful one who reviles you and flaunts the love you give, driving it back into your very teeth, you do ill? I tell you nay; for though it be far from him, he will one day remember and perhaps look for the proffered gift. By expressions of hatred and shame, men mar the surface of their own souls; by expressions of virtue and honor, they lay up in heaven a wreath of victory on behalf of all Life.[5]

In the final analysis, certain things can only be done by the individual seeker of truth. Although immortality is offered to every living soul, it needs to be consciously sought and claimed by each soul.

Jesus continues with advice on sharing the Way with others:

Beloved, you are wayshowers even as I am; therefore, in drawing men unto the Father, you yourself must first draw very close to the Father. In approaching the Godhead, men must understand that they are not playing a losing game, but that they are winning their own victory.
There is a tendency on the part of the students to believe too much in the reality of the senses and all that they perceive without paying allegiance to the powers of spiritual sensing which belong to the eyes of the soul. To screen out the nebulous (mistlike, hence mystifying) and vicious thoughts of the

serpent mind, to screen out the psychic (astral, mayic) accumulations, which like a kaleidoscopic cinema divert the consciousness from the symmetry of the kingdom of God—is a necessity.[6]

There is a tendency for mankind to attribute human qualities to God or higher beings like the Ascended Masters. The Ascended Masters no longer have human imperfections. All their feelings and thoughts are perfected, for they dwell in the perfect consciousness of Christ. This can be difficult for those on Earth to envision.

Countless people have been frustrated in their search for truth. In some instances, holy books have included misinterpretations of sacred texts that readers have felt pressured or lured to believe. Often these incorrect teachings have been presented by those who truly believe them. Teachings which distort or compromise truth can leave truth-seekers feeling empty.

Fear of the unknown, self-doubt and other self-defeating thoughts and emotions have also held many people back. Dear Kuthumi addresses the roadblock of fear, suggesting that the logic of our conscious existence needs to be considered:

Fear keeps men bound, for they fear to believe lest they be found gullible and they fear to doubt lest heaven spurn them. Teach them to pay homage neither to belief nor doubt but, in being true to themselves, to remember the words of Descartes, who declared, "I think, therefore I am." Let men perceive by logic that inasmuch as they live and affirm "I am," therefore God lives to create and affirm "I AM THAT I AM" and sustain his creation![7]

Let all who read and believe consider how they can best offer loving service in some form. In this new era, every soul is being sent a message containing their immortal destiny—a clear expression of the goal for each soul. Let not any decisions be made from fear, for in time, all will live in peace and harmony. When reaching out to others, we most definitely need to avoid attempting to force them into an exacting cookie-cutter pattern. Freedom and creativity allow for the uniqueness of each soul to develop in its own way.

We need to be sensitive and discerning in our efforts to help friends and acquaintances along the way. Just as too little effort in reaching out is unlikely to get through to a shy fellow or bewildered traveler, so too can an overbearing approach cause the "threatened soul" to erect defense mechanisms and shun your offer of help or encouragement. A person is best served when offered spiritual teachings with a measured approach, without overwhelming anyone with information. Ideally, we offer it to a degree and in a manner as we ourselves would be comfortable accepting it.

It is all a delicate balance. I learned a powerful lesson about this when I was much younger. I was sharing teachings about the Masters and about all of us being sons or daughters of God. The person I was speaking with was excited about what she was hearing. Unfortunately, it was rather late at night, I was speaking on the phone with her, and I was tired. Being on the phone, I couldn't see her reaction to what I was saying. I got carried away and continued to go on and on, not realizing that I had shared too much at that time. I then realized that she hadn't said anything in a while. I could tell that her interest at that point had been lost. I learned then that it is better to say too little than too much. I also learned to not only listen to the other person and understand where they are coming from, but also to listen to my inner guidance.

People's spiritual beliefs are, of course, very sacred to them. Whatever insight comes to mind to share with them can be balanced with a listening ear to hear their experiences and opinions and to empathize with them, loving them and acknowledging their beliefs and feelings. Develop a listening ear and an ever more compassionate presence, and when on the spot, say a silent prayer asking for inner guidance. Then with a smile and/or a lighthearted comment, offer to share some thoughts that you sense can help the person out. Not too much, not too little—always the middle way.

The Holy Spirit is the driving force behind any true conversion. It is like water, ever-present to permeate whatever openings of consideration we allow into our consciousness. Master Kuthumi describes its action within us:

> *Try to realize that the power of conversion is the gift of the Holy Spirit alone; hence, man is compelled by his own spirit to accept the idea of his own immortal existence (which only fools or the godless deny). Out of this initiatic idea of one's immortality—the eternality of self, spanning past, present, and future ages—each day unfolds from within a greater understanding of divine Law.*
> *Do not try to rush your own or your neighbor's comprehension, blessed children of the Light. Let patience have her perfect work as you realize that your diligence in pursuing the Path according to the best within you is God's way of encouraging self-disciplined action in others.*[8]

When sharing spiritual teachings with others, we cannot expect that they will always be well received, much less instantly assimilated. But do not be discouraged in your efforts. In this regard a friend on the Path recently related to me his personal experience soon after encountering the Master's teachings:

> *In my college years and for a time thereafter, I used marijuana and hashish and, regrettably, even some psychedelics. So it was, when I was exposed to the Teachings of the Masters, because of the kindness and love I felt from so many individuals associated with the organization, I realized in my heart, and by the grace of God, that I had found a wonderful spiritual path and a community of active practitioners!*

But I was actually just getting started in my journey. It may sound strange but for at least the first six months, if I sat in a congregation to listen to a teaching, I would quite literally become dazed and fall asleep. People sitting adjacent to me would whisper and gently prod me to wake up, and this could happen many times during a single session. This all became such a distraction to others that, as long as this "condition" persisted, I was asked to be seated in the very back of the congregation.

I am glad to report that with perseverance, fasting, the help of other members and honest self-reflection and prayer, I came through this "period of initiation." To this day—many years later—I am exceedingly grateful that I stuck with it, for these teachings have steadied and sustained me wonderfully through all the challenges and ups and down of my life.

Let each soul develop the habit of regularly affirming what is good and positive, and simultaneously rejecting what is immoral or sinful. Doing so creates a giant momentum of divine power, making it possible to be victorious over all self-induced bondage. And let praise for our loving Christ Self be the key to positive change on Earth. As we build greater habits of good character, we receive reinforcing strength from the Holy Spirit. This results in greater success in all tasks, accompanied by a growing sense of achievement as we move forward on the Path, and an increasing joy of immersion in Loving Light.

Blessed Master Jesus defines the grace of God that can flow from the one Son, the Christ, and that is available in unlimited supply to each one of us:

How futile it is to let a lack of grace deter you from outpicturing the fullness of the light already given you. Grace is a quality of the heart of Christ containing all mercy and forgiveness, love and light. Contrary to the accepted doctrine that grace comes only from myself, you yourself can increase the grace flowing through your heart center (chakra) from your Holy Christ Self. This you accomplish by various loving means, including the multiplication (expansion and refinement) of talents given into your hand instead of burying them in the napkin of despair.

These talents are, in fact, your past momentums of good habit built up in previous lives of service to the God of Truth. Each talent is a developed genius acquired by hard work and diligence to the duty of unfolding the soul's inner potential.[9]

In other words what we are good at doing—our talents—are the result of our efforts both in this life and past lives. These talents are accessible for our continued good use and enhanced development as we share divine truth with all who are open and receptive. It is best to educate ourselves in our chosen fields so that we are really able to help others through the work that we do.

Not only did Jesus say, "Feed my lambs," he also said:

And Jesus said unto them, Come ye after me, and I will make you to become fishers of men.[10]

What can be done by any one of us who aspires to help "teach men the way" is to provide loving guidance and assistance in the most practical manner. In addition, it is important to also pray for every specific individual in your care or within your circle of influence. Let us fully accept the grand opportunities to help all in need on Earth, for this loving action will accelerate our own spiritual progress.

The ideal preference of the Ascended Masters is for us to teach through word and example. This requires that we be grounded in love and humility, being sufficiently bonded to our Holy Christ Self, enabling us to be good stewards of God's Light and love.

Dear Jesus adds to his appeal for helpers with two statements:

Only by taking heroic measures to counteract the apathy and godlessness of the present day can my disciples give to my message and mission of two thousand years ago a new and effective voice in this hour.
Let them win the hearts of today's men and women for the radiant personal love of God, their own Mighty I AM Presence.
Let them win for the worldwide dawn of peace in the golden age, when goodwill shall blaze forth through all hearts from the magnificent cosmic heart of God—who even now loves the whole earth as one great Son (Sun!) So shall it be!
With the entire hosts of heaven, I AM beckoning my Christ-filled soldiers Onward![11]

The goal of your striving, blessed heart, is that the song of the Holy Spirit proclaim its message of goodness and ever-unfolding joy to the world through your own sacred labor, so that through your effort many may be freed from the power of misqualified energy and from a distorted viewpoint of everything and everybody.[12]

To truly learn something, we need to teach it. As we do this, we will receive fresh insights and more expanded understanding, as well as more opportunities to serve. The sincere practitioner soon discovers there is nothing that compares to sharing with others keys to personal, spiritual growth. They realize such sharing leads others to greater immersion in the glorious Light of God, helping souls to remember their true identity in God and all divine Life.

Most people on Earth do not realize the tremendous potential *power* and *intensity* of *divine love* in our feeling world. As we purify our hearts, we clear the way for this intense loving spirit with its powerful energy! All matter has pure loving Light at its core. When this Light is released all who are touched by it are blessed.

Blessed Master Kuthumi shares why it is so natural for us to share this loving Light:

> *The symbology of the Lord's "common table" reminds us that the Law of Love is based on the great unity of Life—a love of Love, by Love and for Love! How can God forget man whom he has created, seeing that he, the Creator, is endowed with infinite grace and mercy? Those who are the true followers of the divine Mind, perceiving his grace and the fullness thereof, must respond in the mode of the Father to the spiritual hungers of his little ones and, in the Master's words, "Feed my lambs!"* [13]

Master Kuthumi provides essential information for us regarding purifying our hearts, which then allows the intense and powerful ecstasy of love's flow through us:

> *Divine Love holds the answer to the release of immortality, and anyone who manifests any feeling less than love for all Life, or any part of Life, is denying himself the secret elixir of immortal Life. Man can no more deceive or thwart the Great Law than he can rise from the earth and ascend bodily into heaven without the assistance of the Almighty and the release of the spiritual energies of his God Self.*
>
> *The earnest student must believe us when we say that so long as a trace of human feelings—mild dislike, including subtle jealousies or hatreds—remains in his consciousness, he will be unable to summon the great love magnet of the Central Sun to assist him in obtaining reentrance into the paradise of God where the Tree of Life spreads its all-enfolding branches of beneficence. The Law makes no exceptions.* [14]

Now is the time in history when many who are "dead" to the realities of divine love and Light due to their ignorance and misqualifications of life energies will finally hear the divine message and begin an earnest spiritual striving—toward the goal of a joyous and eternal future.

All souls have restless minds until they find true peace in God-consciousness. Our task is one of eternal exploration whereby we will continue to discover the many and surely endless facets of God's love for each one of us and all of Creation. Our love is the foundation for empowering new habits in our feeling and thinking worlds, enabling us to forget the darkness of the past. Let us raise ourselves up to behold in ever-greater measure the unimaginably vast, infinite accumulation of Good which comprises the Universe.

Chapter 19

The Holy Grail–Drinking From The Cup Of Light

Our beloved elder brother Jesus would have us drink from his cup. Referring to his biblical statement recorded in Matthew 4:4, he shares with us a powerful view of the pathway he chose to take, and one that he wishes his disciples to follow:

> *My statement "Man shall not live by bread alone, but by every word that proceedeth out of the mouth of God" must be applied to the understanding of God's laws in living as a son of God. Living by material standards, no matter how high, cannot possibly connect our disciples with the pure vibration of spiritual compassion which so reveres the Word of God that every moment is perceived as an opportunity to stand forth as a living example—a living revelator of God, interpreting God unto man not through the vanity of earthly ideas or even the grandeur of cultured prose, but through living successfully as a divine embodiment here and now.*[1]

Let us then drink of this proffered cup of God-identity which is offered to all disciples. When we choose to fully drink, we receive cells and atoms of divine energy, and we will continue to grow in our divinity. The result will be, finally, our freedom from human bondage.

Consider what living on Earth would be like without the enlightening spiritual concepts and hopes that have been and are still being transmitted to us. Without such spiritual concepts and encouragements, a sense of hopelessness and despair could easily prevail. If that were the case, then only the most spiritually sensitive would still be able to have any sense of an eternal, joyful future. What we are blessed with instead is a steady flow of divine illumination from a wealth of inspiration which brings uplifting energy and knowledge of our divine, eternal life.

According to scripture, as prospective disciples, we have access to the gifts of the Holy Spirit. In 1 Corinthians 12:8-10, there are enumerated nine specific gifts, including wisdom, knowledge, empowerment in faith, the power to heal, prophecy, the gift of discernment and the working of miracles.

The Holy Spirit is divine Light. Master Kuthumi emphasizes the power of the divine Light of the Holy Spirit to radically improve our life experience:

> *Upon feeling the regenerative powers of the Christ, the errant knight of the outer self seeks to drink the cup of true Being and to pursue that Light which has never shone on land or sea, for it is the internal nature of all things which has never been profaned by the grossness of outer expression. It is this Light which maketh all things whole, whose shining gleams forth from the Grail and exhorts the lesser radiance to become the greater.*
>
> *No loss is ever the portion of that one who, desiring not to abide in the aloneness of outer self-expression, unites with the all-oneness of God. Supreme questing-fulfillment*

beholds in hope the day-to-day challenge to keep on keeping on—assuredly to find in time and space the priceless, eternal treasure of Being.[2]

Here we recognize that the nature of Light is beyond human comprehension. We know that from the outset of the material Creation itself, it was literally the Words of our heavenly Father, "Let there be Light!" that brought into being the entire physical universe.

Throughout recorded history, philosophers, theologians, mystics and even today's astrophysicists have pondered the nature of Light, and have generally come away with a deep reverence and an equally deep intellectual humility. The brilliant religious scholar Huston Smith refers to the two great scientific accomplishments of the twentieth century—the theory of relativity and quantum mechanics—as both relating to Light. He states that "everything is created from Light," and that all the subsequent interactions after that proceed from Light. He also states how Light "stands outside the matrices of space, time, and matter" which control all creation.[3]

The nature of divine Light is such that, at times, it is pure energy and at other times, it takes the form of matter. Scientific studies of light waves and particles have confirmed this. These dual qualities play a key role in the creation, the nurturing, and the ultimate dissolution of all observable materiality. The greatest minds in human history have yet to completely understand all aspects of the nature of Light. Scripture proclaims the Divinity of Light:

God is Light and in Him is no darkness at all.[4]

Divine Light is the energy, frequency or vibration from the highest level and source of ultimate reality. For those of us in physical embodiment, to the degree that we are immersed in the finite material world, we are to that same degree unable to fully comprehend the nature of divine Light.

The Bible contains numerous examples of the seemingly miraculous power of divine Light. Here is but one:

> *And a certain woman, which had an issue of blood twelve years,*
> *And had suffered many things of many physicians, and had spent all that she had, and was nothing bettered, but rather grew worse.*
> *When she had heard of Jesus, came in the press behind, and touched his garment.*
> *For she said, If I may touch but his clothes, I shall be whole.*
> *And straightway the fountain of her blood was dried up; and she felt in her body that she was healed of that plague.*[5]

Our beloved Master Kuthumi enlightens us on this unlimited power of the Holy Spirit, comprised of Light containing divine Love, Wisdom, and Power:

> *The issue of blood which troubled the woman for many years ere she touched the hem of Christ's garment symbolizes the issuing forth of man's life-energy in wasted years of fruitless existence. The drying up of the "fountain of blood" through the healing power of the living Christ symbolized the redirection of Light flowing from the fount of energy, the Mighty I AM Presence, into the chalice of individuality. The Light, skillfully redirected by the Master Physician, restored the 'woman' (symbolizing the feminine nature of the receptive soul) to her original reason for being.*[6]

This illustrates our ability, as we are progressing along our divine Path, to touch the hem of the garment of our Mighty I AM Presence. As we proceed along this Path of our spiritual evolution, it is wonderful to know that no sense of struggle is necessary. Effort is required, but not with any sense of struggling to achieve goals. All we need to do is ask.

> *Ask, and it shall be given you; seek, and ye shall find; knock, and it shall be opened unto you:*
> *For every one that asketh receiveth; and he that seeketh findeth; and to him that knocketh it shall be opened.*[7]

We are told that if we do not receive an answer of guidance or assistance or see progress on our chosen path, that it is important not to cast doubt on ourselves or upon God's Law. Instead, search to discover what may have been done incorrectly in our submission. Also, adequate time needs to be allowed for answers to come.

Beloved Jesus addresses this issue of asking and not receiving. He explains:

> *"Seek ye first the kingdom of God and his righteousness, and all these things shall be added unto you." This admonition contains the formula of man's eternal covenant with his Maker. It is your first "test question" on your self-examination checklist, if your current results are not all you expect them to be. Ask yourself: "Am I really seeking God's consciousness FIRST—each morning and before every decision—before I get involved in my own human reasoning?" If your answer is not an unqualified "Yes!" then I say, "Mend the nets of your consciousness! Come up higher!"*[8]

Jesus wants us to know how essential it is to be seeking God's consciousness first, as an ever-present priority. And, he also wants us to know that he will help us if we call to him. His aid, and that of other Masters we may call upon, will assist us in understanding divine truth and will help us to experience the comforting Light of the Holy Spirit.

It is important to make an agreement with oneself to live in attunement with our Loving Creator and request that our mind be filled with His holy Light—a divine Light that we will *not allow to be disturbed in any way*. And, to realize that if we make improper use of these new energies bestowed upon us, further progress cannot be made until we re-consecrate ourselves to our pure and perfect dedication to the Light. Those that maintain this dedication are readily helped from above whenever help is requested.

We need to ultimately lose all of our frustrations and anger, all anguish and all doubts concerning our divine potential. These must be transmuted before a total reunion with our Creator can happen. The fire of the Holy Spirit is an unfailing resource, and will transmute anything, including all mortal concepts, that are less than perfection. All Ascended Masters, saints and other members of God's hierarchy join with Jesus in inviting us to drink from the Cup of God-Identity. As we do, we will absorb the divine Light of the Holy Spirit. Every atom and cell in our four lower bodies will be energized and attuned to the greater eternal reality as we free ourselves from our mortal bonds.

Chapter 20

Transfiguration

AUTHOR'S NOTE: I recommend not reading this chapter on Transfiguration until you have had some experience with the flow of Light and love—by reading the previous chapters and at least beginning to "work with the Light" in Part II and the Appendix. Otherwise, reading about our Transfiguration might be just too difficult to believe!

If you haven't jumped ahead, and have read through every chapter before coming to this last one, you have most probably felt joyful, but also in some cases perhaps doubtful, concerning all the blessings our Creator has in store for us. Many of these gifts can be difficult to believe, for they are promises of incredible new life, energy, and purpose.

One of the most astounding and dynamic events that we will someday experience is our Transfiguration. When considered in context with all that has been covered thus far, unless we persistently oppose God's will, our return to spirit is inevitable.

Please do not be dissuaded by doubts that would shut down the divine possibilities. It is vital to remain open-minded to *all* good potentials and not limit God. Consider these opportunities, not allowing doubt or disbelief to creep in before reading this entire chapter. After all, we know our physical bodies won't last long! How can our promised eternal life be possible without fully transitioning ourselves into the world of spirit, where the energy flows are limitless and lift us up to glorious divine realms? Our Transfiguration will be a major step and a permanent change in our being that enables us to receive subsequent initiations.

Beloved Jesus tells us that it is God's sacred fire that can prepare us daily for this blessed event:

> *The power of the Transfiguration to change one life exemplifies the action of the sacred fire, whose transforming Light is the miracle worker day by day, until the soul and four lower bodies of the disciple are prepared for the fullness of the all-enveloping Transfiguration.*[1]

God wants to bless His children, once we prepare adequately, with his great loving gift of the Holy Spirit. After the Transfiguration, our ability to help others significantly increases, for we shall then have much greater knowledge and power to utilize God's loving Light to heal those in need.

Master Jesus shares with us the purpose and method of Transfiguration:

> *Transfiguration is the means devised by the Godhead to free man from (1) all manipulations and degrading changes intended to de-evolutionize the race and (2) all that is not in complete unity with the seed-essence of God himself and with the sacred fire of the Mighty I AM Presence.*
>
> *Through the acceleration of the electronic fire rings of the Presence that occurs during the initiation of the Transfiguration, individuals are "stepped up" in vibration and clothed with the seamless garment of electronic light.*[2]

Transfiguration

We are told that this Light comes from the heart of our Creator and that it is able to pass through all the human density and delusion that hides our divine potential. This divine Light then radiates outward from our heart to fill every cell in the body temple. Once this process is begun by the Presence and fully recognized by a soul, no division of distinct or separate religious affiliation remains in the consciousness. The pure joy of being immersed in God's Light through this initiation of the Holy Spirit takes precedence.

Jesus further describes this experience for us:

The effect of God's Light upon man's consciousness is great joy and peace. When the Light and fire of God flow through him like a crystal-clear river of Life, washing away the former impressions of unhappiness, the glory and freedom he feels are boundless![3]

From the Bible, we learn of Jesus addressing not only his disciples, but the people that were following their group:

Verily I say unto you, That there be some of them that stand here, which shall not taste of death, till they have seen the kingdom of God come with power.[4]

The Bible then reports that six days after Jesus shared this with his disciples, he had his own Transfiguration experience:

And after six days Jesus taketh with him Peter, and James, and John, and leadeth them up into an high mountain apart by themselves: and he was transfigured before them. And his raiment became shining, exceeding white as snow; so as no fuller on earth can white them.[5]

Jesus was so filled with the pure, white Light of God that his human form was enveloped in a shimmering white radiance. This transfiguring energy is available to us and will one day likewise emanate through us when we pursue our personal spiritual destiny. The Transfiguration involves the same Light that created all things in the universe. This Light provides oneness and total connectivity to God's loving energy and prevents any form of discord within our feeling world.

Understand that God wants each of us to be transfigured—ideally in this lifetime. God wants us, every day, to make progress toward that goal, by our good works, our prayers, and by invoking His Light. There is a wonderful decree that can be given to accelerate the Transfiguration process, which is located in Part II, "The Blessing of Transfiguration." The Appendix also contains this decree along with guidance for a call that can be given daily for one's Transfiguration.

Jesus tells us that an important factor to help us on the Path to Transfiguration is to first and always listen for God's voice, and to obey it. We hear this voice in our hearts. Jesus tells us:

> *All of us [all souls who have ever progressed to the point of their Transfiguration initiation] were obedient to God as we made our way up the mount of Transfiguration. We counted it the highest honor to so be and to so attain, and so it is.*[6]

It is also important to contemplate and attune with divine Power and divine Light. It is essential that this is done with the goal in mind of increasing the goodness in life, as well as divine peace, magnetizing Light's power within the very cells of our body temple by meditating on the Light (Appendix, "Meditation on Light").

Think of the power within atomic energy—the potential energy within every cell of our four lower bodies. Divine Power contains even more energy! This power is available for our use in loving and righteous action. Blessed Master Kuthumi directs us to increase the divine Light within us:

In the spirit of infinite peace and goodwill, let all amplify the power of Light within the cells of their whole being. Draw and magnetize the Light, but know that this Light is the balanced action of divine Love, Wisdom, and Power— teaching, cherishing, and directing you always into the paths of righteousness for His name's sake, I AM. How else, blessed ones, can man "be still and know that I AM God"?[7]

It is vital that we not only comprehend these teachings about divine Light from an intellectual level, but that we *feel* and literally incorporate the Holy Spirit's love and blessings into our being. Doing so attracts the Light, not only to ourselves, but to others close to us, as well as others we may encounter for the remainder of our time on Earth. This balanced power of divine energy automatically connects us with God, our Mighty I AM Presence.

To that end, blessed Master Kuthumi offers a valuable checklist for a disciple to follow when considering their future actions:

First, he will take care that any and all acts, including both words and deeds (which always require energy, power, determination, and will to accomplish) are not compromised by human willfulness, rebellion, pride, anger, aggressiveness, ambition or any such abuses of the First Ray of God's powerful Will.
Second, he will balance all his activities by the necessary application of Wisdom's objectivity and equanimity— preceded by forethought, study, research, analysis, and careful consideration that each thrust for a purpose is constructive, well-organized, and of benefit or gain to some part of Life.
Third, he will test every move, project, or plan by the measure of God's Love, purifying motive and intent with charity and compassion, especially examining it for its practicality— "Will it work?" He will enfold his actions with

creativity, devotion, carefulness, unselfishness, and gratitude, giving the glory to God and taking care that the work or word contains the essentials to bear fruit, multiplying grace and increasing the Christ consciousness on earth.[8]

God wants us to follow the examples set by the Ascended Masters, who are our elder brothers and sisters. They are those who have lived on Earth as we are doing, and who have striven diligently and succeeded in balancing their debts to Life. They are now in a blessed state whereby they can utilize God's power for the greater good.

We can follow this same Path taken by the Ascended Masters, though the timetable for each individual soul is dependent on their understanding, diligence and striving. Our I AM Presence can show us the way. We can commune with God as we, in prayer and meditation, attune with Him and His divine, eternal love.

Dear Master Kuthumi also describes for us the ideal goal to pursue:

There is an ideal situation to which all should aspire, and this is the highly spiritual, ecstatic state wherein identification with your Mighty I AM Presence is the high prize to which your total being aspires. This aspiration to Light's ecstasy elevates the inner vision to the point where the white fire core of matter comes under one's conscious control, according the devotee the privilege of increasing his own capacity and power to internalize the sacred fire. Thus, the ultimate Way is approached and the disciple is led step by step through the gates to the Infinite, ever higher on the upward spiral of Being.[9]

The Ascended Masters will help us with this process. It is natural for them to want to, just as it is natural for each one of us to want to help those in need. Calling for their assistance grants them permission to intercede directly on our behalf. They will assist us by working with our Higher Selves, teaching us and enabling us to do greater works than we could do on our own without their guidance and assistance.

Today we have Jesus himself, Master Kuthumi, and countless other Ascended Masters and loved ones on our side! They are rooting for us, guiding and encouraging us to come up higher. Let us be open to their divine assistance and grateful for their love.

Our Creator lovingly acts in a rational, objective, logical and scientific manner—to uplift our souls, to gently guide us as we make progress in our lives, and to raise our consciousness so that we will be happier and grow closer to Him.

Our journey will require effort and striving but this will result in joy beyond description! Let us remember that each one of us will be tested, sometimes severely, along the Way.

Let us also remember to avoid a "sense of struggle." Blessed Jesus avoided that feeling, which contributed to his ability to receive more energy and illumination from the Father. He used this energy to heal others and to transcend ordinary human limits. This made it possible for him to stay constantly attuned with the wisdom of the Father. Jesus accomplished this by periodically fasting, praying and meditating during those times when he removed himself from the crowds to areas of solitude.

Every soul, prior to their Victory of achieving their Ascension, experiences the initiations of the Transfiguration, the Crucifixion, and the Resurrection. These initiations comprise the completion of our spiritual journey into new realms of Life. They are *not* covered in great detail in our source book, The *Corona Class Lessons*. They are addressed in other teachings of the Ascended Masters. It is far more important for as many people as possible to progress through the various stages that lead up to the Transfiguration, for this is where the greatest challenges and work need to be undertaken. For the remainder of this final chapter, we will touch upon some main points about the Crucifixion.

There is a Law of progress. The Light that we receive must be increased for us to advance on the Path. And, a growing amount of divine Light has been and will continue to be increasing on Earth. Its purpose is for our salvation.

Light reveals Truth, exposing lies that have been lodged in darkness. This can precipitate hatred within souls who have harbored such darkness.

Souls who love God accept whatever suffering manifests from the increase of Light. Souls who shake their fists at God in anger for bringing suffering upon them are ignorant of divine Law, which requires the return of karma and soul purification before entering into Higher Realms.

We need to be ready to receive this Light, or spiritual fire, to transmute all karmic and carnal resistance to our spiritual progress, for our joyful future lies in divine Light. What will be relinquished is our lower self, our worldly human ego.

The Crucifixion is a form of death—but merely of the mortal, human life, the repository of one's lower nature. It is our free will choice to choose immortality by "surrendering" ourselves to the purity, protection, peace and goodness of God and His holy Will. *This is the voluntary integration of our personality, not the loss of it, with God. It is the full realization, the absolute union, of the soul with Christ, the Son of God, which is every soul's Real Self.*

God blessed us by offering us "the greatest story ever told" in the life of the son Jesus, who demonstrated the Path of Overcoming in his life as the Christed One. This example clearly delineated the stages of our transitioning to spiritual life... the gradual or the rapid letting go of all that is human, and embracing the Light. The Transfiguration, the Crucifixion, and the Resurrection were all shown in his life as distinct stages, to demonstrate in essential detail the concept of each.

Jesus was and is an extraordinary Being, for he volunteered to make this archetypal demonstration so that for all time we would have an example of what a true Son of God faces when proclaiming his divine sonship on this troubled planet. Crucifixion often involves forms of human rejection, character assassination and extreme emotional distress. It can result in grave losses of love, respect, and understanding in our most cherished relationships. It may also involve an extremely difficult trial that may include degrees of sickness, suffering, and pain.

This is not something any of us would look forward to, but if the Crucifixion is the Gateway to the kingdom of God, then whatever pain or suffering we experience is well worth it. The Masters reveal that whatever pain a soul experiences can be significantly reduced by our spiritual attainment. It is even possible for it to be transmuted into bliss. The Crucifixion rewards us with an eternal future which we, in holy stillness and reflection, can only barely begin to comprehend.

The Crucifixion of Jesus is sometimes referred to as the Passion. Crucifixion is a passionate victory over darkness. It is the intensification of the sacred fire of divine love. Each individual soul can pass this initiation by having an intense love for God and a fiery spirit of victory which entirely eclipses darkness. This passion encompasses the highest, most intense love for all life, a "perfect love that casts out all fear."

Our love is for our Creator, who gives us a Life Path which is divinely designed to lead us through the challenges of earthly existence in such a manner that we develop true self-mastery. During this process, we become wise, courageous, and dignified Sons and Daughters of God.

The Transfiguration is the infilling of our soul with divine Light. After much soul testing we are able to experience the great Light of the Transfiguration in which our soul becomes wed to Christ. The world will then crucify the Christed One because currently so much in this world is carnal and has great hatred of the Christ and will attack the Christed One. This is the Crucifixion.

Faith serves as a shield during our various initiations, including the ultimate initiation of the Crucifixion. We will need to maintain a faith that expects and knows that all divine initiations can be victoriously passed. Again, whatever suffering we endure will be well worth it to achieve our freedom in the Light—to enter into God's kingdom. The result of passing the great initiation of Crucifixion is our subsequent Resurrection and Ascension into magnificent and eternal life. These initiations comprise a completion of our spiritual journey into new higher and sublime realms of Being.

Both the Resurrection and the Ascension involve receiving a great flow of Light, joyous beyond description. The resurrected Jesus, on Easter morning, was the transcendent and wholly Glorified Son of God, Jesus Christ—a pillar of Light and Love crowned with God's omnipotent power.

In the Resurrection state, we are in the world, but we are not of the world. We will be able to teach our brothers and sisters on the Path of Light the great mysteries of God.

The Ascension is the final ritual before achieving permanent freedom from mortality. It is a complete victory over all human imperfection. Whatever our unique mission to life has been, at this point it will have been completed.

The Masters tell us that whenever a soul makes their Ascension, Light is released to all still dwelling in the material realms. At some point in the future of cosmic cycles, all souls created in the Lord's image and likeness, who embrace His divine and loving goodness, will have made their Ascension, thus entering forever the eternal realms of Spirit.

May contemplating and acting upon these teachings, as well as reading Part II and using the power of the spoken word in the Appendix, enable all sincere seekers to be victorious in all future initiations, challenges, tests and karmic situations that will present themselves along the Way.

Our determination and perseverance will, step by step, assuredly bring us ever closer to our divine eternal destiny. We will then enter the Valhalla that saints, avatars, poets and mystics have alluded to since the origins of sentient Life. And we will not merely be returning to the holy, comfortable realms of our origin in God, when, as His innocent children, we ventured forth into this denser physical existence. No, rather we will be, as sacred scripture confirms, His Sons and Daughters, living in the never-ending and ever-evolving Worlds and Universes of Beauty and Creativity altogether impossible to imagine or comprehend in our present blessed, but still very limited, human existence.

> *But as it is written, Eye hath not seen, nor ear heard, neither have entered into the heart of man, the things which God hath prepared for them that love him.*
> —1 Corinthians 2:9

Part Two

WORKING WITH THE LIGHT

KEY TEACHINGS, CALLS, PRAYERS AND DECREES

Working with the Light
Daily Protection
Embracing God's Will and Soul Purification
Meditation on Light
God's Consuming Fire
Heart, Head and Hand Decrees
Strengthening the Heart
Healing and Wholeness
The "I AM" Way of Jesus
Call to Overcome the Lower Self
Call for Forgiveness
Divine Assistance—Asking for Help
Sharing the Light
Humility
Calls for Perfection

SECRETS OF THE INNER LIGHT

Our Unique Being in God
Identification with God
I AM Lord's Prayer—to Raise our Consciousness
Christ Vision and Increasing our Perception
The Power of Faith
The Blessing of Transfiguration
Prayer of Praise for Service
Join with Others
Our Path of Overcoming Darkness

Working with the Light

Part I of this book takes spiritual seekers far beyond common understanding of the journey home. We have learned how very blessed we are by the extent of God's love for His creation and that we are destined to enjoy unlimited love, beauty, peace and fulfillment.

In addition to this knowledge and understanding, we can use the mighty power of the spoken word for our spiritual acceleration. Part II provides helpful information about how we can accomplish this—in the form of decrees, affirmations and prayers. These are uplifting and dynamic exercises. We can use our divine attunement to direct God's Light—divine power, wisdom and love into situations that require it. We are then able to maximize the divine Light flowing through us resulting in dynamic improvements for the good in our own lives, and radiate it outward to our loved ones and into needful situations throughout the world.

Included in Part II are several key teachings as well as some of the calls, prayers and decrees for invoking divine Light presented within the *Corona Class Lessons*. As God's sons and daughters, we are encouraged to work with the Light to bring forth solutions to personal challenges we face. And, we can call forth divine Light to positively affect the many difficult and dire conditions others experience on our planetary home. This is gratifying "work" to do when we are not otherwise going about our daily tasks or out in the field helping others.

The Appendix contains a streamlined list of nearly all of the affirmations, decrees and prayers within the *Corona Class Lessons* plus a few additions. It enables everyone to easily give them in a logical sequence.

Another important benefit to giving these decrees, affirmations and prayers is that our spoken words give permission for those within God's hierarchy who are eager to help to do so. God's hierarchy of Elohim, Archangels, Angels, Masters and Elementals provide us with guidance and assistance whenever possible—they are eager to help us. But due to the Law of free will they can help us even more when we give them our permission with our spoken words—this is God in action.

Divine Light is God's energy and power, and is the animating force behind all Life. This Light also contains divine love and wisdom. According to Master Kuthumi:

> *The power of the Light behind all light: the unfailing Light of God must be invoked and focused in man ere he can rise in consciousness until he actually ascends into that light realm of freedom which is the heavenly home of everyone who has successfully passed Earth's tests and has dared to step beyond the veil of human ignorance. Thus, the glorious flame of illumined obedience to divine Law must express the fullness of Love's immortality within man as his thought and aspiration rise toward God.*[1]

Every soul who has made their Ascension knows that achieving eternal reality is our life's goal. The fundamental key to that achievement is developing, through effective and earnest spiritual practices, a degree of love like our Lord Jesus and other great souls manifested during their earthly lives.

The Master Jesus shares with us the importance of regular prayers and calls to our God Presence, which is always with us and ready to answer:

> *The depths of God's love and wisdom are to the present hour conveyed to hearts of goodwill who make consecrated application to the heart of heaven. The door of communion is never shut, for I AM the door that opens in response to the quiet supplication of the loving heart for more Light, until at last each living soul stands face to face with his own God-identity.*[2]

Jesus also teaches us how we can maintain the necessary balance between an internal peace and composure, while calling forth and deploying the energy required to accomplish our goals with confidence. This helps us to have a cheerful disposition and to be able to spread joy to others.

> *Prayer, fasting, meditation on the Presence—physical exercise, yoga, breathing in fresh air and sunshine, etc.—and, above all, harmony in the feeling world, high-mindedness, proper rest and a wholesome diet will complement your application of the Word for maximum acceleration of the divine memory of the Mind of God within your etheric body and its anchoring in the physical cells of the brain and central nervous system.*[3]

We can make real and tangible spiritual progress as we use these affirmations, prayers and decrees. I say this with a humbled but very sincere confidence, for over the years, I have experienced this progress in my own life, and I have been blessed to witness a similar progress in my dear wife and with many of my friends and acquaintances along the way.

The Masters assure us that what Jesus and the many saints through the ages have achieved is likewise within our reach—even if we still harbor doubts about our ability "to measure up." As we discussed in Part I, it is very much worth remembering that our Creator and the entire divine hierarchy do not expect some sort of brittle perfection from us. We have often been reminded that if a very exalted or near-perfect status would be necessary before we could enter upon the spiritual Path and make progress, most of us would not qualify. Fortunately, that is not the case, or we might not even try!

Blessed Jesus acknowledges the difficult problems that beset souls living on Earth today, but wants us to forsake any sense of hopelessness or depression as well as any momentums in our thought and feeling world that would perpetuate carnal habits or create despair. Instead, we are advised to focus on the highest characteristics of God-goodness and nurture a calm spirit that is aware of the constant, loving watchfulness of our ascended brethren. Jesus asks us to hold these facts in our consciousness:

> *I AM the immortal consciousness of Truth, I AM that Christ Truth which affirms the power of Light and Light's intelligent energy to establish in my world, mind, and affairs the perfection of permanent Good!*[4]

Jesus urges us to know and to feel in our hearts that every discordant or negative habit shall yield to the power of Christ-domination. This is how the Light will expand within us.

Let us apply the power of habits as they were discussed in Chapter 11. Develop the habit of using the power of the spoken word to make calls and prayers daily, as often as needed. They will be a positive force that accelerates our spiritual development because habits, often adopted haphazardly as we go through the hustles and bustles of life, are more powerful than we realize.

Dear Master Kuthumi makes this important point:

Can...the raging heathen energies (of the mass consciousness), or the die of the human thought matrix stay or destroy the perfect beauty of the eternal concepts God has about you? Of course not! But the thoughts God holds for you as an individual i-den-ti-fied with Life (I AM densified, or coalesced, in form) MUST hold sway in your world, and the priceless treasures of heaven MUST become a daily habit BEFORE you can be vested with the power of all Good."[5]

Let us be true children of God. For we are assured we shall not in the slightest miss the carnal habits of this world, which include limited, non-eternal life, when we follow God's Path to spiritual perfection. Master Kuthumi shares with us a powerful call that we can make:

I AM the all-enfolding garment of Light charged with the life, truth, and radiance of God, good! Naught of the human can distress me, for I AM the victorious, all-powerful consciousness of God in action—blessing, guarding, guiding, and directing me in all that I do![6]

Consider pausing here and using this life-affirming affirmation. Use it silently within or, if you are in the privacy of your own home, speak it aloud slowly, with meaning, even repeating it a few times for even deeper effect.

Let your total being become more and more aware of the great Light of God. This Light is always with you in every part of your life and it is integral to the reality of all Life. Dear Jesus describes for us how fully we can experience divine Light:

Sense that you can contact the Light and that it can contact you. Sense that it is the life-force in every budding flower, every sweet scent, every ray of sunshine, every feeling of hope in the human heart. Sense that it is the eternal bond between heart and heart, that it is the avenue of Ascended Master communication, that it is the light of thousands of suns shining in their strength. Sense that God can—by the power of making himself large or small, by the power of the "I AM"—put all of this radiance of himself into every cell of you and into your whole being![7]

Master Kuthumi urges us to call for the Light with the intensity of our being:

As a miner stakes his claim, you must plead for the power of the coronary [encircling like a crown] Light to flow from the heart of God into your world.[8]

By attuning with and working with our inner divine Light, we can become vessels of divine love, transforming our surroundings with each heartfelt action. We can become light beacons offering hope and encouragement. We will be empowered to heal, inspire and uplift those in our world. When we focus on our inner divine Light we can transcend personal limitations and connect with God's wisdom and power. We then become more attuned to the needs of others and more inspired to act selflessly. Through our dedication to doing good works, we increase the joyful flow of Light through ourselves, and bring joy and love to a world in need of both.

Daily Protection

Working with our inner vision, we can say the following "Tube of Light" decree, which clothes us with Light's protection for the day:

Working with the Light

O my constant, loving I AM Presence,
Thou Light of God above me
Whose radiance forms a circle of fire before me to light my way:
I AM faithfully calling to thee
To place a great pillar of Light
From my own Mighty I AM God Presence
All around me right now today!
Keep it intact through every passing moment,
Manifesting as a shimmering shower of God's beautiful Light
Through which nothing human can ever pass.
Into this beautiful electric circle of divinely charged energy
Direct a swift upsurge of the violet fire
Of Freedom's forgiving, transmuting flame!
Cause the ever-expanding energy of this flame
Projected downward into the forcefield of my human energies
To completely change every negative condition
Into the positive polarity of my own Great God Self!
Let the magic of its mercy
So purify my world with Light
That all whom I contact shall always be blessed
With the fragrance of violets from God's own heart
In memory of the blessed dawning day when all discord—
Cause, effect, record, and memory—is forever changed
Into the Victory of Light and the peace of the ascended Jesus Christ
I AM now constantly accepting the full power and manifestation
Of this fiat of Light
And calling it into instantaneous action
By my own God-given free will
And the power to accelerate without limit
this sacred release of assistance from God's own heart
until all men are ascended and God-free
in the Light that never, never, never fails![9]

This powerful recitation is a great way to start the day! We need Light's protection during these challenging times.

God's Will and Soul Purification

As students, we can experience the flow of Light as we attune to God and His Will. As we integrate with His Will we are able to subdue all that is encountered that is less than divine. Acting as extensions of that divine Will, we can regularly affirm:

Not my will but Thine be done![10]

For we are not to think of life so much as formidable or challenging, but rather as a marvelous opportunity to join and mesh with God's perfect plan for each unique individual. And we can be assured this is what will ultimately bring us the greatest joy. Yes, there will be suffering to endure at times for the purposes of learning needed lessons, for our purification, and transmutation of karma. Yet if we maintain and grow our faith and sincerely pursue and embrace the holy Will of our beneficent Creator, it will be the greatest undertaking of our life in the world of form. For we, in this process, become like the faithful Job, who despite the harshest human experiences, never gave up on His Father. Every soul who chooses this Path can achieve a life that is a manifestation of divine joy within God's loving flow of Light.

Many people do not realize how much our Creator loves His Children. What God wants always results in the greatest ultimate good and happiness. Personally, I feel that when I make the following call it helps me to lose any desire I might otherwise have for any unrighteous or selfish action. God's will is in perfect alignment with our true nature, our Higher, Divine Self, and always knows what is best for us.

After giving the preamble, this decree can be given once or as many times as your heart guides you.

Working with the Light

In the name of the I AM THAT I AM, in the name of Jesus Christ, I call to the heart of the Will of God in the Great Central Sun to fan the flame of the will of God throughout my four lower bodies and answer this my call infinitely, presently, and forever:

1. *I AM God's Will manifest everywhere,*
   I AM God's Will perfect beyond compare,
   I AM God's Will so beautiful and fair,
   I AM God's willing bounty everywhere.

Refrain: Come, come, come, O blue-flame Will so true,
   Make and keep me ever radiant like you.
   Blue-flame Will of living Truth,
   Good Will flame of eternal youth,
   Manifest, manifest, manifest in me now!

2. *I AM God's Will now taking full command,*
   I AM God's Will making all to understand,
   I AM God's Will whose power is supreme,
   I AM God's Will fulfilling heaven's dream.

3. *I AM God's Will protecting, blessing here,*
   I AM God's Will now casting out all fear,
   I AM God's Will in action here well done,
   I AM God's Will with Victory for each one.

4. *I AM blue lightning flashing Freedom's love,*
   I AM blue-lightning power from above,
   I AM blue lightning setting all men free,
   I AM blue-flame power flowing good through me.

And in full Faith I consciously accept this manifest, manifest, manifest! (3x) right here and now with full Power, eternally sustained, all-powerfully active, ever expanding, and world enfolding until all are wholly ascended in the Light and free! Beloved I AM! Beloved I AM! Beloved I AM![11]

Blessed Master Kuthumi gives us a simple but valuable exercise for achieving soul purification. He recommends that after we focus on attuning to our Holy Christ Self, that we faithfully call, in our own words, to the heart of God for the purification of our soul.

Meditation on Light

The regular practice of meditation is *crucial* for the necessary attunement with the divine. There are so many names for what meditation connects us with. Here, we have called it our I AM Presence, our Holy Christ Self, the divine Light, our Higher or Divine Self. Some may prefer to call it the One, Universal Mind, the Allness, the Suchness, or even the quantum field. There are many forms of meditation. Just make sure that the one you choose results in experiencing a transcendent state that connects you with Spirit. In that state, you will feel peaceful, balanced and most receptive to spiritual guidance.

Twenty minutes twice a day is ideal. I have, in the past, often rationalized skipping meditation because it would "take too much time." However, I have found, along with many other meditators who speak of this, that the time invested in meditation is easily recouped by more efficiency in thought, more peace, and more appropriateness in various situations. The benefits of regular meditation are numerous and powerful.

Our beloved Master Jesus had this to say about the importance of regular meditation:

So, beloved, change comes by the alchemy of God. It comes by a sudden awareness because you have taken those moments to meditate, to still the mind that you might hear one word from us that we might get in when the mind is finally no longer occupied.
O beloved, we can speak to you, but where is the listening mind and the attuned ear?...
Still the agitated mind.[12]

The Appendix presents the Ascended Master Saint Germain's[13] meditation, which is extremely powerful. It is the one meditation that I chose to include in both my previous books. Although I do this meditation on occasion, on other days I practice a streamlined version. I will sit in a comfortable chair, at a time when the chances of my being disturbed are at a minimum, and just relax. I close my eyes, and often begin by simply saying "O God, You are so Magnificent. Your wonderful Light infills me so!" After saying that a few times, I notice that my breathing (ideally through the nose) is smoother and shallower. I usually then simply observe my breath, which is a form of mantra. Whenever I catch myself having a thought, I gently remind myself that the purpose of what I'm now doing is to give my mind a rest from thinking, and I then switch back to observing my breath.

I will also occasionally, at the beginning of my meditation, focus my intent on any aspects of healing that I or others I know need. Or I may invoke the Light, or God's love and wisdom. I may focus Light and love into various world situations, or personal situations. But after doing so, I settle into the meditation, where freedom from the usual thoughts allows my mind and body to connect to the Light.

Saint Germain has made the following comments about the practice of meditating on Light:

Remember always, "One becomes that upon which he medi-

> *tates," and since all things have come forth from the Light, Light is the Supreme Perfection and Control of all things. Contemplation and adoration of the Light compels Illumination to take place in the mind—health, strength, and order to come into the body—and peace, harmony, and success to manifest in the affairs of every individual—who will really do it, and seeks to maintain it. All the way down the centuries—in every age, under every condition—we are told by all who have expressed the greater accomplishments of Life that—the Light is Supreme—the Light is everywhere—and in the Light—exist all things.*[14]

In the above quotation, the word "Light" was originally in quotes, to denote that it not only encompasses the power or energy of God and His Creation, but also God's consciousness—the kingdom of God—the original source and Creator of all. Every one of us needs to know for ourselves and also teach the truth of the eternal Presence. Our Creator wants to resurrect our thoughts, circumstances and even our physical temples out of their imprisonment, confined as we are by our fears and doubts, so that we can then *know* the truth deep within.

It is important to note that after a while, many people who use these spiritual exercises begin to take them somewhat for granted, becoming lazy in their usage, or feeling so good that they stop doing them. It is better to be regularly reminded of the source of our blessings by daily (or more frequently) invoking the Light.

This book only touches on the benefits of regular meditation. Dawson Church[15] and Dr. Joe Dispenza[16] are but two of several researchers providing additional information about the many scientific findings that establish the benefits of meditation. Just two of these benefits include heart-brain coherence and the balancing of the left and right brain hemispheres, but there are many more!

God's Consuming Fire

We have the reminder from the Apostle Paul:

For our God is a consuming fire.[17]

God's "consuming fire" is not—in the view of numerous adherents to Christianity, including saints and mystics and modern theologians—a hellfire inflicting eternal punishment upon errant souls. What God's consuming fire can do is erase the record and the memory of our sins. It is a forgiveness flame of divine Light. When sincerely invoked, this flame lifts the burden of guilt and self-condemnation from the soul. This new freedom results in a soul's gratitude and inspires them to focus on their spiritual goals.

It has been well established by science that everything in the material universe is composed of vibrations—Light. When under observation, these vibrations can become particles of the smallest size, and they can revert back to frequencies. The components of an atom ultimately consist of frequencies or vibrations. We are reminded of the proclamation in the very first line of Genesis wherein God created the entire physical universe:

And God said, Let there be Light: and there was Light.[18]

Most souls in embodiment can only see a small portion of the entire electromagnetic spectrum of varying wavelengths that include gamma rays, X-rays, infrared radiation, microwaves, radio waves, and visible light. Isaac Newton, the renowned physicist and mathematician of the seventeenth century, observed that white light will refract into the seven colors of the rainbow: red, orange, yellow, green, blue, indigo, and violet. Violet is always the color that is the highest arc in any rainbow. Modern science teaches us that this violet hue is only partially visible to the unaided human eye and that the invisible (to us) portion merges into a higher plane of frequency.

Lamps that radiate ultraviolet light have been used for some time to kill viruses, bacteria and molds in hospitals, as well as used as sanitizers in the food-processing industry.[19] Ultraviolet light has been demonstrably used to kill cancer cells in patients.[20] There are numerous examples of the efficacies of ultraviolet light being used successfully in medical applications in past decades, and new usages have been coming forward in our modern era.[21]

It is clear that violet light is a special divine gift, yielding numerous blessings. Violet Light purifies. It is high frequency spiritual energy. When we invoke and visualize violet flame, we qualify a spectrum of God's Light into a specific characteristic known to transmute and purify past records of error.

We can visualize ourselves standing within this violet fire, utilizing the focus of the third eye and visualizing it streaming forth from our I AM Presence to surround us and penetrate every atom of our four lower bodies. We can especially visualize its power within our heart.

A short general decree to invoke the violet flame is simply:

I AM a being of violet fire
I AM the purity of God's desire!

A longer decree to the violet flame is:

I AM the violet flame
In action in me now
I AM the Violet Flame
To Light alone I bow
I AM the Violet Flame
In mighty Cosmic Power
I AM the Light of God
Shining every hour

I AM the Violet Flame
Blazing like a sun
I AM God's sacred power
Freeing every one[22]

It is possible to actually feel the power of the violet flame dissolve and melt burdens, sorrows, fears and karma. This merciful flame of freedom can help to fulfill an important aspect of your life plan—the total release from any negative or harmful manifestations that you may have created. Invoking the violet flame can also improve a soul's ability to receive divine guidance and inspiration.

You will also find violet flame in several of the following decrees as well.

Heart, Head and Hand Decrees

Another wonderful spiritual exercise that can yield innumerable blessings are the basic and very rhythmic "Heart, Head, and Hand Decrees" which represent the Love of Christ in our hearts; the Wisdom of the Father in our heads, and the Power of the Holy Spirit in our hands.

It is important to have a balanced amount of equal attainment in our Love (Heart), Wisdom (Head), and Power (Hands) to be the most effective and able to progress further along the Path. These particular decrees help us to achieve balance in these most basic elements of our Path, helping us to make steady progress in our spiritual life.

Starting with the heart, we can give the following decree three times:

Violet fire, thou love divine,
Blaze within this heart of mine!
Thou art mercy forever true,
Keep me always in tune with you[23]

As we give this decree, we can intensify this violet light/fire in our heart by visualizing it there. Many people have reported an actual burning sensation that can be felt in the heart, dissolving and transmuting the heart's burdens, its sorrows and fears, as well as any hardness of the heart. This is a most wonderful divine gift, for our hearts can be magnified spiritually to become influential forces for God on Earth by radiating healing love throughout the world!

We can then focus on the transmutation of blockages in the head. For this, we visualize the three spiritual centers or chakras located in the head (the crown chakra at the top of the head for wisdom and illumination; the third eye chakra for intuition, foresight and visualization; and the throat chakra or power center). Ask that this violet fire transmute debris, wrong thinking and wrong concepts, burdensome images and thoughtforms and even any physical obstructions and unhealthy conditions that may be lodged therein. Doing this will help you clear the mind and enable you to connect readily with your Higher Self.

I AM Light, thou Christ in me,
Set my mind forever free;
Violet fire, forever shine
Deep within this mind of mine.
God who gives my daily bread,
With violet fire fill my head
Till thy radiance heavenlike
Makes my mind a mind of Light.[24]

Finally, we can visualize the intensity of the violet flame in our hands, seeing and perhaps even feeling it burning right in the middle of each palm. Our hands have the potential for being great vehicles for healing. With our hearts radiating love, with our heads attuned to the divine wisdom of our Creator, and our hands being the instrument of God's holy Will, we can transmit God's healing to others in our personal circle, as well as out into the world at large.

We can visualize the intense action of the violet flame in our hands as we decree:

> *I AM the hand of God in action,*
> *Gaining victory every day;*
> *My pure soul's great satisfaction*
> *Is to walk the Middle Way*[25]

These calls can be given one after another, whenever we feel the need or a prompting. Ideally, they are repeated in multiples of three (three, six, nine times or more). It is important to remember to include visualizing this violet flame transmuting action as we give the calls.

Strengthening the Heart

In addition to the earlier decree for the violet flame purification of the heart, it is also important to strengthen our heart, which after all, even as sacred scripture indicates, is the altar of God's Light in our being. Giving the following decree helps to magnetize the power of love from our Creator, magnifying it within our heart, so that we can radiate it out to transmute darkness across our planetary home.

> *I AM the Light of the Heart*
> *Shining in the darkness of being*
> *And changing all into the golden treasury*
> *Of the Mind of Christ*
> *I AM projecting my Love*
> *Out into the world*
> *To erase all errors*
> *And to break down all barriers*
> *I AM the power of infinite Love,*
> *Amplifying itself*

Until it is victorious,
World without end![26]

Jesus also wants everyone who strongly desires to experience the richness of God's kingdom to benefit from divine guidance. He asks us to make the following call daily, and tells us that doing so will yield an understanding of life and the knowledge of how to energize your body's cells and uplift your thoughts and feelings. He wants serious disciples to *persistently call for the expansion of the flame of divine illumination* within their hearts.[27]

Healing and Wholeness

When there are concerns for achieving true healing and wholeness, remember that our physical bodies are very much subject to how we consciously engage ourselves in life, as well as how we treat them. Our bodies have intelligence and await our commands!

Through enlightened spiritual disciplines, good health practices and an overall balanced approach in our daily routines, we can optimize our potential to serve life. Our physical bodies are changing constantly, with some cells dying while new ones are being created. Likewise, each of our higher bodies are also evolving and changing. As we grow in emotional maturity, we rise above and move beyond former conditions, jealousies, harsh judgments, prejudices, anger, etc. We see these steadily transformed into goodwill, compassion, and an inner peace that can be silently extended to those around us.

For maximum healing potential, we can choose to keep a vigil of ongoing prayer and meditation. We benefit the most by renewing ourselves daily. We can command our cells to submit to the matrix of our perfect Christ Self, so they will not succumb to taking on patterns of disease

Our mental bodies likewise change and evolve to a higher

degree of functioning as we, by God's grace, begin to open ourselves. As scripture advises us:

> *Let this mind be in you, which was also in Christ Jesus.*[28]

And of course, all of this is ultimately achieved in our etheric body under the tutelage and sponsorship of our Higher Self, as we walk a legitimate path in the Spirit.

A powerful decree to restore perfection in our four lower bodies is included in the Appendix.

The "I AM" Way of Jesus

In Part I, the following quote from John 14 is referred to several times. Jesus said this after Thomas asked him, "Lord, we know not whither thou goest; and how can we know the way?" It has become one of the more well-known passages in the New Testament:

> *Jesus saith unto him, I am the way, the truth, and the life; no man cometh unto the Father, but by me.*
> *If ye had known me, ye should have known my Father also: and from henceforth ye know him, and have seen him.*[29]

Jesus explains for us the deeper, profound meaning of this statement, and he shares a *powerful affirmation* and empowering insights to ultimately help us—in emulation of our Lord— "to go and do likewise."

> *Therefore, in truth ye DO know the Way: for I AM the Way, I AM the Truth, and I AM the Life. No man cometh to the Father (his God Presence) except through me (the Holy Christ Self of each one), and this is the universal plan—the same for all.*

> *Face and overcome sin, condemnation, false conscience, and fear. To all these declare fervently and know that:*
> *I AM the fullness of God/Good!*
> *I AM walking into daily oneness with the Father.*
> *I AM made ever new in God's image, the similitude and likeness of all that is Good.*
> *I AM the justice of the divine Law which reaches out to fulfill the true spirit of both human and divine Law.*
> *I AM the manifestation of that sacred Law, and in the joy of the ascended Jesus Christ consciousness,*
> *I AM illumined to know that this living, inner Law is the Golden Rule!*[30]

It is our responsibility to recognize that God literally lives within us. We need to know and affirm that our identity includes two all-encompassing factors which are a part of the Oneness of God and the totality of Being. These factors are the Son of God (our Holy Christ Self) and God the Father, our Creator (our Mighty I AM Presence). This truth is embodied in the words "I AM." We use the words "I AM" to affirm our true divine nature and the reason for our existence, which is to fully integrate with the goodness, the consciousness and Being of God.

For this reason, it is actually a type of blasphemy—a tragic, self-limiting behavior—to use any version of the verb "to be" in association with lower, limited or negative qualities. God's name, given to Moses on Horeb's height is "I AM THAT I AM!" As God's devoted offspring, we will wisely not affirm negatives by saying "I AM afraid" or "I AM weary," for when we do, we give power to these limiting human attributes. Instead, beloved Jesus suggests:

> *Why not affirm, instead, the immortal truth of Being? "Lo, I AM God in manifestation everywhere!" is a far more accurate statement of your true divine Selfhood. This statement alone, repeated many times a day as a flowing mantra and a*

song of the heart, will swallow up the petty negatives that tear down your spirituality.[31]

Do we become fully attuned with the glory of God after we say this but one time? When, in fact, we have wound our limiting beliefs and our karmic errors around our consciousness for many turns? Naturally, just as the summits of mountains are not climbed by one giant leap but by one wise step after another, by one victory after another, we gain our spiritual freedom and attunement with God gradually when we patiently and lovingly climb one step at a time in His direction. Our focus shall not be looking back or looking down, but rather gazing up to the Summit of our Being in God as our goal!

The blessed Master Jesus shares with us a great key to contemplate. This revelation is deeply rooted in mystical Christianity.

Being itself is the 'AM' of existence, my beloved. But in order for you (the 'I' individualized) to enter in, you must become the 'I' of the 'I AM' and experience for yourself the wonders of the glory of God. Do you see, blessed ones? Oh, do meditate on this point of the Law!"[32]

Beloved Jesus tells us of this grand opportunity that we have to join with him and other Ascended Hosts:

To our holy order of Sons of the Most High, priests of God with Melchizedek[33] *and brothers of Light, I, Jesus, welcome all. Kneel to your own God Presence I AM, drinking daily into the communion of saints. For to this end were all borne by the Holy Spirit from realms of Light—that fair flowers though we may be or become upon earth, fairer still shall we be in the heart of the Father.*

As your hearts now beat with His higher hope, maintain our communion spirit. Hold fast to the image and guidance sent to you daily by your own Holy Christ Self; then shall each day be for you a natal day of cosmic expansion into ever-new birth.[34]

Jesus teaches that we will never be able to improve ourselves and return to higher spiritual life until we *prove the Law* for ourselves. This we do by granting authority, control and dominion to God in our lives. For God grants to each soul the divine Light of illumination when we steadfastly pursue our divine Path.

Making the calls on a regular basis for attunement with our loving Creator (whose nature and vision is always for the highest good) is a powerful way to improve our discernment. Beloved Master Jesus shares with us a great key to his victory, which we are invited to include in our regular declarations:

This is how I attained my own victory. I knew that I came forth from God and that I must return to him. I perceived that the surest way to do so was the I AM way: hence, I declared:
"I AM in the Father and the Father is in me. He that hath seen me hath seen the Father. The words that I speak unto you I speak not of myself: but the Father that dwelleth in me, he doeth the works." [35]
This is the true and only formula for the exemplar who would demonstrate his dominion over "these things" of the earth.[36]

Jesus adds to his explanation of this powerful affirmation:

The disciple in imitation of the Master is expected to assimilate an intense feeling of oneness with his Great God Source. "I AM in the Father and the Father is in me" was the statement which I used often in order to anchor the affirmation of true being within my thinking and feeling worlds. Unlim-

ited good will come to all who faithfully use this statement as a divine decree (mantra) and acknowledge this blessed concept of their cosmic unity with God.[37]

Call to Overcome the Lower Self

Another call that aids in our liberation is a powerful call to overcome the domination of the carnal mind, or lower self—also known as the self-absorbed human ego. (See the complete definition in the Glossary.) It is "the call that compels the answer." Master Jesus instructs us to visualize the radiant, loving Light of God and to loudly declare with all your heart:

The Light of God never fails!
The Light of God never fails!
The Light of God never fails!
And the Beloved Mighty I AM Presence is that Light!

We are instructed to: "Repeat this call four times, expelling the carnal mind from each of your four lower bodies as you do. And accept your freedom and your reality by the authority of the Christ who I AM, who You Are—with you now!"[38]

In other words, give this call four times, consciously ejecting the carnal mind first from our physical body, followed by our emotional body, our mental body and finally our etheric (memory) body as we do. This results in the gradual progression of redemption and transmutation of carnal energies (consisting of past misqualifications and misunderstandings) that are lodged within us.

Call for Forgiveness

Forgiveness is an activity of enormous importance. Consider the parables, stories and direct teachings on forgiveness that Jesus gave us in the New Testament. For example, he told us the stories of the

Prodigal Son, the adulterous woman, and even the forgiveness extended to the repentant criminal crucified alongside Jesus on Golgotha.

It is helpful to occasionally search your memory for past times when undeserved negative feelings and thoughts were sent to another. More serious would be any negative actions taken against another. We can pray for souls we have wronged, and if possible make amends. Afterlife teachings tell us we will have a life review after death when we will momentarily experience, to a certain degree, the harmful effects we caused to another. This is always a huge learning experience and deepens our sense of empathy.

If our Creator's Golden Rule is not followed, either because of ignorance or intent, this results in feelings of emptiness, non-fulfillment, and eventually a deepening despair. An important corollary to the Golden Rule is: *Forgive others as you'd like to be forgiven by others, and as you'd like to forgive yourself.* As we pray for the forgiveness of others, we add to the grace of forgiveness that we ourselves receive for our own past misdeeds.

The lack of forgiveness is a giant roadblock in one's spiritual growth. It is wise to make the calls for forgiveness whenever we engage in a wrong or hurtful act or form of speech, and even when we bring to mind a karmic incident from our near or distant past. Of course, these calls are also helpful to make when someone else acts in a wrong, hurtful, or disrespectful way to you. On such occasions, we can give the following call to transmute and clear away blockages in our etheric/memory body, to transform conscious and subconscious memories of violence or trauma, and to clear our mental body of any false or harmful thoughts and concepts. This also helps to clear our emotions, especially feelings of fear or pain, as well as any associated negative records:

I AM forgiveness acting here,
Casting out all doubt and fear,
Setting men forever free

*With wings of cosmic victory.
I AM calling in full power
For forgiveness every hour;
To all life in every place
I flood forth forgiving grace*[39]

God desires to set free all of life that has borne the burden of error. He wants to repair all damage and replace mistaken human, self-absorbed thinking with a consciousness of divine love and wisdom. Even though no one escapes divine justice by evading any part of the Law, it is possible to accelerate freedom through the invocation of the merciful flame of forgiveness, with intense love for God and others.

Divine Assistance – Asking for Help

If we need help with any challenging situation, or if we start to regress back into former negative habits, help is always available. Blessed Jesus confirms that divine assistance is always available:

*Foremost among the problems men need to solve for themselves is that of the power of habits of negative action.
Let no one's heart be troubled because he has long endured banal habits; let none feel a sense of absolute frustration or loneliness concerning the overcoming of these unwanted conditions. I AM the compassionate Christ anchored above each lifestream, longing to pour the full momentum of my assistance into every waiting consciousness chaliced in the attitude of receptivity.
Beloved ones, you do not walk alone. It is ever foolhardy to insist upon solving your own problems without calling to us for aid.*[40]

Jesus shares with us a beautiful message about life, and his willingness to help us along the way.

> *Life is God, Life is I AM, and it was intended to be beautiful, eternal, powerful, and happy. This can be so only through your outpicturing of all that is the power (will of God), the kingdom (wisdom of God), and the glory (love of God). <u>There is no other way</u>....*
>
> *Do not fail to watch with me, disciples of this hour, for Life ever tests each aspirant, and I AM so willing to assist all who ask!*[41]

When concerned with losing emotional control, when under attack, when being tempted by something you know is unrighteous, when things aren't going the way you want, or when someone is belittling you there is a wonderful, short mantra you can give: *Let God be magnified!* The corollary to it is: *Let the anti-God be diminished, let it be denied!* When giving this mantra, it is important to visualize God's Light being magnified by the Sun in all parts of your body. Giving this mantra when needed will manifest strength and comfort within you. Giving this mantra is your call for all that is *not* of God to be consumed.[42]

The Master Jesus wants us to know that we are greatly loved, to feel welcome to call to him for assistance, and to joyfully anticipate a greater divine life with God. He tells us:

> *You are beloved, whether fully aware of it or not, and I am certain that each one of you who will read these words and look up at me right now and call for my light will feel me standing within your room in my Electronic Presence radiating my light and blessing you with the precious anointing of spiritual assistance and my Christ-victory which overcomes the world.*[43]

We are urged to make this call in our own words. An example is given in this section of the Appendix.

Thousands of our elder brothers and sisters who have gone before us and climbed the steps of their spiritual evolution are standing by ready to assist us in joining them to rise up higher. These Masters are eager to assist, for love is the byword of all true hearts of Light. Nothing pleases them more than to help us when we allow it and call for it. The Appendix for this section gives an example.

More than just saying the words, see and feel his Light fully surrounding and penetrating every cell of your being. Picture him just above you, radiating his Presence into and around you! If you have a picture of Jesus nearby, use it to help tangibly experience his great love and care for your lifestream, and send back a current of your own sincere love in return. Let your total being become more and more aware of the great Light of God. Remember that this Light is always with us in every part of life and that it is integral to the reality of life. Jesus urges us to:

> *Sense that it [Light] is the life-force in every budding flower, every sweet scent, every ray of sunshine, every feeling of hope in the human heart. Sense that it is the eternal bond between heart and heart, that it is the avenue of Ascended Master communication, that it is the Light of thousands of suns shining in their strength.... Sense that God can... put all of this radiance of himself into every cell of you and into your whole being!*[44]

Dear Master Kuthumi urges us to call for the Light with the intensity of our being:

> *Plead for the power of the coronary [encircling like a crown] Light to flow from the heart of God into your world.*[45]

Jesus encourages us with his words:

Beloved ones, be of good cheer! Because I have overcome the world, you can hope to do so, too. For you also are one with the Father and myself as you embrace the Life within you which is God, the Mighty I AM Presence, in obedient action everywhere toward all hearts.[46]

Scripture also reveals how we can multiply the heavenly aid we seek. This comes about when we join with others. (See "Join with Others.")

Sharing the Light

Aspiring disciples will greatly benefit from a regular practice of meditation, as well as contemplation and focus on developing a *sense* of what their advancing spiritual progression will feel like. This is also developed by daily prayer, making calls for the Light to descend and for guidance, assistance and energy, not only for ourselves but for the benefit of world situations and individuals in need.

The Master Jesus describes the Path for spiritual evolution:

Initially, you must establish a hallowed sense of the reality and the tangibility of the blessing you can obtain and bestow on others as a true disciple of God's great Brotherhood of Light. Let your hearts be humble yet unafraid, desiring to perceive your errors only enough to correct them and your virtues only enough to express gratitude for them. Then I am certain you will find the grossness of the human condition giving way to the refinement of eternal values within you—and as your views change to those of heaven, the reality of the kingdom shall enfold you as a mantle of power.[47]

An example call is given in this section of the Appendix.

Dear Master Jesus has told us of his request to our Father for us to share in the great blessing of Christ consciousness:

Long ago, as I expanded my soul into the essence of communion with the Holy Christ Self of all through the universal Christ, I sent forth the call on wings of Light to the eternal Father, to His heart of creation and being, to flood the essence and consciousness of Himself into the hearts of His children so that all who did hunger and thirst after righteousness might drink of the water of Life freely.
Blessed ones, the water of Life flows freely from your I AM Presence charged with the feeling of the unlimited and unmeasured current of God's being, imparted unto each son and daughter in accordance with his capacity to receive. It is this full quality and power of God's immortality and intelligence in the very 'water' (energy) of Life which quickens in every son and daughter of Life the sense of the soul's eternal mission.[48]

We can share the blessings of God with others by making such a call. An example is given in this section of the Appendix.

Humility

Beloved Jesus set forth his own eternal standard for true leadership involving both genuine humility and sincere innocence. When the disciples asked Jesus who was the greatest in the kingdom, Jesus gave these answers:

And whosoever of you will be the chiefest, shall be servant of all.[49]

Verily I say unto you, Except ye be converted, and become as little children, ye shall not enter into the kingdom of heaven. Whosoever therefore shall humble himself as this little child, the same is greatest in the kingdom of heaven.[50]

The powerful simplicity and innocence of a sunbeam, and a child, is addressed in the following affirmation, given to us by both Jesus and Kuthumi:

I AM a created ray from the very heart of God. I AM shining each day with the lifting, living light of resurrection's eternal flame, awakening my divine memory to the infinite wisdom in a sunbeam, a ray-o-light within me, within all God's children!
I glory in Light's apparent simplicity, knowing that therein lies locked the mightiest power, most profound wisdom, and greatest love of eternity.[51]

Many people pass by and don't utilize the divine teachings. Instead, they quarrel about things even when God proclaims that all discord should end. At this time on Earth, we have such deep, widespread conflict and crises which only divine intercession can truly mend. One simple but powerful thing we can do is to remember what it felt like to be an innocent child and to create our own simple melody to sing:

Jesus wants me for a sunbeam to shine for him each day.[52]

And do join in, no matter what you think your singing voice is like, whenever the opportunity arises to sing beautiful and uplifting songs in a group. We know that religious traditions the world over, since the earliest recorded times have used songs, sacred chants and hymns as a means of strengthening love and devotion, helping disciples and devotees to uplift their spirits and persevere through hard times. Even at the conclusion of the Last Supper, Jesus sang hymns with the apostles.[53]

Calls for Perfection

As we strive for perfection, this good intent, along with our prayers for guidance and assistance, is noticed. Over time we will be able to attain more wisdom and strength. This process is of great benefit and provides a loving service to all on Earth, for it magnifies the message of Christ—for good will and living in harmony.

Although we are not expected to be perfect at this point in our eternal lives, we are to strive toward that goal, particularly in our intentions. Jesus suggests another powerful call for our pursuit of the Path:

When you call with all the intensity of your being for your own perfection in the Light, believing beloved [Ascended Master] Victory when he tells you that your own victory is possible today—there and then you make it possible![54]

An example is given in this section of the Appendix.

Jesus advises us to focus on the higher characteristics of Heaven and nurture a calm spirit that is aware of the constant loving watchfulness of our spiritual brethren, and to hold these facts in our consciousness as we give the following affirmation:

I AM the immortal consciousness of Truth, I AM that Christ Truth which affirms the power of Light and Light's intelligent energy to establish in my world, mind, and affairs the perfection of permanent Good![55]

Our Unique Being in God

Beloved Master Kuthumi shares the importance of discovering our true being and identity:

> *Every lifestream has a matrix, or God-design, which he ought to outpicture each day. Unless this is made known to the outer self of the seeker, it is difficult for him to cooperate with the mighty plan of the inner life.*[56]

Master Kuthumi explains that we can learn more about who we really are, our unique qualifications, talents and interests by invoking guidance from above. As this is accomplished, we can move forward and bring about our "particular plan of action." And, our calls for divine guidance can also yield *how* necessary change can be implemented, so that we can fully achieve our purpose. This is how we can contribute the greatest good in our lifetimes. An example call is located in this section of the Appendix.

Jesus wants everyone to benefit from divine guidance. To "persistently call for the expansion of the flame of divine illumination within their hearts."[57] Doing so will yield an understanding of life and the knowledge of how to energize our body's cells and control our thoughts and feelings. An example call is in this section of the Appendix.

Identification with God

If, during your daily life, you experience a dip in energy, a sense of burden or letdown, try the following simple, yet powerful, call. It will take you to an immediate identification with God by declaring:

I AM Good![58]

Working with the Light

This is a beautiful reinforcement of the original declaration made by our Creator when He observed His original creation.

And God saw every thing that He had made, and, behold, it was very good.[59]

This "I AM Good!" declaration can contribute to the transmutation by divine fire of any remaining corrupt aspects within our consciousness.

Our blessed Master Kuthumi has shared with us that once we have transmuted all that is less than perfection, we will enjoy the supreme benefits of *fully* attuning with the Mind of God.

This unity with the universal Mind is a pearl of great purity and great price, affording solace, harmony, and restoration to the soul. In this lovely consciousness every child of God shall find his heaven, his peace, his victory.[60]

Master Kuthumi reminds us again to be childlike, but to also be warned (and warn others) of the tricks and deceits of devilish minds waiting to entrap us. As long as we are here below in the "footstool kingdom," there is always the danger of falling back into old, familiar habits that we have previously succeeded in freeing ourselves from. Although God's mercy and compassion have helped us escape from many binding habits, the potential still exists for carelessness, whereby a soul reverts back to tired and unwanted habits and lesser states of consciousness. Never forget that divine assistance is always available for those who ask!

Dear Master Kuthumi leaves with us a powerful affirmation to lead us to our goal:

Of all this, say to yourself: I AM apart from manifestation, for I AM the all of God—the all-ness of God, the wholeness of God. The I AM is my Father, and the I AM and I are one![61]

I AM Lord's Prayer

Master Kuthumi tells us of the steps that are essential to raising our consciousness. The first is obedience to the voice of God. The second is thinking about Light, and the third is thinking about power (not human power, but the omnipotence of God). If we focus on these three things while we repeat the I AM Lord's Prayer, we can, over time, free ourselves from what is holding us back.

> *Our Father who art in heaven, Hallowed be thy name,*
> *I AM.*
> *I AM thy kingdom come*
> *I AM thy will being done*
> *I AM on earth even as I AM in heaven*
> *I AM giving this day daily bread to all*
> *I AM forgiving all Life this day even as I AM all Life forgiving me*
> *I AM leading all men away from temptation*
> *I AM delivering all men from every evil condition*
> *I AM the kingdom*
> *I AM the power and*
> *I AM the glory of God in eternal, immortal manifestation—*
> *All this I AM*[62]

Christ Vision–Increasing our Perception

Remember that our vision is what we picture in our mind's eye and also shapes and focuses our thoughts, feelings and actions. It is crucial to always carry the highest and best vision for the greatest good, beauty and love. The other aspect of our vision also refers to our level of discernment—our ability to distinguish between good and evil. As our senses are attuned to the Christ consciousness, they have the potential to protect us by helping us avoid any situations that do not promote the greater good. Through practice, it is possible to train oneself to be aware of and to exclude all things not belonging in our perfect vision.

One dynamic way to increase our sense perception is to regularly make the affirmation recommended by beloved Master Jesus, who states:

> *The affirmation "I AM the Resurrection and the Life of my perfect seeing, hearing, feeling, tasting, and smelling now made manifest!" should be repeated often in order to raise the senses to their natural and spiritual perfection—sharper than a two-edged sword when probing the physical dimensions.*
>
> *The purified consciousness when put to its best use is ever so effective in quickly changing the thought from the shadows of error-inducing unhappiness to pure Christ-vision. Thus cleansed, the student observes the Great Law producing eternal joy within his members whenever that Law is called into action.*[63]

The Power of Faith

As we know, the power of faith is extraordinary. Jesus told us it can move mountains! It ultimately led Moses to accept his mantle and lead the children of Israel to the promised land. It gave the shepherd boy, David, the conviction to challenge and slay the giant, Goliath. It empowered the Prophets Samuel and Jeremiah and the other brave men of God to stand before the various kings of Israel—and the errant high priests who supported them—risking their lives for the defense of truth and honor, thus saving Israel again and again from certain destruction by its many enemies.

And there are countless examples from conventional history.

Faith gave George Washington the enormous determination needed to sustain the ragtag band of revolutionaries through seven long years of battle against the pre-eminent military force of the eighteenth century. Faith inspired Mother Teresa to forego all possible material comforts and embark upon an astounding life of merciful service to untold thousands of the poorest and most suffering souls, transforming their lives and founding the Missionaries of Charity, a continuing worldwide mission for Life.

Beloved Master Jesus shares with us powerful guidance for building our individual faith and our spiritual practices, and thereby steadily advancing on the Path:

> *If you believe that you can draw forth from God the desired qualities of Life, I tell you they are yours already. It is doubt that dilutes the essence of manifestation until it is so dim as to be unrecognizable.*
> *You need to (1) Shut out unwanted thoughts and conditions from your world firmly. (2) Call for the protection of your tube of light faithfully. (3) Use the violet fire of freedom daily, and (4) Call for the protection of heaven, the radiance and the power of the Archangels and Ascended Masters constantly—without fail. No matter what men may declare to the contrary, without the assistance of many of these wonderful beings of Light, I would never have been successful in my own mission!*[64]

The Blessing of Transfiguration

A major goal in our endeavors to return to God and His Light is the attainment of our Transfiguration, as discussed in Part I. The preparation for this initiation can occur on a daily basis, as disciples daily strengthen their positive habits, focusing on their goal of spiritual growth. Perseverance toward the goal of the Transfiguration can result in this glorious initiation being experienced while still in embodiment, which has been accomplished by Jesus and other advanced saints.

To transfigure means to "change the form or appearance of." Beloved Jesus has told us of the intensity of the glorious, transforming, white fire which fills our being and consciousness during this grand initiation of Light. Once a soul experiences this wondrous Light, they are a new man, a new woman, clothed in the wedding garment that is a necessary preparation for a soul's entry into the true heaven world. This is also referred to as the "alchemical marriage."

We may call for the transfiguring Light by first meditating upon it to attune with it. When we do so, it amplifies God's consciousness within us. This entire process utilizes the Word of our Father, literally granting us the power to co-create greater goodness with our Creator!

Happily, we can ultimately achieve the Transfiguration, even though we may currently be aware of vestiges of impurity, or be assaulted by memories of past error and karma that remain within us. We know we can use the various rituals of the spoken word to purify and re-energize our four lower bodies and by invoking the divine and transmuting violet fire given to us by God.

Beloved Kuthumi describes the Transfiguration process for us:

To transfigure *thus connotes the shedding of the human image as the soul identity is accelerated in the putting on of a tangible electronic garment, or life-essence, which can never be requalified (or lowered in vibration) to the level of the former state. In the ongoing transfiguration process our disciples experience the spiritual substitution of every human failure with God-dominion, God-creativity, and God-victory, as every manifest virtue and attribute of the Godhead displaces habitual submission to the synthetic programming of the human....*

In transfiguration there is an actual expansion of the light of

> *God that never fails. From within every cell and atom of the physical body, this expansion occurs under circumstances whereby the mud of one's former sullied state is itself dissolved and cannot cling longer round the atoms and cellular structure, for it is permanently changed by the Light.*[65]

In the beautiful process of Transfiguration, every thought results in bliss. Our vast quantity of thoughts become chalices of Light, overflowing with divine joy and wisdom. Every individual that is blessed with the Transfiguration radiates the empowering Light of God-thoughts out to all of Life. This is what our Creator desires.

During this Transfiguration process, our Holy Christ Self, which is both above and within us, will pour into our heart's chalice its beautiful and perfect Life properties. This sacred fire cleanses all areas of the mind of anything that is not in resonance with Life's goodness, love and wisdom. As this occurs, there is a joyous release of Light to all other beings that are near to the one transfigured. This Light surges to its peak, at which level it remains until the electronic structure of the soul has adjusted to the higher range of frequencies.

Relatively few people have succeeded in achieving the outer and visible Transfiguration initiation while in embodiment on Earth. Yet it is an important step for all who walk the Path of Personal Christhood. For when our diligent striving gets to a certain level of intensity, the magnetic attraction of the Light inside our every cell expands outward to connect with the Light of our individual Christ Self, and we are readied for an even deeper communion with the Lord Jesus and the heavenly hosts.[66]

Our loving Creator loves us so much that it is His deep desire for each one of us to experience this blessed and holy Transfiguration. Dear Jesus confirms for us how beautiful and simple this transformation can be.

It is a perfectly natural spiritual manifestation—as simple and sweet as the sunshine itself. It is quite effortless, for once you get the full realization of just what your own Mighty I AM God Presence can actually do for you, you just stand back and let the Presence act in your world as it is wont to do.

Then, when you call to your own dear God Presence, you will sense God's interest in you as your own heavenly Father —even as I did—and you will know, first of all, that God wants to transfigure you. Being convinced that this is so will help you journey from the consciousness of possibility to the state of realization.[67]

The Transfiguration grants us a giant expansion of Light throughout each of our four lower bodies. Let all who truly desire this initiation call and pray for assistance. We are taught that we need to ask for the treasures of Heaven before we can receive them. Jesus reminds us how essential it is to be persistent in our quest, to have unshakeable faith, and to combine heartfelt gratitude with love for our life blessings. And, he acknowledges that the challenges he personally faced at his trial and Crucifixion were significantly easier due to his own prior Transfiguration.

The following decree can be of great assistance in the process of a person's "divine transformation," taking us step by step closer to our own Transfiguration. Once again, we will use the name of God, I AM, which was given to Moses long ago, when he received the task of leading the Children of Israel out of bondage and to the Promised Land.

I AM changing all my garments,
Old ones for the bright new day;
With the sun of understanding
I AM shining all the way.
I AM Light within, without;

I AM Light is all about.
Fill me, free me, glorify me,
Seal me, heal me, purify me!
Until transfigured they describe me:
I AM shining like the Son,
I AM shining like the sun![68]

Blessed Master Jesus urges us to become more fully conscious of God's divine Light, to be aware that this Light is a reality and that it is always around us and in us, for it is the "reality of existence." It was surely the I AM Light which empowered Moses and the Israelites when, against all human odds, they were enabled to escape the might of the Egyptian Pharaoh and his vast army. This divine Power parted the Red Sea for them and fed them in the wilderness, helping them to eventually establish a new nation in a land "flowing with milk and honey." And just as the I AM Presence was the ultimate source of success for the Israelites, just so it can lead us forward on the Path which enables each one of us to manifest our true potential. The stream of our higher states of consciousness and the source of our energy comes to each of us from our I AM Presence flowing down our crystal cord as the River of Life.

We are so profoundly blessed! Our body temple, as well as our mind, is meant to be a vessel for the Holy Spirit. And we may call upon our God to use our temple and our soul to transmit Light from our I AM Presence to others who are in need.

Jesus urges us to call for Transfiguration:

Call for the intensification of the cosmic flame of the transfiguration and for the amplification of your faith in it. Be constant in your application. And then, with heartfelt devotion and gratitude, await the sudden expansion of the perfect love and light that casts out all fear.
Welcome into your lifestream with open arms and grateful heart the flow of God's light without limit until, like me, you

> *abide in God's arms of transfiguring mercy where you always know the full meaning of God-freedom which all of you should share—and one day shall!*
> *All blessings of the cosmic dawn to you!*[69]

A simple example of how this call can be made can be found in the Appendix, which contains a presentation of all the calls we have been encouraged to make.

Prayer of Praise for Service

Beloved Master Kuthumi graces us with his inspirational overview of how to live life. He then shares the following prayer of praise for service:

> *Your immortality is attained here and now, blessed ones of the Light. It is won in your joyous use of the shining hours, in your radiant, God-expressed harmony, in paeans of praise released to the heart of God from your own wonderfully charged, beating hearts, swelling with the love-tide of gratitude for life.*[70]

Here is Kuthumi's lovely Prayer of Praise for Service:

O Love of God immortal Love,
Enfold all in thy ray,
Send compassion from Above
To raise them all today!
In the fullness of thy power
Shed thy glorious beams
Upon the earth and all thereon
Where life in shadow seems.
Let the Light of God blaze forth
To cut men free from pain.

Raise them up and clothe them, God,
With thy Mighty I AM Name![71]

Join with Others

We can significantly increase the power of our calls and prayers if we join with others. We can multiply the heavenly aid we seek.

> *If two of you shall agree on earth as touching any thing that they shall ask, it shall be done for them of my Father which is in heaven.*
> *For where two or three are gathered together in my name, there am I in the midst of them.*[72]

Many of us have, no doubt, already experienced the blessed, heightened atmosphere of a prayer session given together with a group of kindred souls. I know for myself, I have experienced prayer sessions in a congregational setting in which both the power and grace were almost indescribable, and such feelings stayed with me for hours and sometimes days after.

Not every group prayer session has had the same effect for me. This experience, however, has occurred often enough that I can personally confirm the truth of this passage from the Apostle Matthew.

If you are facing a very serious personal challenge, whether it is your health, or a family member in crisis, do consider seeking out others close to you who respect the power of prayer and join your prayer requests together. Saying them aloud together is very powerful, but just enlisting others for prayerful assistance in any form is helpful.

Our Path of Overcoming Darkness

If the sacred texts were not so misinterpreted, we would have a clearer understanding of the Path we are all destined to follow. We would not have become so clouded. Confusion, even deliberate obfuscation, has hidden God's divine plan from His creation.

Master Kuthumi advises us to be aware, and even perhaps to expect, that past experiences and distant memories of our misqualifying God's Light and abusing our free will may arise as we go forward on our spiritual journey. He gives us this warning so that when we encounter these thoughts or memories, we will not be overwhelmed by guilt. Instead, we can use the tools presented here for their transmutation and continue to move ahead.

Because sin can have no real existence in the consciousness of God or, for that matter, within the divine nature of his offspring, it retains its quasi [pseudo] reality only in the memory process. In the human sense, the record of sin which is semi-permanent is merely a chronology of the negative, or anti-Christ, acts of each lifestream.[73]

"AntiChrist" means whatever is against the Light. It originates in the godless rebellion of the fallen angels who refused to recognize the wisdom and the all-goodness of our Creator. It refers to lower levels of vibration which coalesce into darkness, or "densified shadow." This darkness contains fear, unrighteous desire and habit, doubt, and vanity, which all contribute to the "re-creation" of sin and which magnetizes more of the same to keep souls in bondage.

These dark, negative and evil forces are not considered ultimately real. Rather, from the higher perspective, they are a temporary illusion to be transmuted into good.

By using the calls and prayers herein and by developing better habits, we can purge ourselves of the seeds of darkness. Let us strive, for our salvation, to experience the Mind of God, the kingdom of God, the memory of God's All-Goodness! Master Kuthumi tells us how:

> *The memory of man is at present not the memory of God, for the old patterns and records of sin occupy its compartments. It must likewise be recognized that the memory of man can become the complete memory of God, the repository of the original blueprint: and in this possibility is the hope of salvation in the Light, the Christ who lighteth (illumines by his Mind) every man who comes into the world. Those who willingly open the door to this Mind/memory bank, containing the original patterns of things perfect in the heavens of one's Higher Consciousness, admit the inflow of every good and perfect influence of the Holy Spirit.*[74]

Let us listen for the "still, small voice," which is the vibratory action of the voice of God that can be heard by all true disciples who are attuned with their Higher Self. Let us daily go out into the world to sow the seeds of goodness wherever we are! Let our new thinking and feeling habits empower our love for all in our world, no longer disturbed by memories of past errors. Let us be the Good Samaritan and the Good Shepherd, and thus be victorious, like all the wonderful saints and devotees who have gone before us. With eyes of childlike innocence, let us gaze into the limitless good throughout the universe.

APPENDIX

This Appendix revisits some of the most important teachings in Parts I and II and also contains some new material. Present are nearly all of the decrees, prayers and affirmations within the *Corona Class Lessons* plus a few additions.

It is designed to efficiently guide the reader through a logical sequence of those decrees, prayers and affirmations. Feel free to refer back to Part II or Part I for more information about the various topics covered here. For your convenience, those who would like to run through the calls, affirmations, decrees, and prayers on a regular basis can give them by simply jumping from one set of italics to the next, once the teachings about them have been learned.

The exact wording has been given from the Masters for many of the following calls and decrees. These are shown in **bold italics.** In other cases, we are asked to make the calls in our own words. For convenience, examples are presented in some, but not all, cases. These examples are shown in *italics*, but they are *not in bold*. Using your own words, whenever it is recommended, is preferable to using the examples shown.

SECRETS OF THE INNER LIGHT

Regarding the giving of decrees, they usually consist of three parts:

1. A greeting called the "preamble." Here, we can address Ascended Masters and Angels specifically. Here, we give them authority to take action, if our request is given with love and is aligned with God's will. We can only command these energies when we are operating from our Higher, Divine Self. Decree preambles can begin in several ways. One way can be *In the name of the beloved mighty victorious Presence of God, I AM in me, and my very own beloved Holy Christ Self....* After giving a preamble, any personal calls can then be made.
Preambles are not always required, especially when giving short affirmations, fiats (commands) or mantras.

2. The body of a decree is your actual statement of what you want, and is usually composed of the words directly given by Ascended Masters or Angels through their messengers.

3. The closing is given after the body of the decree is given one or more times. It seals the decree with God, and it expresses our acceptance of God's answer to us. A general closing that is commonly used is:
And in full Faith I consciously accept this manifest, manifest, manifest! (3x) *right here and now with full Power, eternally sustained, all-powerfully active, ever expanding, and world enfolding until all are wholly ascended in the Light and free! Beloved I AM! Beloved I AM! Beloved I AM!* [1]

These are "action steps," powerful tools that help us to be fully within the flow of divine and perfect Light, our Creator's purity,

APPENDIX

healing, love, protection, wisdom, peace, and power. These calls invoke purification of past errors, cutting us free from the energies of past misdeeds. The committed student can undertake them to reinforce the ideal mindset of expectations and vision, and magnetize the Light into all areas directed by divine wisdom.

In addition to the abundant personal benefits that result from incorporating these calls into our life, using the power of the spoken word helps to reduce the stress of planetary challenges and situations that we now face. We can make a significant contribution to help raise the Earth and her people out of current misunderstandings, suffering, and despair, by the grace of God.

WORKING WITH THE LIGHT

Remember that divine Light is God's energy and power, and it is the animating force behind all of life.

Blessed Master Jesus shares with us the importance of regular prayers and calls to our God Presence, which is always with us and ready to answer. "The depths of God's love and wisdom are to the present hour conveyed to hearts of goodwill who make consecrated application to the heart of heaven. The door of communion is never shut, for I AM the door that opens in response to the quiet supplication of the loving heart for more Light, until at last each living soul stands face to face with his own God-identity."[2]

Therefore, let us apply the power of habits as they were discussed in Chapter 11. Develop the habit of making these calls daily, as often as needed. They will mightily assist you in your spiritual development.

Master Kuthumi makes this important point: "The priceless treasures of Heaven MUST become a daily habit BEFORE you can be vested with the power of all Good."[3]

Practicing these exercises before a personal altar, in a sacred space set aside for your inner spiritual work, can boost your sense of divine contact and help in forming positive habits as you go about your daily life.

DAILY PROTECTION

We need to pray for God's protection every morning. As we visualize God's divine Light beaming down to surround us, we can give the following "Tube of Light" decree:

O my constant, loving I AM Presence,
Thou Light of God above me
Whose radiance forms a circle of fire before me
to light my way:
I AM faithfully calling to thee
To place a great pillar of Light
From my own Mighty I AM God Presence
All around me right now today!
Keep it intact through every passing moment,
Manifesting as a shimmering shower of God's
beautiful Light
Through which nothing human can ever pass.
Into this beautiful electric circle of divinely
charged energy
Direct a swift upsurge of the violet fire
Of Freedom's forgiving, transmuting flame!
Cause the ever expanding energy of this flame
Projected downward into the forcefield of my
human energies
To completely change every negative condition
Into the positive polarity of my own Great God
Self!
Let the magic of its mercy
So purify my world with Light

*That all whom I contact shall always be blessed
With the fragrance of violets from God's own heart
In memory of the blessed dawning day when all discord—
Cause, effect, record, and memory—is forever changed
Into the Victory of Light and the peace of the ascended Jesus Christ
I AM now constantly accepting the full power and manifestation
Of this fiat of Light
And calling it into instantaneous action
By my own God-given free will
And the power to accelerate without limit
this sacred release of assistance from God's own heart
until all men are ascended and God-free
in the Light that never, never, never fails!*[4]

There is also a short "Traveling Protection" call that can be made daily, and especially when traveling, to our Beloved Archangel Michael. Doing this call adds a layer of protection from negative forces:

*Lord Michael before, Lord Michael behind,
Lord Michael to the right, Lord Michael to the left,
Lord Michael above, Lord Michael below
Lord Michael, Lord Michael, wherever I go
I AM His love protecting here
I AM His love protecting here
I AM His love protecting here!*[5]

The following is a beautiful decree from Master Kuthumi, "I AM Light," from his book, "Studies of the Human Aura." Giving this decree one or more times daily will help to magnetize more of God's Light into your world.

> *I AM Light, glowing Light*
> *Radiating Light, intensified Light.*
> *God consumes my darkness,*
> *Transmuting it into Light.*
> *This day I AM a focus of the Central Sun.*
> *Flowing through me is a crystal river,*
> *A living fountain of Light*
> *That can never be qualified*
> *By human thought and feeling.*
> *I AM an outpost of the divine.*
> *Such darkness as has used me is swallowed up*
> *By the mighty river of Light which I AM.*
> *I AM, I AM, I AM Light;*
> *I live, I live, I live in Light.*
> *I AM Light's fullest dimension;*
> *I AM Light's purest intention.*
> *I AM Light, Light, Light*
> *Flooding the world everywhere I move,*
> *Blessing, strengthening, and conveying*
> *The purpose of the kingdom of heaven.*[6]

EMBRACING GOD'S WILL AND SOUL PURIFICATION

An excellent way to begin the day is by attuning to God's will. Remember that many people do not realize how much our Creator loves His Children. What God wants always results in the greatest ultimate good and happiness. Personally, I feel that when I make the following call it helps me to lose any desire I might otherwise have for any unrighteous or selfish action. God's will *is* in perfect alignment with our true nature, our Higher, Divine Self; and what it needs and wants to do. After giving the preamble, this decree can be given once or as many times as your heart guides you:

In the name of the I AM THAT I AM, in the name of Jesus Christ, I call to the heart of the Will of God in the Great Central Sun to fan the flame of the will of God throughout my four lower bodies and answer this my call infinitely, presently, and forever:

1. I AM God's Will manifest everywhere,
I AM God's Will perfect beyond compare,
I AM God's Will so beautiful and fair,
I AM God's willing bounty everywhere.

Refrain: Come, come, come, O blue-flame Will so true,
Make and keep me ever radiant like you.
Blue-flame Will of living Truth,
Good Will flame of eternal youth,
Manifest, manifest, manifest in me now!

2. I AM God's Will now taking full command,
I AM God's Will making all to understand,
I AM God's Will whose power is supreme,
I AM God's Will fulfilling heaven's dream.

*3. I AM God's Will protecting, blessing here,
I AM God's Will now casting out all fear,
I AM God's Will in action here well done,
I AM God's Will with Victory for each one.*

*4. I AM blue lightning flashing Freedom's love,
I AM blue-lightning power from above,
I AM blue lightning setting all men free,
I AM blue-flame power flowing good
through me.*

And in full Faith I consciously accept this manifest, manifest, manifest! (3x) right here and now with full Power, eternally sustained, all-powerfully active, ever expanding, and world enfolding until all are wholly ascended in the Light and free! Beloved I AM! Beloved I AM! Beloved I AM![7]

True disciples love the flow of Light as they attune to God and His Will. This is how they are able to subdue all that is less than divine. They act as though they are extensions of that divine Will, and regularly affirm:

Not my will but Thine be done![8]

For we are not to think of life as formidable, but rather as a marvelous opportunity to join with the perfect divine love and wisdom of God, who always knows what will ultimately bring us the greatest joy. Every soul can live a life that is a manifestation of divine joy within love's flow.

Blessed Master Kuthumi tells us that another valuable call to make is for soul purification. He recommends that after we focus on attuning to our Holy Christ Self, that we call, with total faith, and *in our own words*, to immortal Life and to the heart of God, for the purification of our soul. For example, we could say:

> *In the name of my Mighty I AM God Presence and Holy Christ Self, I call to immortal Life and to the heart of God, for God's purifying Light to transmute all darkness within my soul and four lower bodies.*

MEDITATION ON LIGHT

The Ascended Master Saint Germain has shared with us a powerful meditation that directs divine Light into every cell of our four lower bodies.

"The first step to the control of yourself—is the stilling of all outer activity—of both mind and body. Fifteen to thirty minutes—at night before retiring and in the morning before beginning the day's work—using the following exercise—will do wonders for anyone—who will make the necessary effort.

"For the second step, make certain of being undisturbed, and after becoming very still—picture and feel your body enveloped in a Dazzling White Light. The first five minutes—while holding this picture—recognize—and feel intensely—the connection between the outer self and Your Mighty God Within—focusing your attention upon the heart center—and visualizing it—as a Golden Sun.

"The next step is the acknowledgment—***I now joyously accept—the Fullness of the Mighty God Presence—the Pure Christ.*** Feel—the Great Brilliancy of the Light and intensify It—in every cell of your body for at least ten minutes longer.

"Then close the meditation by the command, ***I am a Child of the Light—I Love the Light—I Serve the Light—I Live in the Light—I am Protected, Illumined, Supplied, Sustained by the Light, and I Bless the Light.***" [9]

Remember that "one becomes that upon which he meditates."

And, that "the Light is Supreme—the Light is everywhere—and in the Light—exist all things.[10]

Also remember that the Light is the kingdom of God—God's consciousness.

GOD'S CONSUMING FIRE

Violet Light purifies. It is a high frequency spiritual energy. In addition to our prayers for divine assistance and calls, we can invoke and visualize divine violet flame. This qualifies the flow of Light we receive into a specific vibration known to transmute and purify past records of error.

We can visualize ourselves standing within this violet fire, utilizing the focus of the third eye and visualizing it streaming forth from our I AM Presence to surround us and penetrate every atom of our four lower bodies. We can especially visualize its power within our heart. Using the following decrees, it is possible to actually feel the power of this violet flame dissolving and melting our karma, burdens, sorrows, and fears. This merciful flame of freedom helps to fulfill what is required of us: the total release from any negative or harmful manifestations that we may have created or which have been done to us, or even witnessed. It also helps pave the way for our acceptance of guidance from our Higher, Divine Christ Self.

A short general decree to invoke the violet flame is simply:

I AM a being of violet fire
I AM the purity of God's desire!

A longer decree to the violet flame is:

I AM the violet flame
In action in me now
I AM the Violet Flame

To Light alone I bow
I AM the Violet Flame
In mighty Cosmic Power
I AM the Light of God
Shining every hour
I AM the Violet Flame
Blazing like a sun
I AM God's sacred power
Freeing every one[11]

You will find violet flame in several of the following decrees as well. Also, if you're interested in working with more violet flame decrees and songs, they can be found at www.summituniversitypress.com.

CALLS FOR THE HEART, HEAD, AND HAND

These represent the Love of Christ in our hearts; the Wisdom of the Father in our heads, and the Power of the Holy Spirit in our hands. It is important to have a balanced amount of equal attainment in our Love (Heart), Wisdom (Head), and Power (Hands) to be the most effective and able to progress further along the Path.

FOR THE HEART:

We can call to Almighty God to transmit the violet flame for the purification and intensification of the Light in our heart by giving the following decree three or more times:

Violet fire, thou love divine,
Blaze within this heart of mine!
Thou art mercy forever true,
Keep me always in tune with you[12]

As we give this decree, we can further attract this violet Light/fire in our hearts by visualizing it there. This can be done until an actual burning sensation can be felt in the heart, dissolving and transmuting the heart's burdens, its sorrows and fears, and any hardness of the heart.

FOR THE HEAD:

We can then focus on the transmutation of blockages in the head, which contains three spiritual centers or chakras (the throat chakra or power center; the crown chakra at the top of the head for wisdom and illumination; and the third eye chakra for intuition, foresight and visualization). We can now call for this violet fire to transmute all darkness or concepts that are not clear or truthful in the mind. Doing this will help cleanse the mind, enabling entry of the Christ mind.

> *I AM Light, thou Christ in me,*
> *Set my mind forever free;*
> *Violet fire, forever shine*
> *Deep within this mind of mine.*
> *God who gives my daily bread,*
> *With violet fire fill my head*
> *Till thy radiance heavenlike*
> *Makes my mind a mind of Light.*[13]

FOR THE HAND:

Next, we can visualize the intensity of the violet flame in our hands, seeing it burning right in the middle of each palm. Our hands have the potential for being great vehicles for healing. With our hearts radiating love, with our heads hosting the divine wisdom of our Creator, and our hands being the instrument of power, we can transmit God's healing to others in our world.

I AM the hand of God in action,
Gaining victory every day;
My pure soul's great satisfaction
Is to walk the Middle Way[14]

STRENGTHENING THE HEART:

Our hearts are the altars of God's Light. The following decree helps us to magnetize the power of love from our Creator, magnifying it within our hearts. Then, we can radiate it outward to transmute darkness on our planet.

I AM the Light of the Heart
Shining in the darkness of being
And changing all into the golden treasury
Of the Mind of Christ

I AM projecting my Love
Out into the world
To erase all errors
And to break down all barriers

I AM the power of infinite Love,
Amplifying itself
Until it is victorious,
World without end![15]

Also, Beloved Jesus wants us to experience the richness of God's kingdom by a greater attunement with divine guidance. He suggests that we persistently call for the expansion of the flame of divine illumination within our hearts.[16] We could simply repeat:

Beloved Jesus, I call for the expansion of the flame of divine illumination within my heart!

HEALING AND WHOLENESS

Our bodies have intelligence and await our commands. Our bodies change constantly, with some cells dying and new ones being created. For maximum healing ability, we can choose to keep a vigil of ongoing prayer and meditation. We benefit the most by renewing ourselves daily. We can command our cells to submit to the matrix of our perfect Christ Self, so they will not succumb to taking on patterns of disease. Before beginning the following decree, a prayer or preamble can be given, such as:

In the name of my Mighty I AM Presence and Holy Christ Self I call to thee, beloved Jesus and the healing angels for strength and wholeness.

In addition, more specific calls can be made for specific ailments you may have or on behalf of someone else.

The following decree helps to restore the matrix of perfection in our body temple:

1. *I AM God's perfection manifest*
In body, mind, and soul—
I AM God's direction flowing
To heal and keep me whole!

Refrain: (repeat after each verse)
O atoms, cells, electrons
Within this form of mine,
Let heaven's own perfection
Make me now divine!
The spirals of Christ wholeness
Enfold me by his might—
I AM the Master Presence
Commanding, "Be all Light!"

2. I AM God's perfect image:
My form is charged by love;
Let shadows now diminish,
Be blessed by Comfort's Dove!

3. O blessed Jesus, Master dear,
Send thy ray of healing here;
Fill me with thy life above,
Raise me in thine arms of love!

4. I AM Christ's healing Presence,
All shining like a mercy sun—
I AM that pure perfection,
My perfect healing won!

5. I charge and charge and charge myself
With radiant I AM Light—
I feel the flow of purity
That now makes all things right![17]

Decrees can be ended or sealed with any number of statements that express gratitude, or simply by making the following statement:

According to God's holy Will may it be done.
AMEN.

For healing and also general spiritual progress, the following call is helpful:

I invoke the mind of Christ in healing
action now!

NOTE: Although this book includes most of the calls, decrees and affirmations contained within the *Corona Class Lessons*, some information about specific healing situations within its section "Healing Through the Transfiguration" has not been included in this book. If you like this book, you can't go wrong buying your own copy of *Corona Class Lessons*.

THE "I AM" WAY OF JESUS

To come closer to God requires the belief that He exists, and the belief that God is in you, right where you now are. We are encouraged to declare His name, as He did on the mountain top to Moses:

I AM THAT I AM![18]

Jesus explains: "I knew that I came forth from God and that I must return to him. I perceived that the surest way to do so was the I AM way. Hence, I declared: 'Believest thou not that I am in the Father, and the Father in me? The words that I speak unto you I speak not of myself: but the Father that dwelleth in me, He doeth the works.'"[19]

"Unlimited good will come to all who faithfully use this [the following] statement as a divine decree (mantra) and acknowledge this blessed concept of their cosmic unity with God."

Therefore, proclaim on a regular basis:

I AM in the Father, and the Father is in me![20]

Jesus shares a powerful affirmation and empowering insights to help us in the emulation of the life he led. "Therefore, in truth ye DO know the Way: for I AM the Way, I AM the Truth, and I AM the Life. No man cometh to the Father (his God Presence) except through me (the Holy Christ Self of each one), and this is the universal plan—the same for all.

"Face and overcome sin, condemnation, false conscience, and fear. To all these declare fervently and know that...

I AM the fullness of God/Good!
I AM walking into daily oneness with the
Father.
I AM made ever new in God's image, the similitude and likeness of all that is Good.
I AM the justice of the divine Law which reaches out to fulfill the true spirit of both human and divine Law.
I AM the manifestation of that sacred Law, and in the joy of the ascended Jesus Christ consciousness,
I AM illumined to know that this living, inner Law is the Golden Rule!"[21]

Therefore, based on this explanation from Jesus, we too may affirm:

I AM the Way, I AM the Truth, and I AM the
Life.

Beloved Master Kuthumi shares with us a powerful call that we can make:

I AM the all-enfolding garment of Light charged with the life, truth, and radiance of God, good!
Naught of the human can distress me, for I AM the victorious, all-powerful consciousness of God in action—blessing, guarding, guiding, and directing me in all that I do![22]

The simplest yet quite powerful call we can make to announce our identification with God is declaring:

I AM Good! [23]

This reinforces the original declaration made by our Creator when He observed His original creation. This declaration also contributes to the transmutation by divine fire of any remaining corrupt aspects within our consciousness.

Beloved Jesus urges us to contemplate what is deeply rooted in mystical Christianity. "Being itself is the 'AM' of existence, my beloved. But in order for you (the 'I' individualized) to enter in, you must become the 'I' of the 'I AM' and experience for yourself the wonders of the glory of God. Do you see, blessed ones? Oh, do meditate on this point of the Law!"[24]

We will wisely not affirm negatives by saying "I AM afraid" or "I AM weary," for when we do, we give power to these limiting human attributes. Instead, beloved Jesus suggests "Why not affirm, instead, the immortal truth of Being?"

Lo, I AM God in manifestation everywhere!

"[This proclamation] is a far more accurate statement of your true divine Selfhood. This statement alone, repeated many times a day as a flowing mantra and a song of the heart, will swallow up the petty negatives that tear down your spirituality."[25]

CALL TO OVERCOME THE LOWER SELF

Another call that aids in our liberation is a powerful cry for divine assistance for transmuting the domination of the lower or materialistic mind—also known as the self-absorbed human ego. It is "the call that compels the answer." Master Jesus instructs us to visualize the radiant, loving Light of God and to loudly declare with all your heart:

The Light of God never fails!
The Light of God never fails!
The Light of God never fails!
And the Beloved Mighty I AM Presence is that Light!

We are also instructed to: "Repeat this call four times, expelling the carnal mind from each of your four lower bodies as you do. And accept your freedom and your reality by the authority of the Christ who I AM, who You Are—with you now!"[26]

Not only is this a powerful call for help, giving this call on a regular basis results in the gradual progression of redemption and transmutation of carnal energies that consist of misqualifications and misunderstandings lodged within us.

CALL AND PRAYER FOR FORGIVENESS

It is helpful to occasionally search your memory for past times when undeserved negative feelings and thoughts were sent to another. More serious would be any negative actions taken against another. We can pray for souls we have wronged, and if possible, make amends. Afterlife teachings tell us we will have a life review after death when we will momentarily experience, to a certain degree, the harmful effects we caused others. This is always a huge learning experience and deepens our sense of empathy.

If our Creator's Golden Rule is not followed, either because of ignorance or intent, this results in feelings of emptiness, non-fulfillment, and eventually a deepening despair. An important corollary to the Golden Rule is: "Forgive others as you'd like to be forgiven by others, and as you'd like to forgive yourself."

We can visualize our entire body filled with violet Light, and give the following decree to transmute and clear away blockages in our etheric/memory body, to transform conscious and subconscious memories of violence or trauma, to clear our mental body of any false or harmful thoughts and concepts, to clear our emotions, especially feelings of fear or pain, as well as any negative records connected to them.

I AM forgiveness acting here,
Casting out all doubt and fear,
Setting men forever free
With wings of cosmic victory.
I AM calling in full power
For forgiveness every hour;
To all life in every place
I flood forth forgiving grace[27]

Divine Light can be magnetized by steadfastly holding our divine vision. As we pray for the forgiveness of others, we add to the grace of forgiveness that we ourselves receive for our own past misdeeds.

God desires to set free all of life that has borne the burden of error. He wants to repair all damage and replace mistaken human, self-absorbed thinking with a consciousness of divine love and wisdom. Even though no one escapes divine justice by evading any part of the Law, it is possible to accelerate freedom through the invocation of the merciful flame of forgiveness, with intense love for God and others. For example:

In the name of my Mighty I AM Presence and my Holy Christ Self, I invoke God's merciful flame of forgiveness for:

DIVINE ASSISTANCE—ASKING FOR HELP

We are not alone. We can and should ask for help, which is

often needed to prevail over powerful negative habits and forces. It is worth repeating what Jesus told us in Part II: "I AM the compassionate Christ anchored above each lifestream, longing to pour the full momentum of my assistance into every waiting consciousness chaliced in the attitude of receptivity.

"Beloved ones, you do not walk alone. It is ever foolhardy to insist upon solving your own problems without calling to us for aid."[28]

When concerned with losing emotional control, when under attack, when being tempted by something you know is unrighteous, when things aren't going the way you want, or when someone is belittling you, the following short mantra can be given:

Let God be magnified!

The corollary to it is: **Let the anti-God be diminished, let it be denied!**[29]

When giving this mantra, visualize God's Light being magnified by the Sun in all parts of your body.

Thousands of our elder brothers and sisters who have gone before us are standing by ready to assist us. These Masters are eager to assist, for love is the byword of all true hearts of Light. Nothing pleases them more than to help us when we allow it and call for it. For example, we could make the following call:

In the name of the Christ, I call to thee beloved Jesus,
Ascended Masters, and Angels of Light who would assist me
to help me with

_____.

The great Master Jesus wants us to know that we are greatly loved, and to feel free to call to him for assistance, and to joyfully anticipate a greater divine life with God. "I am certain that each one of you who will read these words and look up at me right now and call for my light will feel me standing within your room in my Electronic Presence radiating my light and blessing you with the precious anointing of spiritual assistance and my Christ-victory which overcomes the world.

"You also are one with the Father and myself as you embrace the Life within you which is God, the Mighty I AM Presence, in obedient action everywhere toward all hearts."[30]

For example:

Beloved Master Jesus Christ, I call for thy blessed Light to saturate me and for thy spiritual assistance so that I may achieve my Christ-victory over...[state your situation that needs divine assistance]. I am so very blessed and grateful for thy love.

See and feel his Light fully surrounding and penetrating every cell of your being. Picture Jesus just above you, radiating his Presence into and around you! If you have a painting of Jesus nearby, use it to help tangibly experience his great love and care for your lifestream, and send back a current of your own sincere love in return. Let your total being become more and more aware of the great Light of God.

Jesus urges us to: "Sense that it [Light] is the life-force in every budding flower, every sweet scent, every ray of sunshine, every feeling of hope in the human heart. Sense that it is the eternal bond between heart and heart, that it is the avenue of Ascended Master communication, that it is the Light of thousands of suns shining in their strength.... Sense that God can... put all of this radiance of himself into every cell of you and into your whole being!"[31]

Dear Master Kuthumi urges us to call for the Light with the intensity of our being: "Plead for the power of the coronary [encircling like a crown] Light to flow from the heart of God into your world."[32]

For example:

Beloved heavenly Father/Mother God, I invoke the power of Thy coronary Light to flow from Your Heart into my world!

Beloved Master Jesus shares with us powerful guidance for advancing on the Path. "If you believe that you can draw forth from God the desired qualities of Life, I tell you they are yours already. It is doubt that dilutes the essence of manifestation until it is so dim as to be unrecognizable.

"You need to (1) Shut out unwanted thoughts and conditions from your world firmly. (2) Call for the protection of your tube of light faithfully. (3) Use the violet fire of freedom daily, and (4) Call for the protection of heaven, the radiance and the power of the Archangels and Ascended Masters constantly—without fail. No matter what men may declare to the contrary, without the assistance of many of these wonderful beings of Light, I would never have been successful in my own mission!"[33]

For those choosing to be disciples, we are already doing 1,2 and 3. Jesus recommends that we also constantly ask for protection and empowerment. For example, we could make the following call:

In the name of Jesus Christ, I call for Heaven's protection, and for the radiance and power of the Archangels and Ascended Masters. I am grateful!

Because we often need help, it seemed important to repeat most of what was presented in that section of Part II, and add additional information. Also, don't forget the previously listed call if you need help, under "CALL TO OVERCOME THE LOWER SELF!"

SHARING THE LIGHT

It is worthwhile to basically repeat this information from Part

II. Beloved Master Jesus described for us the Path for our spiritual evolution: "Initially, you must establish a hallowed sense of the reality and the tangibility of the blessing you can obtain and bestow on others as a true disciple of God's great Brotherhood of Light. Let your hearts be humble yet unafraid, desiring to perceive your errors only enough to correct them and your virtues only enough to express gratitude for them. Then I am certain you will find the grossness of the human condition giving way to the refinement of eternal values within you—and as your views change to those of heaven, the reality of the kingdom shall enfold you as a mantle of power."[34]

The following is an example call (usable when not choosing the preferred method of using your own words):

In the name of my Mighty I AM Presence and Holy Christ Self, I call to thee, beloved Jesus and all Masters and Angels who would assist me, to infill me with Light for divine guidance, help and energy. And I ask that this Light also blaze through the following world situations and individuals:_____.

Dear Master Jesus has told us:

"Blessed ones, the water of Life flows freely from your I AM Presence charged with the feeling of the unlimited and unmeasured current of God's being, imparted unto each son and daughter in accordance with his capacity to receive. It is this full quality and power of God's immortality and intelligence in the very 'water' (energy) of Life which quickens in every son and daughter of Life the sense of the soul's eternal mission."[35]

Therefore, we can share the blessings of God with others by making the following call (or something similar):

In the name of the Christ, I call to thee beloved Lord God, to Your Heart of creation and Being, to flood the essence and consciousness of Thyself into the hearts of Thy children so that all who are hungry and thirst after righteousness might drink of the water of Life freely.

HUMILITY

Regarding humility, we see from Part II that Jesus advised us to be a "servant of all," and to "become as little children."

The powerful simplicity and innocence of a sunbeam, and a child, is addressed in the following affirmation, given to us by Jesus and Kuthumi:

I AM a created ray from the very heart of God. I AM shining each day with the lifting, living light of resurrection's eternal flame, awakening my divine memory to the infinite wisdom in a sunbeam, a ray-o-light within me, within all God's children!

I glory in Light's apparent simplicity, knowing that therein lies locked the mightiest power, most profound wisdom, and greatest love of eternity. My own I AM Presence ever unlocks for me this wisdom-balanced power in daily manifestation of all the ascended Jesus Christ love, beauty, grace, and perfection now made manifest.

In childlike humility, I sit at the feet of the gracious Ascended Masters until, sweetly crowned by them, I AM ever the sunbeam-ray which shines for them each day![36]

Also, spending time with small children helps us to remember what child-like innocence is all about. It is suggested that we offer up song like a child to attract divine intervention. This is because Earth currently has such deep, widespread conflicts and crises that only such intercession can truly restore righteous living. And God has proclaimed that all discord should end.

One suggestion is to sing:

Jesus wants me for a sunbeam to shine for him each day.[37]

CALLS FOR PERFECTION

As we strive for perfection, this good intent, along with our prayers for guidance and assistance, is noticed. Over time we will be able to attain more wisdom and strength. This process is of great benefit and provides a loving service to all on Earth, for it magnifies the message of Christ—for good will and living in harmony.

For example, we can make the following call, or something like it:

Beloved heavenly Father, please help and guide me as I strive to overcome all imperfect thoughts, words, emotions and deeds in my life. I am grateful.

Jesus suggests another powerful call, to be made in your own words with all the intensity of your being for "your own perfection in the Light," with belief "that your own victory is possible today—there and then you make it possible!"[38]

For example:

Beloved heavenly Father, I call for Thy grace to bless me with my own perfection in the Light! And I accept my Victory here and now!

Jesus advises us to focus on the higher characteristics of Heaven and nurture a calm spirit that is aware of the constant loving watchfulness of our spiritual brethren, and to hold these facts in our consciousness as we give the following affirmation:

I AM the immortal consciousness of Truth, I AM that Christ Truth which affirms the power of Light and Light's intelligent energy to establish in my world, mind, and affairs the perfection of permanent Good![39]

OUR UNIQUE BEING IN GOD

Beloved Master Kuthumi shares the importance of discovering our true being and identity. "Every lifestream has a matrix, or God-design, which he ought to outpicture each day. Unless this is made known to the outer self of the seeker, it is difficult for him to cooperate with the mighty plan of the inner life."[40]

Master Kuthumi explains that we can learn more about who we really are, our unique qualifications, talents and interests by invoking guidance from above. As this is accomplished, we can move forward and bring about our "particular plan of action." And, our calls for divine guidance can also yield *how* necessary change can be implemented, so that we can fully achieve our purpose. This is how we can contribute the greatest good in our lifetimes. For example, the following call can be used, or something based on the above teaching, that is in your own words:

> *In the name of the Christ, I call to thee beloved Father/Mother God and ask that you reveal to me my God-design and all secrets of my being, including the spiritual means to change what must be changed. Please reveal my unique talents so that I may manifest a wise plan of action, including how necessary change can be implemented to enable my achievement of all righteous projects and goals.*

Jesus wants everyone to benefit from divine guidance. To "persistently call for the expansion of the flame of divine illumination within their hearts."[41]

This call was already given in the earlier "Strengthening the

Heart" section. It is so important it is worth repeating, here in a more formal example:

> *In the name of my Beloved Mighty I AM Presence and Holy Christ Self, I call for the expansion of the flame of divine illumination within my heart! And I am grateful for this divine blessing.*

Jesus states that we will be rewarded when we give this, for when we give it "comes the understanding of Life and the instruction on how to energize the cells of the physical body and how to control the bodies of thought and feeling."[42]

IDENTIFICATION WITH GOD

To counter a dip in energy or a sense of letdown or burden, let us remember the short but powerful affirmation we first saw in "The I AM Way of Jesus," for an immediate identification with God:

I AM Good!

Blessed Master Kuthumi has pointed out that once we have transmuted all that is less than perfection, we shall enjoy the supreme benefits of being able to *fully* attune with the Mind of God. "This unity with the universal Mind is a pearl of great purity and great price, affording solace, harmony, and restoration to the soul. In this lovely consciousness every child of God shall find his heaven."[43]

Master Kuthumi leaves us with a powerful affirmation to lead us to our goal:

I AM apart from manifestation, for I AM the all of God—the all-ness of God, the wholeness of

God. The I AM is my Father, and the I AM and I are one![44]

I AM LORD'S PRAYER

Master Kuthumi tells us of the steps that are essential to raising our consciousness. The first is obedience to the voice of God. The second is thinking about Light, and the third is thinking about power (not human power, but the omnipotence of God). If we focus on these three things while we repeat the I AM Lord's Prayer, we can, over time, free ourselves from what is holding us back.

Our Father who art in heaven,
Hallowed be thy name, I AM.
I AM thy kingdom come
I AM thy will being done
I AM on earth even as I AM in heaven
I AM giving this day daily bread to all
I AM forgiving all Life this day even as I AM all
Life forgiving me
I AM leading all men away from temptation
I AM delivering all men from every evil
condition
I AM the kingdom
I AM the power and
I AM the glory of God in eternal, immortal
manifestation—
All this I AM[45]

CHRIST VISION—INCREASING OUR PERCEPTION

It is crucial to always carry the highest and best vision for the greatest good, beauty and love. The other aspect of our vision also refers to our level of discernment—our ability to distinguish between good and evil.

Beloved Master Jesus states that the following affirmation

"should be repeated often in order to raise the senses to their natural and spiritual perfection....

"The purified consciousness when put to its best use is ever so effective in quickly changing the thought from the shadows of error-inducing unhappiness to pure Christ-vision. Thus cleansed, the student observes the Great Law producing eternal joy within his members whenever that Law is called into action.[46]

I AM the Resurrection and the Life of my perfect seeing, hearing, feeling, tasting, and smelling now made manifest!

CALLING FOR THE TRANSFIGURATION

We may call for the transfiguring Light by first meditating upon it to attune with it. When we do so, it amplifies God's kingdom or consciousness within us. This consciousness is pure love and Light, all-power. This entire process that utilizes the Word of our Father is granted to us so that we may co-create greater goodness *with* our Creator.

We are urged to meditate on Light within our members. Beloved Jesus has told us of the intensity of the glorious, white fire which will fill our consciousness with divine joy and freedom once the Transfiguration is achieved. Master Kuthumi describes the ongoing Transfiguration process when "disciples experience the spiritual substitution of every human failure with God-dominion, God-creativity, and God-victory, as every manifest virtue and attribute of the Godhead displaces habitual submission to the synthetic programming of the human."[47]

In the beautiful process of Transfiguration, every conscious and subconscious thought is transformed into a joyous state of divine bliss. Our vast quantity of thoughts become chalices of Light, overflowing with divine joy and wisdom. Every individual that is blessed with their Transfiguration radiates the empowering Light of

APPENDIX

divine God-thoughts out to all of Life. This is what our Creator desires.

Our call can be made in our own words for "the intensification of the cosmic flame of the transfiguration and for the amplification of your faith in it." We are urged to be persistent in making this call. "And then, with heartfelt devotion and gratitude, await the sudden expansion of the perfect love and Light that casts out all fear."[48]

One example of how this call could be made is:

In the name of my Mighty I Am Presence and Holy Christ Self, I now call for the intensification of the Cosmic flame of Transfiguration, and for the amplification of my faith in it. My heart is filled with a deep gratitude, and I now await the expansion of perfect love and Light that casts out all fear.

The following decree is for one's Transfiguration:

I AM changing all my garments,
Old ones for the bright new day;
With the sun of understanding
I AM shining all the way.
I AM Light within, without;
I AM Light is all about.
Fill me, free me, glorify me,
Seal me, heal me, purify me!
Until transfigured they describe me:
I AM shining like the Son,
I AM shining like the sun![49]

Let all who truly desire the Transfiguration call and pray for assistance. We need to ask for the treasures of Heaven before we can receive them. Jesus reminds us how essential it is to be persistent in our quest, to have unshakeable faith, and to combine heartfelt gratitude with love for our present and future life blessings.

PRAYER OF PRAISE FOR SERVICE

Beloved Master Kuthumi graces us with his inspirational overview of how to live life:

"Your immortality is attained here and now, blessed ones of the Light. It is won in your joyous use of the shining hours, in your radiant, God-expressed harmony, in paeans of praise released to the heart of God from your own wonderfully charged, beating hearts, swelling with the love-tide of gratitude for Life."[50]

Here is Kuthumi's Prayer of Praise for Service:

O Love of God immortal Love,
Enfold all in thy ray,
Send compassion from Above
To raise them all today!
In the fullness of thy power
Shed thy glorious beams
Upon the earth and all thereon
Where life in shadow seems.
Let the Light of God blaze forth
To cut men free from pain.
Raise them up and clothe them, God,
With thy Mighty I AM Name![51]

It seems fitting to repeat dear Kuthumi's earlier affirmation, located in "Identification with God." This is a powerful affirmation that will lead us to our goal:

I AM apart from manifestation, for I AM the all of God—the all-ness of God, the wholeness of God. The I AM is my Father, and the I AM and I are one![52]

JOIN WITH OTHERS

We can significantly increase the power of our calls and prayers when we join with others.

"If two of you shall agree on earth as touching any thing that they shall ask, it shall be done for them of my Father which is in Heaven.

"For where two or three are gathered together in my name, there am I in the midst of them."[53]

If you are facing a serious personal challenge, whether it is your health, or a family member in crisis, do consider seeking out others close to you who respect the power of prayer.

OUR PATH OF OVERCOMING DARKNESS

To maximize our chances of achieving our ultimate spiritual freedom, there is one habit we should seriously consider adding to our daily routine. Our dear elder brother Jesus tells us:

> "Rise fifteen minutes early and with full concentration upon my teaching take one of my books.[54] Read for fifteen minutes. Carry that book with you and remind yourself of what you read. Embody it for the day. A morsel will suffice for the divine alchemy. Where there is no morsel I, then, have nothing to multiply, no wavelength of meditation whereby to enter.
> "Neglect not, beloved, for in days in the future and in the hereafter salvation is far, far more difficult than in the eternal Now. The tools are before you. Let them not rust upon the bench."[55]

By using the calls and prayers herein and by developing better habits, we can purge ourselves of the seeds of darkness. Let us strive, for our salvation, to experience the Mind of God, the kingdom of God, the memory of God's All-Goodness! Master Kuthumi tells us how:

> "The memory of man can become the complete memory of God, the repository of the original blueprint: and in this possibility is the hope of salvation in the Light, the Christ who lighteth (illumines by his Mind) every man who comes into the world. Those who willingly open the door to this Mind/memory bank, containing the original patterns of things perfect in the heavens of one's Higher Consciousness, admit the inflow of every good and perfect influence of the Holy Spirit."[56]

Let us listen for the "still, small voice." Let us daily go out into the world to sow the seeds of goodness wherever we are!

AUTHOR'S NOTE: If you find you are starting to forget the magnificent joys and energy that God has designed for us, consider re-reading Chapters 1-3.

Glossary

Angels. Spiritual, celestial beings, obedient to the will of God and superior to human beings in power and love. Angels are the helpers of mankind. In the scriptures, they appear as God's messengers. Angels serve under their hierarchs, the Archangels, and perform specialized tasks such as bringing healing, protection or comfort to souls in need.

Apocryphal. Spurious; of doubtful or questionable origin. In Christianity, the term "apocryphal books" refers to certain early witness accounts about Jesus Christ and gnostic experiences recorded by his followers that were deemed questionable by Church Fathers and were not included in the official canon of the New Testament.

Ascetic. A person who lives an austerely simple life in self-denial of the normal pleasures of life, often for the purpose of spiritual discipline.

Atlantis. A lost continent that once existed in the Atlantic Ocean.

Glossary

Atlantis was first mentioned by the philosopher Plato in his books *Timaeus* and *Critias,* described as a large island beyond the Pillars of Hercules (the Strait of Gibraltar). Atlantis sunk around 11,500 years ago, its demise being ascribed to extreme misuses of science and power by its inhabitants. The sinking of Atlantis is believed to have given rise to legends of a catastrophic flood found in many cultures around the world.

Attune. To bring into harmony; to adjust to the same frequency. In a spiritual sense, attunement refers to the practice of elevating the vibration of one's consciousness so one is able to connect with beings in higher realms and be receptive to their intimations.

Ascended Masters. Highly advanced spiritual beings who once lived in physical embodiment on Earth, succeeded in balancing their debts to life, were liberated from the wheel of birth and rebirth, and gained their immortal freedom in the ritual of the **ascension.** They are now in a blessed state where they can wield God's power for greater good. Ascended Masters have risen from every race and nation and are often recognized as great spiritual leaders, visionaries, mystics, saints and sages before attaining their ascension. Deeply concerned with human evolution, Ascended Masters are our elder brothers and sisters who teach mankind the way to the same state of immortal grace they themselves have attained. *See also:* **Ascension.**

Ascension. The ultimate reunion of the soul with its Divine Source or **I AM Presence.** Considered to be the last of the final four initiations on the path to union with one's **Divine Self,** conferring immortality on the soul and qualifying the victorious one to be called an **Ascended Master.** The initiation of the ascension was demonstrated publicly by Jesus Christ after his resurrection, when he ascended to heaven in the presence of many witnesses: "And when he had spoken these things, he was taken up;

and a cloud received him out of their sight." [*See* Mark 16:19; Acts 1:9-10.] *See also:* **Crucifixion; Resurrection; Transfiguration.**

Bija Mantras. The word *bija* means "seed" in Sanskrit. Bija mantras, also called "seed syllables," are short words or syllables such as AIM, HRIM or HUM associated with specific deities and chanted repeatedly to invoke the presence, power and action of those deities. Spiritual focuses such as the seven chakra centers may also be associated with unique bija mantras; when chanted, these mantras are understood to purify and accelerate those spiritual centers.

Bliss. The highest degree of happiness; blessedness; exalted felicity; heavenly joy.

Brotherhood, the. The collective body of those who are part of the heavenly hierarchy for this planet and beyond. The Brotherhood, consisting of ascended beings and some of their most advanced students on Earth, is also referred to as the **Hierarchy** and as the Great White Brotherhood ("white" is a reference to the halo of while light that surrounds these immortal beings). See also: **Chela.**

Call. A type of quick spoken prayer; a specific and clearly worded request for assistance, given aloud and directed to one of the heavenly **hierarchy.**

Carnal Mind. The human **ego.** The mind of the **lower self** or materialistic self, as opposed to the mind of the **Higher Self.** The self-created, self-absorbed human ego that is opposed to and unable to comprehend higher truths. The carnal mind of a human being will rationalize its selfish desires and decisions and do its best to preserve the status quo, using misconceptions and lies. When indulged in and not dealt with, the carnal mind is a morass of artificial standards and values that can block any spiritual progression and would keep the soul bound in chains of mundane mediocrity and illusion. Advancing on the spiritual path means slaying the carnal mind through love for and devotion to the higher principles of God, and assimilating and expressing the **Christ consciousness** in one's daily life.

Center. *See* **Chakra.**

Chakra. (Sanskrit: "wheel," "disc.") Chakras are centers of spiritual light located in the body. There are seven main chakras, situated along the spine and in the head. Their Western names are base-of-the-spine chakra; seat-of-the-soul chakra; solar-plexus chakra; heart chakra; throat chakra; third-eye chakra; and crown chakra. Chakras take in spiritual light and distribute it through the body to sustain the functions of life. They also act as transmitters of spiritual light into the world around the individual. When one purifies one's chakras, they can act as orifices for the release of spiritual blessings to all life.

Chela. (Hindi *cela,* Sanskrit *ceta,* "slave," meaning servant.) In Hinduism, a chela is a student or disciple of a guru or accomplished spiritual teacher. In exchange for selfless striving and loving obedience on the part of the chela, the guru imparts spiritual knowledge and helps the chela balance his karma and attain higher consciousness. Ascended Masters speak of their students as chelas once they have made a firm inner commitment to walking the spiritual path and serving their Ascended Master guru in exchange for divine assistance in attaining the goal of the **Ascension.**

Christ. (From the Greek *christos,* meaning "anointed one," used in the Septuagint to translate the Hebrew term *messiah,* "one who is anointed.") The appellation "Christos" was given to Jesus, the

Messiah or Savior, at the beginning of the Christian era. The term "Christ" also refers to the Universal Christ, meaning the universal consciousness of God that went forth as the Word, the **Logos** that God used to fire the pattern of His divine identity in His sons and daughters and to write His laws in their inward parts. Each individualization of the Universal Christ is unique, because each individual was ordained by God to reflect a particular facet of the Universal Christ. Also, simply "God in man." *See also:* **Christ consciousness; Christ Self.**

Christ consciousness. Higher consciousness. An intermediate stage of consciousness between that of everyday life and what is known as the divine consciousness of the **I AM Presence.** Someone who has developed his Christ consciousness has reached the advanced level of awareness of Self and of life that was demonstrated by Jesus **Christ.** Christ consciousness manifests as a balanced control and wise, benevolent use of the forces of power, wisdom and love in one's being. *See also:* **Christ Self.**

Christ Self. A segment of one's **Higher Self** that acts as the intermediary between the soul and its **Divine Self** or **I AM Presence**. Just as the individualized Divine Self is created out of the Universal Divine Consciousness and is essentially one with it, the individual Christ Self is a portion of the Universal Christ. Whereas one's Divine Self dwells in realms of purity, perfection and light, the Christ Self is aware of both that realm of perfection and the world of imperfection that is the temporary abode of the soul in incarnation. This enables the Christ Self to act as teacher of the soul and as mediator between the soul and its Divine Source, until the soul is purified and ready to behold its Divine Self face to face. On the journey to the **Ascension,** the soul first bonds with its Christ Self—attaining **Christ consciousness**—and then, ultimately, reunites with its Divine Self, thereby attaining divine consciousness and access to the full power, wisdom, love and all other divine attributes of its I AM Presence.

Conscience. The faculty, power or inner principle of righteousness that evaluates the nature and quality of one's own actions, purposes and affections, warning against that which is wrong and prompting that which is right; the moral faculty that passes judgment on one's self; the moral sense.

Contemplation. Considering something with more than usual attention; reflection; continued attention of the mind to a particular subject. Taking into account all sides or perspectives of something. In a spiritual sense, contemplation is the act of deeply reflecting on an aspect of the divine in order to understand it profoundly, as in contemplating the nature and actions of a **saint** in order to assimilate the qualities of sainthood one admires in that person.

Corona. (Latin: "wreath," "garland," "crown.") A halo, such as the luminous circle surrounding the sun and moon.

Crucifixion. An ancient Roman capital punishment consisting of being nailed to a wooden cross and left to die. Symbolically, the laying down or surrendering of the physical form while carrying the weight of the world, simultaneously maintaining one's connection to Spirit in anticipation of a higher resurrection. Considered to be the second of the final four initiations on the path to union with one's **Higher Self**. The initiation of the Crucifixion was demonstrated by Jesus Christ after his arrest and trial by Pontius Pilate. [See Matthew 27; Mark 15; Luke 23; John 19.] See also: **Ascension; Resurrection; Transfiguration.**

Disciple. Follower or adherent; especially, a follower who believes in the truth of the doctrine of his teacher, as the disciples of Gautama Buddha or Jesus Christ.

Glossary

Divine. Pertaining to divinity; related to God, the Supreme Being or the Universal Divine Consciousness.

Divine Hierarchy. *See* **Hierarchy.**

Divine Self. *See* **I AM Presence.**

Ego. One's awareness of one's own identity, as distinct from others or from the world at large. Also: egotism, conceit; an exaggerated sense of self-importance.

Etheric Body. The highest vibrating of the four lower bodies of man, which are the physical, emotional, mental and etheric bodies or vehicles used by the soul to navigate the material world. The etheric body, also known as the fire body and the memory body, is imprinted with the divine blueprint of the evolving soul; this original imprint acts as a magnet for the soul's ultimate self-realization. The karmic records of particular embodiments are also stored in the etheric body; these are carried over from incarnation to incarnation to help the soul remember and transmute unresolved emotional and mental energies and patterns from previous lifetimes.

Elohim. In Hebrew, *Elohim* is the plural of the word *El*, "god." The Elohim or "gods" are mentioned in Genesis as the divine beings who made the world and created mankind in their own image: "And God said, Let us make man in our image, after our likeness: and let them have dominion over the fish of the sea, and over the fowl of the air, and over the cattle, and over all the earth, and over every creeping thing that creepeth upon the earth. So God created man in his own image, in the image of God created he him; male and female created he them."[Genesis 1:26-27.] The Elohim are the builders of form, including the vastness of the universe, the material objects found in nature, and the physical forms of plants, animals and human beings. They hold the highest offices in the **hierarchy** of those beings that are responsible for creating the material universe, in perfect oneness with God's plan.

Faith. That which is believed in any subject, whether in science, politics or religion; in particular, a system of religious belief of any kind. Also: belief; trust.

God. The Supreme Being; the eternal and infinite Spirit, the Sovereign of the universe. The Creator of all good. The Universal Field of Loving Intelligence—All Love, All Light.

Grace. The divine favor of God toward man; the mercy of God, as distinguished from His justice; also, any benefits that His mercy imparts; divine love or pardon; a state of acceptance with God; divine assistance.

Great Central Sun. The center of the cosmos; the principal source of life, energy and **Light** for the physical/spiritual universe. Also called the Great Hub, it is the center point or nexus of the cosmos where Spirit become Matter and Matter becomes Spirit.

Heaven. The realm above Earth. The dwelling place of God and of the blessed after death. The realm of **Spirit** where **angels** and **Ascended Masters** abide. A place of supreme happiness, joy and tranquility; the abode of **bliss**.

Hierarchy. A system of persons or things that are ranked one above the other. In government, business and religion, the placing of officials in successive ranks that carry increasing responsibility. In spiritual teachings, "the Hierarchy" refers to the organized body of ascended, spiritual and cosmic beings who are ranked according to their levels of spiritual attainment. Based on their office or stature in Hierarchy, they are vested with different levels of accountability for those below them in this great cosmic chain of being, as well as for unascended souls evolving on inhabited planets such as Earth.

Higher Self. A term used to denote a level of conscious awareness in man that is elevated in vibration above one's everyday state of being (characterized by ego awareness and imperfection). An evolving soul may glimpse its Higher Self during spiritual experiences such as intuitive knowing, premonition, inspiration, divine direction and vision. Many belief systems acknowledge the existence of the Higher Self and associate it with the individual's eternal or divine inner being. The Ascended Masters teach that what is commonly called the Higher Self consists of two distinct yet interconnected levels of higher consciousness: (1) the **Christ Self,** and (2) the **Divine Self** or **I AM Presence.**

Holy. Spiritually whole or pure; of unimpaired innocence and virtue; free from sinful affections; pure in heart; godly; acceptable to God; worthy of veneration as sacred; hallowed.

Holy Christ Self. See **Christ Self.**

Holy Spirit. In Christianity, the Third Person of the Trinity (Father, Son, and Holy Spirit). The outpouring of vital energy originating from God the Father and permeating the visible and invisible aspects of creation, infusing all with the divine presence and connecting every part of the creation.

I AM Presence. The individualized presence of God. The name "I AM" is derived from the self-identification of the Godhead to Moses when appearing to him in a bush that burned but was not consumed: "I AM THAT I AM." [See Exodus 3:1-15.] The I AM Presence of Divine Presence abides in the realm of Spirit. It creates a separate, smaller reflection of its divine nature called the soul, and cyclically sends this extension of itself into physical embodiment for the purpose of increasing individual self-awareness. The Presence, hovering over the soul and connected to it by means of what is called the "crystal cord," remains untainted by the impure thoughts, feelings and creations of the soul while in a state of lower consciousness. As the soul evolves and matures, it increases in higher consciousness and ultimately reunites with its I AM Presence in the ritual of the **Ascension** as a self-realized divine identity.

Joy. A state of great delight or happiness; felicity.

Karma. (Sanskrit: "deed," "action.") In Hinduism, karma is seen as the total of one's thoughts, words and actions that acts as the causative factor in determining one's fate in life. Negative or "bad" karma underlies experiences of difficulties and challenges; positive or "good" karma manifests as benevolent or helpful experiences and opportunities. Though in traditional Eastern religions karma is often regarded as fate or punishment, the Ascended Masters teach that karma is an impartial cosmic mechanism that teaches the evolving soul how to use its life energy wisely for purposes of learning, reflection and self-transcendence.

Kingdom. Realm. Used to describe distinct domains of being, such as the angelic kingdom, the elemental kingdom and the human kingdom. In the New Testament, used to denote the consciousness of God or Spirit, as in "enter the kingdom of God," and "the kingdom of God is within you." [See Matthew 6:33; Mark 10:15; Luke 17:21, etc.]

Light. A cosmic energy that has both visible and invisible aspects. In a spiritual sense, "Light" can mean divine energy and power; vital force; wisdom; illumination; **Christ consciousness** or divine consciousness; the energy of creation.

Logos. (Greek: "word.") In philosophy, logos refers to the rational principle or law that governs and regulates the universe. In Christianity, Logos is a term used for Jesus Christ as the Son of God, described in the Gospel of John as the Word of God that created the world: "In the beginning was the Word, and the Word was with God, and the Word was God. The same was in the beginning with God. All things were made by him; and without him was not any thing made that was made. In him was life; and the life was the light of men." [John 1:1-4.] In esoteric teachings, Logos refers to the knowledge and wisdom aspect of God that infuses the universe with intelligent understanding and action.

Love. Due gratitude and reverence to God. Affection; kind feeling; friendship; strong liking or desire; fondness, good will; tenderness; as, the love of brothers and sisters.

Lower Self. The unreal self; the not-self; the human self. The carnal mind; the body of desires; the illusion of an existence separate from God that ultimately will pass away. The lower self is the origin of selfishness, harmfulness and destructiveness, as opposed to the Real Self or **Christ Self,** which is God in manifestation in human beings. *See also:* **Christ Self; Higher Self; I AM Presence.**

Master. One who has attained great skill in the use or application of anything. In a spiritual sense, a master is one who has achieved total mastery of life and may function as a sacred conduit for wisdom and as a teacher or helper to those who seek self-realization. In the context of this book, the term "Master" usually refers to **Ascended Masters**.

Maya. Illusion. In Hinduism and Buddhism, the notion that the ever-changing world we experience through the five senses is not real; it is an illusion that covers over the realm of spiritual reality and must be overcome to enter into that higher realm of true existence and Reality.

Meditation. The process of concentration of the mind by means of engaging in a repetitive or singular mental activity that helps the mind to disengage it from its usual random thought patterns. The practice of meditation facilitates the opening of the mind to receive spiritual revelation. It also enhances the ability of the mind to "see" beyond the physical dimension of life and to become a co-creator of constructive patterns and thoughtforms that can elevate life.

Mystic. A person who experiences direct interaction with the divine Spirit, thereby acquiring a knowledge of God and of spiritual things unattainable by the intellect alone.

Mysticism. A religious and spiritual doctrine that presupposes the human ability to approach or interact with the divine by means of deep contemplation or other spiritual practices that lead to a state of ecstasy; a sense of blissful union with the divine Spirit while retaining individual self-awareness.

Nirvana. In Buddhism, the state of the highest, enduring, transcendental happiness and calmness that flows from enlightenment. Liberation of the soul from the wheel of birth and rebirth and from worldly existence. Absorption into the Divine.

Prayer. The act of addressing supplication to God; the offering of adoration, confession, supplication, and thanksgiving to the Supreme Being. May manifest as private prayer or public prayer.

Pride. The quality or state of being or feeling proud; a sense of satisfaction of having accomplished a difficult or challenging task; inordinate self-esteem; conceit of one's own superiority in talents, appearance, wealth, station in life, etc., which may manifest as a sense of being better than or elevated above others and may result in contempt of others.

Prophet. One who speaks by divine revelation or acts as spokesperson for God or for a deity. A prophet may foresee or foretell the future and warn of calamity if certain behaviors or states of being out of alignment with or acting contrary to the laws of God are not corrected.

Propitiation. Conciliation; appeasement; atonement. Often used in connection with the concept of making amends for sinful acts: propitiation or atonement for one's sins.

Reincarnation. The process of souls taking embodiment in successive physical bodies during a long span of time, for the purpose of the evolution and spiritualization of the individual's consciousness.

Resurrection. The raising of the physical body from a state of having died. Considered to be the third of the final four initiations on the path to union with one's **Higher Self.** Symbolically, the overcoming of the "last enemy" of death, which in a spiritual sense denotes the entombment of the soul in the material world. The initiation of the Resurrection was demonstrated by Jesus Christ after his crucifixion, when he rose from the tomb on the third day as a radiant light being. [See Matthew 28:1-9; Mark 16:1-11; Luke 24:1-9; John 20:1-18.] *See also:* **Ascension; Crucifixion; Transfiguration.**

Righteousness. The quality or state of being righteous; rectitude, uprightness. Righteous conduct.

Glossary

Sacred. Venerable; consecrated; holy; revered; not profane or common.

Saint. A person characterized by an unusual or exceptional level of virtue, kindness or holiness. A person so recognized by an established religion after death, often subject to veneration, celebration and prayers for divine intercession.

Self. In psychology, the ego or superficial self; the personality. In a spiritual sense, the Self refers to one's **Higher Self** or True Self or to the "Observing Self:" a point of pure consciousness or awareness that is untainted by one's lower mental and emotional states. See also: **Christ Self.**

Spirit. The highest vibrating, most intelligent and illumined, non-material and immortal part of a human being, distinct from both the body and the soul. Many religions and spiritual traditions believe that the individual Spirit in a human being is a drop or spark of the Universal Divine Spirit that permeates the universe, animating, inspiring and guiding a human being in embodiment.

Spiritual Center. *See* **Chakra.**

Spiritual Hierarchy. *See* **Hierarchy.**

Transcend. To go beyond; to exceed; to rise above; to surmount. A term used to pass beyond a former or current state of consciousness to a higher state of awareness and realization.

Transmute. To change from one nature, form, or substance into another; to transform. The word "transmutation" is often used to describe the process of cleaning up one's negative **karma**.

Transfiguration. The changing of the physical body into a radiant light body. Considered to be the first of the final four initiations on the path to union with one's **Higher Self**. The initiation of the Transfiguration was demonstrated by Jesus Christ in the presence of his disciples Peter, James and John: "And he was transfigured before them: and his face did shine as the sun, and his raiment was white as the light." [See Matthew 17:2; Mark 9:2.] *See also:* **Ascension; Crucifixion; Resurrection.**

Truth. Pertaining to that which is true; a verified or verifiable fact. The real state of things; reality.

Violet Flame. A high frequency spiritual energy that purifies and transmutes past records of error. *See also: Saint Germain on Prophecy,* a book by Elizabeth Prophet.

Wisdom. The quality or state of being wise or enlightened; possessing knowledge of the best or most virtuous ends and means, and the capacity to make good use of this knowledge; more than average insight, discernment and judgment; sagacity.

Acknowledgements

Secrets of the Inner Light would not have been possible without the profound teachings lovingly shared with us from beloved Masters Jesus and Kuthumi through the Messenger Elizabeth Clare Prophet. This was made possible by the kind permission of the Summit Lighthouse, which allowed the use of key quotations from the *Corona Class Lessons*.

Many thanks go to my beautiful friends who contributed to this joyful project.

My heartfelt gratitude goes to Timothy Connor, who drew upon his knowledge of these teachings to add numerous contributions and helpful edits to the original manuscript.

We were also blessed by Nigel Yorwerth, who provided several helpful suggestions for the text as well as his guidance for the book's title and subtitle decision. He has since made his transition and is loved and missed by many. Nigel loved the manuscript and his enthusiasm and encouragement helped drive this project to its completion. We are also grateful to Nigel's wife, Patricia Spadaro, for her helpful insights on the book and for her title and subtitle ideas.

Linda Locke also did a superb job proofreading the manuscript and providing some excellent editorial suggestions. Yet despite her best efforts and those of all my editing friends, I'll never ever be absolutely sure about my comma placements!

Thanks to Janette and John Paul Mathis for their enthusiastic support providing editorial suggestions and creating beautiful front and back book covers.

We are grateful to Carla Groenewegen, who provided many helpful suggestions for the book and was the primary contributor and editor for our Glossary.

Gregory Bodwell provided loving support by assisting us several times with excellent legal and editorial advice and encouragement throughout the entire process.

Our thanks go to Patrick Rogers who assisted with the book's typesetting as well as ideas for marketing the book.

Finally, my dear wife, Gretchen, provided the patience and her excellent editorial skills to, time and time again, read the newest versions of the manuscript and recommend helpful improvements. We were amazed how, even after several iterations, new ideas could still be found to make the book more insightful and readable. And, God knows when I would have completed this project without her regular reminders to get it done!

All Glory to God and His Hierarchy for providing loving encouragement and guidance in their sublime and beautiful manner, and for blessing all of us with a beautiful, eternal life plan.

Notes

The Source for this Book

1. Prophet, Elizabeth Clare, *The Word—Mystical Revelations of Jesus Christ Through His Two Witnesses, Volume 6*, (Gardiner, MT, The Summit Lighthouse, Inc., 2022), 170-171.

Introduction

1. Jesus and Kuthumi, dictated to the Messengers Mark and Elizabeth Prophet, *Corona Class Lessons,* (Livingston, MT; Summit University Press; 1986), 223-224.
2. Lundberg, C. David, *Unifying Truths of the World's Religions,* (New Fairfield, CT; Heavenlight Press; 2010)
3. *The Holy Bible—Authorized King James Version,* (London; Oxford University Press; 1611), Mark 4:34.
4. Jesus and Kuthumi, *Corona Class Lessons,* 349-350.
5. *King James Bible,* John 14: 2-3.
6. Jesus and Kuthumi, *Corona Class Lessons,* 400-401.

1. God's Grand Design

1. Jesus and Kuthumi, *Corona Class Lessons,* 277-278.
2. Jesus and Kuthumi, *Corona Class Lessons,* 38-39.
3. Lundberg, *Unifying Truths,* Chapters 1-2.
4. Jesus and Kuthumi, *Corona Class Lessons,* 36-37.
5. Wikipedia: Galaxy.
6. sciencehowstuffworks.com/dictionary/physics-terms/frequency-wavelength-light.htm
7. Jesus and Kuthumi, *Corona Class Lessons,* 401.
8. Jesus and Kuthumi, *Corona Class Lessons,* 33.
9. Jesus and Kuthumi, *Corona Class Lessons,* 334.

2. Misunderstandings Concerning Jesus

1. Jesus and Kuthumi, *Corona Class Lessons,* 70.
2. *King James Bible,* Matthew 5:45 and numerous other passages.
3. *King James Bible,* 1 John 3:1-2; Philippians 2:15; Romans 8:14; John 1:12.
4. *King James Bible,* James 2:5.

Notes

5. *King James Bible*, Matthew 5:48.
6. *King James Bible*, John 14:6.
7. *King James Bible*, John 1:9.
8. Jesus and Kuthumi, *Corona Class Lessons*, 71.
9. *Corona Class Lessons*, 71.
10. *King James Bible*, Matthew 12:48-50.
11. *King James Bible*, John 14:20.
12. *King James Bible*, John 14:23.
13. Jesus and Kuthumi, *Corona Class Lessons*, 72-73.
14. *King James Bible*, John 14:1-6.
15. *King James Bible*, John 14:7-9.
16. *King James Bible*, John 14:10-14.
17. Jesus and Kuthumi, *Corona Class Lessons*, 52.
18. Jesus and Kuthumi, *Corona Class Lessons*, 52.
19. *King James Bible*, Philippians 4:13.
20. Caldwell, Taylor, *Great Lion of God*, (New York, NY; Open Road Integrated Media; 1970)
21. Jesus and Kuthumi, *Corona Class Lessons*, 162-163.
22. *Corona Class Lessons*, 163-164.
23. *Corona Class Lessons*, 178-179.
24. *King James Bible*, 1 John 4:1.
25. Jesus and Kuthumi, *Corona Class Lessons*, 230-231.
26. Jesus and Kuthumi, *Corona Class Lessons*, 229.
27. Jesus and Kuthumi, *Corona Class Lessons*, 334.

3. Losing All Fears

1. *King James Bible*, John 8:44, Matthew 23:33.
2. Jesus and Kuthumi, *Corona Class Lessons*, 391.
3. *King James Bible*, Deut.32:35, Rom. 12:19, Heb. 10:30.
4. *King James Bible*, Revelation 20:15.
5. *King James Bible*, Matthew 18:22.
6. Lundberg, C. David, *Our Magnificent Afterlife*, (Bozeman, MT, Heavenlight Press, 2019).
7. Jesus and Kuthumi, *Corona Class Lessons*, 412-413.
8. Jesus and Kuthumi, *Corona Class Lessons*, 356.

4. Faith Rules

1. *King James Bible*, John 20:29.
2. Jesus and Kuthumi, *Corona Class Lessons*, 311.
3. Jesus and Kuthumi, *Corona Class Lessons*, 311-312.
4. *King James Bible*, Matthew 6:10.
5. *King James Bible*, Matthew 17:20.
6. *King James Bible*, Exodus 3:14.

7. *King James Bible*, John 1:4,9.
8. Jesus and Kuthumi, *Corona Class Lessons*, 368.

5. We Are God's Children With Unlimited Potential

1. *King James Bible*, John 14:6.
2. *King James Bible*, Matthew 16:15,16.
3. *King James Bible*, 1 John 3:1-3.
4. www.adishakti.org/_/great_cover_up_of_reincarnation.htm; www.reluctant-mesenger.com/aquarian_gospel.htm; or just Google "fifth general counsel of the church."
5. Prophet, Elizabeth Clare, *Reincarnation: The Missing Link in Christianity*, (Corwin Springs, MT, Summit University Press, 1997).
6. Jesus and Kuthumi, *Corona Class Lessons*, 230.
7. Jesus and Kuthumi, *Corona Class Lessons*, 53.
8. Jesus and Kuthumi, *Corona Class Lessons*, 55.
9. Jesus and Kuthumi, *Corona Class Lessons*, 66.

6. The Christ Consciousness

1. Jesus and Kuthumi, *Corona Class Lessons*, 300.
2. *King James Bible*, Matthew 28:20.
3. Jesus and Kuthumi, *Corona Class Lessons*, 269.
4. Jesus and Kuthumi, *Corona Class Lessons*, 269-270.
5. *King James Bible*, John 8:11.
6. *King James Bible*, Luke 17:21.
7. *King James Bible*, Genesis 19:26.
8. Chakras are centers of spiritual Light located in the body. See the Glossary for additional information.

7. Empowering Humility

1. *King James Bible*, Matthew 18:3-4.
2. Jesus and Kuthumi, *Corona Class Lessons*, 64.
3. Jesus and Kuthumi, *Corona Class Lessons*, 64.
4. Jesus and Kuthumi, *Corona Class Lessons*, 103.
5. *King James Bible*, Matthew 20:26,27.
6. Jesus and Kuthumi, *Corona Class Lessons*, 407.
7. *King James Bible*, John 3:17.
8. Jesus and Kuthumi, *Corona Class Lessons*, 100-101.
9. *King James Bible*, Proverbs 16:18.

Notes

8. Freedom From Sin

1. *King James Bible*, Ex. 21:23-25; Lev. 24:19,20; Deut. 19:21; Eph. 6:8; Col. 3:25.
2. *King James Bible*, Matthew 5:38-42.
3. Jesus and Kuthumi, *Corona Class Lessons*, 154.
4. Jesus and Kuthumi, *Corona Class Lessons*, 307.
5. Jesus and Kuthumi, *Corona Class Lessons*, 157-158.
6. Jesus and Kuthumi, *Corona Class Lessons*, 169-170.
7. Jesus and Kuthumi, *Corona Class Lessons*, 171-172.
8. Jesus and Kuthumi, *Corona Class Lessons*, 161.
9. *King James Bible*, Luke 15:11-32.
10. Jesus and Kuthumi, *Corona Class Lessons*, 409-410.
11. "Mercy's flames give freedom to all through the diligent application of the violet fire and through hearts burning with eternal love which imputes not sin to any who truly love God and care for his flock." Jesus and Kuthumi, *Corona Class Lessons*, 175.
12. Jesus and Kuthumi, *Corona Class Lessons*, 161.

9. The Perfect You

1. Jesus and Kuthumi, *Corona Class Lessons*, 390.
2. *King James Bible*, Matthew 5:48.
3. Lundberg, *Unifying Truths of the World's Religions*, in chapter 18, "Perfection and Purity," pages 201-209 give excerpts from the sacred texts of world religions teaching that perfection is possible and should be our goal.
4. Jesus and Kuthumi, *Corona Class Lessons*, 99. Referring to Psalm 23:4.
5. Jesus and Kuthumi, *Corona Class Lessons*, 295.
6. *King James Bible*, Exodus 3:11-12.
7. Elizabeth Clare Prophet on February 26, 1974, shared the story of how Jesus once reassured Mark Prophet as to his calling, and included this referenced quote from Jesus.
8. Jesus and Kuthumi, *Corona Class Lessons*, 116-117.
9. Lundberg, *Our Magnificent Afterlife*, Chapter 16, "The Spiritual Body," 69-74.
10. Jesus and Kuthumi, *Corona Class Lessons*, 63.
11. Jesus and Kuthumi, *Corona Class Lessons*, 84-85.
12. Jesus and Kuthumi, *Corona Class Lessons*, 87.
13. Jesus and Kuthumi, *Corona Class Lessons*, 89.
14. Jesus and Kuthumi, *Corona Class Lessons*, 95.
15. Jesus and Kuthumi, *Corona Class Lessons*, 95-96.
16. Jesus and Kuthumi, *Corona Class Lessons*, 96-97.
17. Jesus and Kuthumi, *Corona Class Lessons*, 396-397.

Notes

10. You Are Unique

1. Jesus and Kuthumi, *Corona Class Lessons*, 277-278.
2. Jesus and Kuthumi, *Corona Class Lessons*, 282-283.
3. Jesus and Kuthumi, *Corona Class Lessons*, 392-393.
4. Jesus and Kuthumi, *Corona Class Lessons*, 394.
5. Jesus and Kuthumi, *Corona Class Lessons*, 395.
6. Jesus and Kuthumi, *Corona Class Lessons*, 395-396.
7. Jesus and Kuthumi, *Corona Class Lessons*, 109.
8. The collective body of those who are part of the heavenly hierarchy. See Glossary.
9. Jesus and Kuthumi, *Corona Class Lessons*, 329.
10. Jesus and Kuthumi, *Corona Class Lessons*, 105-106.
11. Jesus and Kuthumi, *Corona Class Lessons*, 410.
12. Jesus and Kuthumi, *Corona Class Lessons*, 411.
13. *King James Bible*, John 8:11.
14. *King James Bible*, Luke 10:37.
15. Jesus and Kuthumi, *Corona Class Lessons*, 412.
16. *King James Bible*, Philippians 4:7.
17. Jesus and Kuthumi, *Corona Class Lessons*, 343.
18. Jesus and Kuthumi, *Corona Class Lessons*, 356.

11. The Power Of Habits

1. Jesus and Kuthumi, *Corona Class Lessons*, 265.
2. *King James Bible*, Acts 9:17.
3. Jesus and Kuthumi, *Corona Class Lessons*, 267-268; 271.
4. Lundberg, *Our Magnificent Afterlife*, "Mind Power in the Afterlife."
5. Recollection of T.J. Conner, a student of Mark Prophet.
6. *King James Bible*, Matthew 16:23.
7. *King James Bible*, Matthew 23:33.
8. Jesus and Kuthumi, *Corona Class Lessons*, 275-276.

12. Discipleship And Mastery

1. https://en.wikipedia.org/wiki/josephine_bakhita.
2. Jesus and Kuthumi, *Corona Class Lessons*, 211.
3. Jesus and Kuthumi, *Corona Class Lessons*, 32.
4. Jesus and Kuthumi, *Corona Class Lessons*, 250.
5. Jesus and Kuthumi, *Corona Class Lessons*, 210.
6. Jesus and Kuthumi, *Corona Class Lessons*, 211-212.
7. Jesus and Kuthumi, *Corona Class Lessons*, 297.
8. Jesus and Kuthumi, *Corona Class Lessons*, 215.
9. Jesus and Kuthumi, *Corona Class Lessons*, 253.

10. Jesus and Kuthumi, *Corona Class Lessons,* 255-256.
11. Jesus and Kuthumi, *Corona Class Lessons,* 234.
12. Jesus and Kuthumi, *Corona Class Lessons,* 50.
13. Jesus and Kuthumi, *Corona Class Lessons,* "Healing through the Transfiguration" section. (8th page).
14. *King James Bible,* 1 John 4:18.
15. *King James Bible,* Luke 10:30-37.
16. *King James Bible,* Matthew 25:40.
17. *King James Bible,* John 10:14-18.
18. Jesus and Kuthumi, *Corona Class Lessons,* 223-224.
19. Jesus and Kuthumi, *Corona Class Lessons,* 237.
20. Jesus and Kuthumi, *Corona Class Lessons,* 240-241.
21. *King James Bible,* Matthew 18:12.
22. Jesus and Kuthumi, *Corona Class Lessons,* 214.
23. Jesus and Kuthumi, *Corona Class Lessons,* 51.
24. *King James Bible,* John 14:12.
25. Jesus and Kuthumi, *Corona Class Lessons,* 52.
26. Redfield, James, https://www.goodreads.com/quotes/816367-where-attention-goes-energy-flows-where-intention-goes-energy-flows.

13. Our Empowering Beautiful Vision

1. Jesus and Kuthumi, *Corona Class Lessons,* 228.
2. Jesus and Kuthumi, *Corona Class Lessons,* 225.
3. Jesus and Kuthumi, *Corona Class Lessons,* 296.
4. *King James Bible,* Prof 23:7. Exact Bible wording is: "For as he thinketh in his heart, so *is* he: Eat and drink, saith he to thee; but his heart *is* not with thee."
5. Jesus and Kuthumi, *Corona Class Lessons,* 331.
6. Jesus and Kuthumi, *Corona Class Lessons,* 332.
7. Jesus and Kuthumi, *Corona Class Lessons,* 260.
8. Jesus and Kuthumi, *Corona Class Lessons,* 259, 261.
9. Jesus and Kuthumi, *Corona Class Lessons,* 228-229.
10. Jesus and Kuthumi, *Corona Class Lessons,* 298.
11. Jesus and Kuthumi, *Corona Class Lessons,* 393.
12. Jesus and Kuthumi, *Corona Class Lessons,* 218-219.
13. Jesus and Kuthumi, *Corona Class Lessons,* 177.

14. Jesus Dying For Our Sins

1. *King James Bible,* Hebrews 9:22.
2. Fertile Crescent: A crescent-shaped region that includes Jordan, Israel, Iraq, Lebanon, Palestine, Syria, along with portions of south-eastern Turkey, western Iran and northern Kuwait. Some also count northern Egypt and Cyprus. This area held a number of our earliest civilizations.
3. Jesus and Kuthumi, *Corona Class Lessons,* 179.

4. Jesus and Kuthumi, *Corona Class Lessons,* 181.
5. Jesus and Kuthumi, *Corona Class Lessons,* 181-182.
6. Jesus and Kuthumi, *Corona Class Lessons,* 183.
7. *King James Bible,* Matthew 3:17.

15. Transcending Mortality—Being "Born Again"

1. *King James Bible,* John 3:3-6.
2. Jesus and Kuthumi, *Corona Class Lessons,* 349.
3. Jesus and Kuthumi, *Corona Class Lessons,* 351.
4. Jesus and Kuthumi, *Corona Class Lessons,* 384.
5. Jesus and Kuthumi, *Corona Class Lessons,* 351-352.
6. Jesus and Kuthumi, *Corona Class Lessons,* 353.
7. *King James Bible,* John 14:6.
8. *King James Bible,* Philippians 4:7.
9. *King James Bible,* 1 Corinthians 3:3.
10. *King James Bible,* 1 Corinthians 9:11.
11. *King James Bible,* Psalms 19:14.
12. *King James Bible,* Genesis 1:27.
13. Jesus and Kuthumi, *Corona Class Lessons,* 199.

16. Losing Life To Find It

1. *King James Bible,* Matthew 10:39.
2. Bija Mantras. The word *bija* means "seed" in Sanskrit. Bija mantras, also called "seed syllables," are short words or syllables such as AIM, HRIM or HUM associated with specific chakra centers in the body, or deities that represent different divine qualities of God. When chanted, these mantras are understood to purify and accelerate our spiritual chakra centers.
3. Jesus and Kuthumi, *Corona Class Lessons,* 384.
4. Jesus and Kuthumi, *Corona Class Lessons,* 163.
5. Jesus and Kuthumi, *Corona Class Lessons,* Chapter 20, "Transfiguration."
6. Jesus and Kuthumi, *Corona Class Lessons,* 17.
7. Jesus and Kuthumi, *Corona Class Lessons,* 133.
8. Jesus and Kuthumi, *Corona Class Lessons,* 133-134.
9. Jesus and Kuthumi, *Corona Class Lessons,* 192-193.
10. *King James Bible,* 1 John 3:1-3.
11. *King James Bible,* Philippians 2:5.
12. Jesus and Kuthumi, *Corona Class Lessons,* 138-139.
13. Jesus and Kuthumi, *Corona Class Lessons,* 139.
14. Jesus and Kuthumi, *Corona Class Lessons,* 323-324.
15. *King James Bible,* John 14:1-3.
16. Jesus and Kuthumi, *Corona Class Lessons,* 325-326.

17. The River Of Life

1. Jesus and Kuthumi, *Corona Class Lessons*, 369.
2. Jesus and Kuthumi, *Corona Class Lessons*, 234.
3. Jesus and Kuthumi, *Corona Class Lessons*, 235-236.
4. *King James Bible*, Isaiah 11:6.

18. Sharing The Light

1. Jesus and Kuthumi, *Corona Class Lessons*, 398-399.
2. Jesus and Kuthumi, *Corona Class Lessons*, 371.
3. Jesus and Kuthumi, *Corona Class Lessons*, 81-82.
4. Jesus and Kuthumi, *Corona Class Lessons*, 364.
5. Jesus and Kuthumi, *Corona Class Lessons*, 409.
6. Jesus and Kuthumi, *Corona Class Lessons*, 365.
7. Jesus and Kuthumi, *Corona Class Lessons*, 239.
8. Jesus and Kuthumi, *Corona Class Lessons*, 240.
9. Jesus and Kuthumi, *Corona Class Lessons*, 290.
10. *King James Bible*, Mark 1:17.
11. Jesus and Kuthumi, *Corona Class Lessons*, 83.
12. Jesus and Kuthumi, *Corona Class Lessons*, 97.
13. Jesus and Kuthumi, *Corona Class Lessons*, 319.
14. Jesus and Kuthumi, *Corona Class Lessons*, 338.

19. The Holy Grail—Drinking From The Cup Of Light

1. Jesus and Kuthumi, *Corona Class Lessons*, 211.
2. Jesus and Kuthumi, *Corona Class Lessons*, 406.
3. Smith, Huston, *Why Religion Matters*, (New York, HarperCollins, 2001), 140.
4. *King James Bible*, 1 John 1:5.
5. *King James Bible*, Mark 5:25-29.
6. Jesus and Kuthumi, *Corona Class Lessons*, 405.
7. *King James Bible*, Matthew 7:7-8.
8. Jesus and Kuthumi, *Corona Class Lessons*, 244-245.

20. Transfiguration

1. Jesus and Kuthumi, *Corona Class Lessons*, 120.
2. Jesus and Kuthumi, *Corona Class Lessons*, 118-119.
3. Jesus and Kuthumi, *Corona Class Lessons*, 119.
4. *King James Bible*, Mark 9:1.
5. *King James Bible*, Mark 9:2-3.
6. Jesus and Kuthumi, *Corona Class Lessons*, 138.

Notes

7. Jesus and Kuthumi, *Corona Class Lessons,* 343.
8. Jesus and Kuthumi, *Corona Class Lessons,* 341.
9. Jesus and Kuthumi, *Corona Class Lessons,* 251.

Working with the Light

1. Jesus and Kuthumi, *Corona Class Lessons,* 340.
2. Jesus and Kuthumi, *Corona Class Lessons,* 347.
3. Jesus and Kuthumi, *Corona Class Lessons,* 330.
4. Jesus and Kuthumi, *Corona Class Lessons,* 287.
5. Jesus and Kuthumi, *Corona Class Lessons,* 294.
6. Jesus and Kuthumi, *Corona Class Lessons,* 293.
7. Jesus and Kuthumi, *Corona Class Lessons,* 128.
8. Jesus and Kuthumi, *Corona Class Lessons,* 55.
9. Https;//www.summitlighthouse.org/your-tube-of-light/.
10. Jesus and Kuthumi, *Corona Class Lessons,* 236.
11. Store.summitlighthouse.org/decrees-and-songs-of-the-first-ray.
12. Prophet, Elizabeth Clare, *The Word: Mystical Revelations of Jesus Christ Through His Two Witnesses, Volume 7,* (Gardiner, MT, Summit University Press, 2022), 259.
13. Saint Germain is the hierarch of the Aquarian age. He is the sponsor of freedom's flame. His name comes from the Latin *Sanctus Germanus,* meaning "Holy Brother." For much more information visit the Summit Lighthouse at: Ascendedmasterencyclopedia.org/w/Saint_Germain.
14. King, Godfre Ray, *Original Unveiled Mysteries,* (Schaumburg, IL, Saint Germain Press, 1982), 12.
15. Church, Dawson, *Mind to Matter,* (Carlsbad, CA, Hay House, 2019).
    Church, *Bliss Brain,* (Carlsbad, CA, Hay House, 2020).
16. Dispenza, Dr. Joe, *Becoming Supernatural,* (Carlsbad, CA, Hay House, 2017).
    Dispenza, *Evolve Your Brain,* (Deerfield Beach, FL, Health Communications, Inc., 2007).
17. *King James Bible,* Hebrews 12:29.
18. *King James Bible,* Genesis 1:3.
19. Medicalxpress.com/news/2020-05-uvc-lamps-virus.html.
20. Imrpress.com/journal/TBS/14/4/10.31083/just.fbs1404027/htm.
    Pubmed.ncbi.nlm.nih.gov/36575836/#.
21. https://en.wikipedia.org/wiki/blood_irradiation_therapy.
22. Summitlighthouse.org/i-am-the-violet-flame/.
23. Jesus and Kuthumi, *Corona Class Lessons,* "Healing Through the Transfiguration" section.
24. Jesus and Kuthumi, *Corona Class Lessons,* "Healing Through the Transfiguration" section.
25. Jesus and Kuthumi, *Corona Class Lessons,* "Healing Through the Transfiguration" section.

Notes

26. Jesus and Kuthumi, *Corona Class Lessons*, "Healing Through the Transfiguration" section.
27. Jesus and Kuthumi, *Corona Class Lessons*, 328.
28. *King James Bible*, Philippians 2:5.
29. *King James Bible*, John 14:6-7.
30. Jesus and Kuthumi, *Corona Class Lessons*, 164-165.
31. Jesus and Kuthumi, *Corona Class Lessons*, 350-351.
32. Jesus and Kuthumi, *Corona Class Lessons*, 128.
33. Melchizedek, member of the ancient sacred-fire priesthood of the Order of Melchizedek, which combines the perfect religion and the perfect science. See ascendedmasterencyclopedia.org/w/Melchizedek. Also, Gen.14:18, Ps. 110-114, Web. 5:5-10, 6:20, 7.
34. Jesus and Kuthumi, *Corona Class Lessons*, 110.
35. *King James Bible*, John 14:10.
36. Jesus and Kuthumi, *Corona Class Lessons*, 81.
37. Jesus and Kuthumi, *Corona Class Lessons*, 225.
38. Jesus and Kuthumi, *Corona Class Lessons*, 388.
39. Jesus and Kuthumi, *Corona Class Lessons*, "Healing Through the Transfiguration" section.
40. Jesus and Kuthumi, *Corona Class Lessons*, 284.
41. Jesus and Kuthumi, *Corona Class Lessons*, 39.
42. Handout for Song 8, *Let God Be Magnified*, The Summit Lighthouse, 2023.
43. Jesus and Kuthumi, *Corona Class Lessons*, 290-291.
44. Jesus and Kuthumi, *Corona Class Lessons*, 128.
45. Jesus and Kuthumi, *Corona Class Lessons*, 55.
46. Jesus and Kuthumi, *Corona Class Lessons*, 291.
47. Jesus and Kuthumi, *Corona Class Lessons*, 215.
48. Jesus and Kuthumi, *Corona Class Lessons*, 269.
49. *King James Bible*, Mark 10:44.
50. *King James Bible*, Matthew 18:3-4.
51. Jesus and Kuthumi, *Corona Class Lessons*, 57-58.
52. Jesus and Kuthumi, *Corona Class Lessons*, 57. From the hymn "I'll Be a Sunbeam," words by Nellie Talbot, music by Edwin O. Exceli (1900).
53. *King James Bible*, Mark 14:26.
54. Jesus and Kuthumi, *Corona Class Lessons*, 19-20.
55. Jesus and Kuthumi, *Corona Class Lessons*, 287.
56. Jesus and Kuthumi, *Corona Class Lessons*, 277.
57. Jesus and Kuthumi, *Corona Class Lessons*, 328.
58. Jesus and Kuthumi, *Corona Class Lessons*, 354.
59. *King James Bible*, Genesis 1:31.
60. Jesus and Kuthumi, *Corona Class Lessons*, 190.
61. Jesus and Kuthumi, *Corona Class Lessons*, 303.
62. Jesus and Kuthumi, *Corona Class Lessons*, 138-139.
63. Jesus and Kuthumi, *Corona Class Lessons*, 228.
64. Jesus and Kuthumi, *Corona Class Lessons*, 291.
65. Jesus and Kuthumi, *Corona Class Lessons*, 122-123.

Notes

66. Jesus and Kuthumi, *Corona Class Lessons*, 130
67. Jesus and Kuthumi, *Corona Class Lessons*, 127.
68. Jesus and Kuthumi, *Corona Class Lessons*, "Healing Through the Transfiguration" section.
69. Jesus and Kuthumi, *Corona Class Lessons*, 128-129.
70. Jesus and Kuthumi, *Corona Class Lessons*, 325.
71. Jesus and Kuthumi, *Corona Class Lessons*, 325-326.
72. *King James Bible*, Matthew 18:19-20.
73. Jesus and Kuthumi, *Corona Class Lessons*, 185-186.
74. Jesus and Kuthumi, *Corona Class Lessons*, 186.

APPENDIX

1. *Prayers, Meditations, Dynamic Decrees for the Coming Revolution in Higher Consciousness*, (Gardiner, MT, The Summit Lighthouse, 1984), 4.02.
2. Jesus and Kuthumi, *Corona Class Lessons*, 347.
3. Jesus and Kuthumi, *Corona Class Lessons*, 294.
4. Https://www.summitlighthouse.org/your-tube-of-light/.
5. Summitlighthouse.org/traveling-protection-archangel-michael/.
6. Kuthumi, *Studies of the Human Aura*, (Gardiner, MT, Summit Publications, 1962) 51-52.
7. Store.summitlighthouse.org/decrees-and-songs-of-the-first-ray.
8. Jesus and Kuthumi, *Corona Class Lessons*, 236.
9. King, *Original Unveiled Mysteries*, 11-12.
10. King, *Original Unveiled Mysteries*, 12.
11. Summitlighthouse.org/i-am-the-violet-flame/.
12. Jesus and Kuthumi, *Corona Class Lessons*, "Healing Through the Transfiguration" section.
13. Jesus and Kuthumi, *Corona Class Lessons*, "Healing Through the Transfiguration" section.
14. Jesus and Kuthumi, *Corona Class Lessons*, "Healing Through the Transfiguration" section.
15. Jesus and Kuthumi, *Corona Class Lessons*, "Healing Through the Transfiguration" section.
16. Jesus and Kuthumi, *Corona Class Lessons*, 328.
17. Jesus and Kuthumi, *Corona Class Lessons*, "Healing Through the Transfiguration" section.
18. *King James Bible*, Exodus 3:14.
19. Jesus and Kuthumi, *Corona Class Lessons*, 81. And John 14:10.
20. Jesus and Kuthumi, *Corona Class Lessons*, 225.
21. Jesus and Kuthumi, *Corona Class Lessons*, 164.
22. Jesus and Kuthumi, *Corona Class Lessons*, 293.
23. Jesus and Kuthumi, *Corona Class Lessons*, 354.
24. Jesus and Kuthumi, *Corona Class Lessons*, 128.
25. Jesus and Kuthumi, *Corona Class Lessons*, 350-351.

26. Jesus and Kuthumi, *Corona Class Lessons,* 388.
27. Jesus and Kuthumi, *Corona Class Lessons,* "Healing Through the Transfiguration" section.
28. Jesus and Kuthumi, *Corona Class Lessons,* 284.
29. Handout for Song 8, *Let God Be Magnified,* Summit Lighthouse, 2023.
30. Jesus and Kuthumi, *Corona Class Lessons,* 290-291.
31. Jesus and Kuthumi, *Corona Class Lessons,* 128.
32. Jesus and Kuthumi, *Corona Class Lessons,* 55.
33. Jesus and Kuthumi, *Corona Class Lessons,* 291.
34. Jesus and Kuthumi, *Corona Class Lessons,* 215.
35. Jesus and Kuthumi, *Corona Class Lessons,* 269.
36. Jesus and Kuthumi, *Corona Class Lessons,* 57-58.
37. Jesus and Kuthumi, *Corona Class Lessons,* 57.
38. Jesus and Kuthumi, *Corona Class Lessons,* 19-20.
39. Jesus and Kuthumi, *Corona Class Lessons,* 287.
40. Jesus and Kuthumi, *Corona Class Lessons,* 287.
41. Jesus and Kuthumi, *Corona Class Lessons,* 328.
42. Jesus and Kuthumi, *Corona Class Lessons,* 328.
43. Jesus and Kuthumi, *Corona Class Lessons,* 190.
44. Jesus and Kuthumi, *Corona Class Lessons,* 303.
45. Jesus and Kuthumi, *Corona Class Lessons,* 138-139.
46. Jesus and Kuthumi, *Corona Class Lessons,* 228.
47. Jesus and Kuthumi, *Corona Class Lessons,* 122-123.
48. Jesus and Kuthumi, *Corona Class Lessons,* 128-129.
49. Jesus and Kuthumi, *Corona Class Lessons,* "Healing Through the Transfiguration" section.
50. Jesus and Kuthumi, *Corona Class Lessons,* 325.
51. Jesus and Kuthumi, *Corona Class Lessons,* 325-326.
52. Jesus and Kuthumi, *Corona Class Lessons,* 303.
53. *King James Bible,* Matthew 18:19-20.
54. Jesus and Kuthumi, *Corona Class Lessons;* Jesus and Kuthumi, *Prayer and Meditation;* Elizabeth Clare Prophet, *The Word: Mystical Revelations of Jesus Christ through his two Witnesses* (this is a most wonderful series of books, containing the teachings of Jesus Christ over many years). All these and other teachings from Jesus are available from The Summit Lighthouse, Gardiner MT. Info@SummitUniversityPress.com. SummitLighthouse.org.
55. Elizabeth Clare Prophet, *The Word: Mystical Revelations of Jesus Christ,* Volume 6, (Gardiner, MT, The Summit Lighthouse, 2022) 275.
56. Jesus and Kuthumi, *Corona Class Lessons,* 186.

About the Author

C. David Lundberg is a lifelong independent spiritual seeker. He was raised in a family business of inspirational publishing. His research has included sacred texts across the religious spectrum, active membership in spiritual/religious organizations, prayer, meditation, powerful spiritual experiences, and an undeniable prompting to establish God's universal truths.

He is the winner of multiple book awards for his highly acclaimed *Unifying Truths of the World's Religions,* and *Our Magnificent Afterlife,* and is pleased to finally be releasing *Secrets of the Inner Light,* based on the secret teachings of Jesus to his disciples.

David is also the publisher of goldenagenow.com, presenting a wealth of cutting-edge information about the latest positive advances in various areas of society. Such information provides realistic, workable solutions for the world's problems. David feels strongly that everyone needs the essential, basic spiritual truths as well as the knowledge about our coming Golden Age which is now being built.

David lives with his wife Gretchen in beautiful Montana, and enjoys hiking, kayaking, and road trips all around the country. He also loves playing the piano, singing and composing.

Made in the USA
Columbia, SC
02 June 2025